Japanese and Chinese Poems to Sing

Translations from the Asian Classics

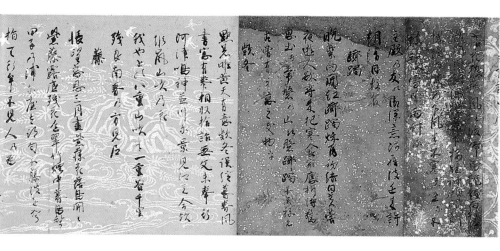

Wakan rōei shū (Kansubon manuscript). Attributed to Fujiwara no Kintō. Two handscrolls, ink on colored paper with mica, gold, and silver; 25.8 × 1292.6 cm, 21.8 × 1133.2 cm. Imperial Household Agency, Sannomaru Shōzōkan.

Japanese and Chinese Poems to Sing

The *Wakan rōei shū*

Translated and Annotated by J. Thomas Rimer and Jonathan Chaves

with contributions
by Jin'ichi Konishi, Stephen Addiss, and Ann Yonemura

Columbia University Press   New York

Columbia University Press
Publishers Since 1893
New York   Chichester, West Sussex
Copyright © 1997 Columbia University Press
All rights reserved

Columbia University Press wishes to express its appreciation for funds given by
the Japan Foundation toward the cost of publishing this volume.

Library of Congress Cataloging-in-Publication Data
Wa-Kan rōeishū. English.
    Japanese and Chinese poems to sing : the Wakan rōei shū /
translated and annotated with introductions by J. Thomas Rimer and
Jonathan Chaves: with contributions by Jin'ichi Konishi, Stephen
Addiss, and Ann Yonemura.
        p.   cm. — (Translations from the Asian classics)
    Includes bibliographical references.
    ISBN 0–231–10702–1 (cloth : alk. paper).
    1. Japanese poetry—To 1185—translations into English.   2. Waka—
Translations into English.   3. Chinese poetry—Translations into
English.   I. Rimer, J. Thomas, 1933– .   II. Chaves, Jonathan, 1943–
III. Konishi, Jin 'ichi, 1915– .   IV. Addiss, Stephen, 1935– .
V. Yonemura, Ann, 1947– .   VI. Title.   VII. Series.
PL763.2.W313   1997
895.6'11408—dc21   97–10277

Casebound editions of Columbia University Press books are printed on
permanent and durable acid-free paper.
Printed in the United States of America
c 10 9 8 7 6 5 4 3 2 1
p 10 9 8 7 6 5 4 3 2 1

This volume is dedicated to Donald Keene

In whose class the plan to undertake this translation was first conceived many years ago

Contents

Preface

As readers of our translation of the *Wakan rōei shū* will soon discover, this important Japanese Heian period anthology was a source of both Chinese and Japanese poetry for Japanese readers, and it played an important part in the development of the visual arts and calligraphy for nearly a millennium. Given its complex linguistic composition, the *Wakan rōei shū* required two translators, Jonathan Chaves and J. Thomas Rimer, and we were happy that we could add essays on various aspects of this work and its importance by such distinguished scholars as Jin'ichi Konishi, now retired from Tsukuba University; Stephen Addiss of the University of Richmond; and Ann Yonemura of the Freer/Sackler Gallery, all of whom wrote these essays specifically for this volume. We are grateful that they share our enthusiasm for the collection, and we know that their contributions will underscore the importance and beauty of the *Wakan rōei shū*.

We also would like to thank Jennifer Crewe of Columbia University Press for her continuous encouragement, as well as our editors Margaret B. Yamashita and Ronald C. Harris, who did so much to give the manuscript its final shape. We give special thanks to Kelly Worley, whose typing and computer skills were crucial to preparing the final drafts, and Ms. Sachie Noguchi of the University of Pittsburgh's East Asian Library, who was able to supply valuable background material in Japanese for both the translation and the accompanying essays.

In addition, we would particularly like to thank the Asian Studies Program at the University of Pittsburgh for the generous grant that made possible the color frontispiece of this book.

J. T. R.

J. C.

Japanese and Chinese Poems to Sing

Introduction

J. Thomas Rimer

At the climactic moment in the fifteenth-century *nō* play *Takasago*—attributed to Zeami and one of the most performed and admired plays of the whole canon—the deity of the Sumiyoshi shrine begins his sacred dance as the chorus intones the words "Plum blossoms, like spring snows, fall on my robe."

This line, which in translation blends into the larger contours of the text, is a series of Chinese characters from a poem written in the classical Chinese language by the Japanese poet Tachibana no Aritsura. Although spoken in the play using the Japanese rather than the Chinese pronunciation of those characters, the reference stands out from the surrounding Japanese text through the precision, elegance, and compactness of the Chinese original.

A contemporary audience would surely have recognized the citation, for this phrase can be found as part of the thirtieth entry in the *Wakan rōei shū* (Collection of Japanese and Chinese poems to sing), of which this volume is a complete translation. Compiled in about 1013, the *Wakan rōei shū* still served some four hundred years later—when the play *Takasago* was written—as a central sourcebook for dramatists. Indeed, the *Wakan rōei shū* was memorized, memorialized, and used as a text for calligraphers, poets, and artists in every period until the early years of this century, giving both pleasure and service for virtually a thousand years.

If the *Collection*, as I shall call it for convenience's sake, is less well known now, it is because the replacement of classical Chinese by European languages (French, English, and the like) in the modern Japanese school curriculum has resulted in fewer and fewer people who can read and appreciate these elegant texts. The *Collection* has receded from the public consciousness in much the same way that, say, John Milton's poems written in Latin—however important they were to him and to his generation—have, so that they are now seldom, if ever, consulted. When in the 1660s, Milton decided to write *Paradise Lost* in English rather than Latin, he changed the development of English literature by giving high cultural expression a strong push toward the vernacular language. A parallel change was not, however, made in Japanese literature until the Meiji period, in the middle of the nineteenth century. Poets and writers thus continued to write in classical Chinese until the time when elderly Japanese now still living were young children.

Because these texts written in Chinese have almost completely slipped away from the contemporary reading public, it is up to us to discover this phantom literature, a set of texts parallel to the acknowledged classics, that has informed the development of Japanese literature in general and poetry in particular from the sixth century onward. It was during this period that written Chinese texts—ranging from Buddhist sutras to poetry, historical documents, and philosophy—became increasingly significant in the development of the indigenous Japanese literary culture. As a result, although Japanese intellectuals may now quote Rimbaud, Baktin, or Foucault, for almost a thousand years they looked to the Lotus Sutra, Confucius, Chuang-tzu, and such poets as Po Chü-i and (later) Tu Fu for understanding and enlightenment. In that genealogy, the *Collection* played a crucial role for virtually a millennium.

What pleasures and enlightenment can be expected for modern readers who read the *Collection* in translation? Two areas of interest strike Jonathan Chaves and me as significant. The first involves our cultural understanding, the second our personal responses as readers of poetry.

The first is broader than what might be expected from a purely literary standpoint. The *Collection* is a felicitous example of the ways in which Japanese have long made use of cultural artifacts they admire that come from abroad. Indeed, the patterns set in place in the eleventh century and before can still be found in Japanese responses to foreign cultures.

The *Collection* contains three kinds of poems. The first was written in classical Chinese by Chinese poets, works that became known to highly educated readers (through the aristocratic classes, since they had the opportunity and leisure to master the difficulties of reading in the original Chinese). The second was written in classical Chinese by Japanese poets, who, through their training in Chinese and a genuine admiration of the original Chinese poems known to them, learned to write within the linguistic and stylistic parameters of classical Chinese verse. The third was those written in Japanese, in the form predominant at the time, the thirty-one-syllable *waka* (literally, a "Japanese poem," as opposed to a Chinese one) or *tanka* (literally, a "short poem," as opposed to the longer Chinese forms). Reading the *Collection* makes it clear that these Japanese poems pay a more sustained homage to Chinese history and literature than we often realize, deprived as we are of the relevant Chinese examples with which to compare them.

The same process of assimilation and adaptation can be seen in literary works created during this century. A well-known example from our own tradition, the poetry of T. S. Eliot, first became known in Japan in the 1920s, at least among those whose linguistic skills allowed them to read the difficult originals. Eliot's work, with its Christian religious overtones, must have been as far removed from ordinary modern Japanese culture as Chinese Buddhist religious texts were from the mentality of the Japanese in the sixth or seventh century, who approached them first in terms of their own Shintō mentality. In the 1920s the brilliant young Japanese poet Nishiwaki Junzaburō (1894–1982), began writing poems in English in imitation of Eliot's (and Ezra Pound's) example. In his maturity, he created a superb rendering into Japanese of Eliot's lengthy and metaphysical "Four Quartets." In the 1930s Nishiwaki also began to write modernist verse of his own in the Japanese language, and of the highest quality. In 1947, he combined both his modernist impulses and his own deepening interest in the insights available from traditional Japanese culture, in his remarkable book-length sequence *Tabibito kaerazu* (No traveler returns).[1] The process of assimilation has been the same: foreign works are admired, studied, absorbed, and then used as an inspiration for creative strategies in the Japanese context. Those who know modern Japanese literature often see this process at work. The *Collection* can show them the power of precedent.

Despite the subsequent fame and wide distribution of the *Collection*, precise details concerning its compilation were not recorded. The generally accepted view is that it was compiled by Fujiwara no Kintō as a wedding gift for his daughter in about the year 1013.

Kintō himself was, by common consent among his contemporaries, the premier poet of his time and a supreme arbiter of taste. Given the fact that he was a member of the Fujiwara family—so influential in court circles during that period—it is not surprising that he rose to high rank. Kintō lived during a remarkable period in the history of Japanese literature. From informal references in the diary of Murasaki Shikibu, who wrote the *Tale of Genji* and in the *Pillow Book* of Sei Shōnagon, it is clear that Kintō was known and apparently respected by all at court. Indeed, it was just such writers and poets who made up his principal audience. Along with the composition of his own poetry, in both Chinese and Japanese, Kintō was responsible for assembling an imperial poetry anthology, the *Shūishū* (Recollection of gleanings) as well as composing several treatises on waka poetics, among them the *Waka kyūhon* (Nine styles of waka), much consulted at that time and since.

Given Kintō's erudition and sense of discrimination, it is not surprising that he was widely accepted as an arbiter in the evaluation of Chinese and Japanese court poetry. In addition, as Earl Miner pointed out, Kintō's fascination with all forms of poetry was such that he chose to include in the *Collection* a few examples of other poetic traditions. Even though those he chose are written in the thirty-one-syllable form, they draw on more popular or folk elements, such as *kagura*, *saibara*, and *imayō*, and including them helped elevate the stature of these forms.[2]

One of Kintō's prevailing enthusiasms was for the work of the great T'ang dynasty Chinese poet Po Chü-i (772–846). Jonathan Chaves discusses this phenomenon at some length in his chapter in this book, so I note here only that Kintō's inclusion of so much poetry by the Chinese master in the *Collection* confirmed a whole new focus in the Japanese appreciation of Chinese poetry. Po's own comparative plainness of diction and sense of the dignity of ordinary humanity (qualities that have also attracted many Western readers to his work[3]) opened new possibilities for court poets of waka in the mid-Heian period (that is, in the early eleventh century), when Kintō was active. He also reaffirmed for his generation the value of those prior Japanese poetic traditions going back to the earlier *Man'yōshū* period of the sixth century, when poets, often using much longer poetic forms than the waka, sometimes wrote of life observed outside the court, chronicling the kinds of subjects—the rigors of travel, the death of loved ones, or the pain of exile. But such topics were later seen, perhaps not surprisingly, as ill suited for treatment within the confines of the increasingly dominant thirty-one-syllable waka poetic form. Kintō's inclusion of poems from the *Man'yōshū* therefore helped maintain their importance in the Japanese tradition.

In one sense, it might be said that the example of Po Chü-i helped free Japanese poets from paying too much attention to questions of style in Chinese poetry and provided them with a cultural example of a poet whose interests seemed to shift in the direction of significant content. In that regard, the injection into Japanese literature of the example of Po's work helped foster the power of many moving moments in a work like the *Tale of Genji*, in which, as Jonathan Chaves points out, Po is often quoted. His influence extends as well to the humane and moving works of medieval Japanese literature, from the memoirs of Kamo no Chōmei and Yoshida Kenkō to the refined austerities of the nō plays of Zeami and Zenchiku.

Kintō was enthusiastic about and interested in more traditional and formal qualities of Chinese poetry as well. His fascination, shared with many of his contemporaries, with the composition and appreciation of parallel couplets in Chinese is often reflected in his choices of couplets included in the *Collection*. These kinds of poetic structures often strike modern readers, unfamiliar with the appropriate conventions, as elaborate word games with little larger significance. And although it is true that this aesthetic remains distant from our modern sense of what the authentic urgency of poetry may require, the inclusion of such sequences serves to remind us that the qualities of intellectual skill, literary recognition, and, on occasion, wit, have long legacies in the Western poetic tradition as well.

I should also mention, as the noted Japanese scholar Konishi Jin'ichi has pointed out elsewhere,[4] that the force of the classical Chinese example, even before Kintō's time, had become all-powerful, even though Japan's contacts with China were becoming far less frequent, due in part to internal troubles in China at the time of the fall of the T'ang dynasty in about 907. In Konishi's view, one of the purposes of assembling the *Collection* was to attempt to lift the art of waka, in terms of both poetic skill and cultural prestige, to that of *shi*, or Chinese poetry, whether written by Chinese or Japanese poets.

The second reason for translating the *Collection* concerns the pleasure of reading the poems themselves. Despite the inevitable flattening out of the verses in translation, so that they lose some of their distinctive and differing linguistic contours, it is clear, even from modern English versions, that the quality of the poems is high. For those readers already acquainted with the waka tradition of this period, the familiar poetic virtues of elegance, gentle introspection, and the use of nature as human metaphor will quickly become apparent. The poems in Chinese by Japanese poets use rhetorical stances that may be less familiar but nonetheless have their own intellectual and emotional appeal.

When reading the *Collection*, the reader is continually exposed to juxtapositions of three types of poetry, and we have underscored these differences by having the present English versions set in a different typeface for the poetry by Chinese authors, the poetry in Chinese by Japanese authors (*kanshi*), and the poetry in Japanese (*waka*). Each category contains works of skill and elegance, still capable of giving pleasure to readers today. Readers also can compare the three forms of poems that concern roughly the same subject matter to observe at close hand the processes of cross-cultural admiration and assimilation at work within the confines of a single topic.

Jonathan Chaves points out in his chapter a number of salient features concerning the work of the Chinese poets that Kintō included in the *Collection*, their general aesthetic stance, and their influence on Japanese poets writing in either language.

The examples of kanshi, that is, poems written in classical Chinese by Japanese poets, in the *Collection* are of particular interest, since so much of this material has never been before made available in English. Because Kintō intended the *Collection* to be an anthology of the best of such poetry available—at least in accordance with his taste and that of the court of his time— these translations put us in touch with works deemed of great importance during a period of several centuries.

The *Collection* was by no means the first collection to include poetry written in Chinese by Japanese. The first anthology of such material is doubtless the *Kaifūsō* (Fond recollections of poetry), presumably compiled by members of the court in 751. Scholars familiar with the contents of the *Kaifūsō* indicate that there is little of lasting value to be found there; most of the poems are exercises in the language and express no personal sentiments, so the anthology had no permanent influence.

The first significant Japanese poet to compose in Chinese was the Buddhist monk Kūkai (774–835), who himself visited China. Despite his preeminence as a poet for Buddhist subjects and as a noted connoisseur of Chinese poetry himself, tastes in kanshi had changed in Kintō's time to the extent that none of his works were even included in the *Collection*. Insofar as the *Collection* represented a final establishment of the canon of Heian kanshi poetry, these early experiments were not deemed worthy of inclusion.

On the other hand, Kintō included almost no kanshi written in his own time; most of his chosen poets were several generations older. The work of the earliest kanshi poet included, Fujiwara no Atsumochi, goes back to the end of the eighth century, and some of the most prominent names included in the *Collection* wrote in the ninth century.

A number of these literary figures, shadowy as they may be to us, held powerful reputations, combining high court rank with impressive talents in composing in classical Chinese. Their names were, if anything, more revered in their times than those of the poets who restricted themselves to composing waka. Among them were Ono no Takamura (802–852) (twelve poems included in the *Collection*), famous among other things for the fact that in 838 he feigned illness in order to avoid the dangerous travel to China as a member of an official mission to the T'ang court. An early enthusiast for the work of Po Chü-i, Takamura wrote both waka and kanshi, and his poetry was so highly regarded that an early medieval prose work, the *Takamura monogatari* (Tale of Takamura), which gives a somewhat fanciful view of his life, uses waka that Takamura reportedly wrote as a basis for the tale. Miyako no Yoshika (834–879) (thirteen kanshi included in the *Collection*) was a civil servant, a distinguished poet, and an accomplished student of classical Chinese, who served as university examiner, then later as a rival, to the brilliant young Sugawara no Michizane (845–903), the greatest of all the kanshi poets included in the *Collection*.

Sugawara no Michizane, with thirty-seven entries, has the most kanshi in the *Collection*. By common agreement even during his lifetime, Michizane was the most accomplished of the Japanese poets to compose in classical Chinese, fusing elegance of diction with highly personal and often emotionally sophisticated sentiments. In a sense, he represented all that an education in the Chinese classics might accomplish in Japan's Heian society, both artistically and politically. When he was forty-nine, Michizane was given the highest reward available, a chance to lead a diplomatic mission to the T'ang court, an honor that he declined, however; seven years later, he was accused of treason and sent in exile to Kyushu, the southernmost island of Japan, where he died several years later.

A series of untoward incidents at court that followed Michizane's death suggested to many that his wrathful spirit was seeking vengeance. A shrine was soon built in his honor in Kyoto, and in time he became recognized as the patron saint of literature, learning, and calligraphy. His exile was pictured in works of art, and his character served as a model for many forms of drama, among them the nō play *Raiden* (Thunder and lightning) and the famous *Sugawara denju tenarai* (Sugawara and the secrets of calligraphy) one of the great Tokugawa puppet plays that still remains a central pillar of the *bunraku* and *kabuki* repertory.[5]

Whatever Michizane's enduring fame as a cultural figure, his poetry—by common consent—was of the highest level of accomplishment, so that the inclusion of many of his works in the *Collection* is not surprising. Nor, perhaps, should it be a surprise that there are twenty-two entries for his disciple and, eventually, his friend and close associate, Ki no Haseo (845–912), another kanshi poet with an enduring reputation. It was Haseo who received Michizane's poetry sent from his place of exile, and because of his generally high literary skills, Haseo is often credited with other works of importance in early Japanese literature, among them the *Taketori monogatari* (Tale of the bamboo cutter),[6] the delightful prototype for the Heian *monogatari* (tale) which found its climax in the *Tale of Genji*, written some hundred years or so later.

A number of poems by Michizane's father-in-law and advocate, Shimada no Tadaomi (828–891), can also be found in the *Collection*, as well as several by Michizane's son Atsushige (d. 926). The most important descendant of Michizane to be included is his grandson Sugawara no Funtoki (sometimes rendered as Fumitoki) (899–981), with thirty-nine entries, whose prose and poetry were highly appreciated and can be found in a number of important collections of Japanese writing in the Chinese language, such as the *Honchō monzui* (Literary essence of our country), compiled in about 1060. Another prestigious poet included in that assemblage was Ōe no Asatsuna (886–957), with thirty entries in the *Collection*. Minamoto no Shitagō (911–983), a gifted kanshi and waka poet of the period, who has some thirty entries, has been credited with the composition of the delightful Heian monogatari the *Tale of Ochikubo*, generally thought to have been written during the latter half of the tenth century. The work is full of deft humor and wry commentary on the society of the time.[7] Shitagō's kanshi "Song of the Tailless Ox"[8] is a well-known and amusingly couched complaint concerning his lack of recognition in court circles.

The only important kanshi poet close to Fujiwara Kintō's own generation to be included in the *Collection* is Yoshishige no Yasutane (?–997), with nineteen entries, who nevertheless died a decade or so before the manuscript was assembled. Yasutane is perhaps best known today for his essay written in classical Chinese, entitled "Record of the Pond Pavilion,"[9] in which he describes his quiet retreat far from the bustle of the capital, where he is able to meditate and pursue his spiritual life. It seems clear that Yasutane's essay provided an important source for the well-known and much loved account by the poet of the succeeding Kamakura period, Kamo no Chōmei (1155–1216), entitled the *Hōjōki* (An account of my hut), in which Chōmei also discusses his retirement from the capital and his need to seek an ever simpler life capable of permitting a search for spiritual detachment.

All these details are worth mentioning because it is clear that to those who consulted the *Collection*, these kanshi poets loomed as major figures in the literary history of Japan during the Heian and succeeding periods. Despite their relative obscurity today, with the obvious exception of Michizane, the undisputed genius of kanshi, it may well profit us to read their work with some close attention and respect, both for its own literary merit and in order to observe the long shadows that this work has cast over the work of many later generations of Japanese poets and writers.

Although in some cases, Kintō has included in the *Collection* poems written in both Chinese and Japanese by the same author, these are relatively few in number. Even so, most of the poets so identified are primarily kanshi poets. Thus, although a few waka can be found in the *Collection* by such poets as Ono no Takamura, Minamoto no Shitagō, and Ōe no Asatsuna, in addition to more minor figures as Tachibana no Naomoto or Fujiwara no Yoshitaka, no kanshi by a major waka poet is included.

Anong the waka poets to be found in the *Collection*, perhaps the most important is Ki no Tsurayuki—one of the four compilers of the first classic waka anthology, the *Kokinshū* (Collection of poems, ancient and modern) in about 905—was by most accounts the most respected poet and critic of his period. His Japanese-language preface to the *Kokinshū* represented the first major articulation of poetic aesthetics for the art of waka, one that continued to be quoted and acted on for many hundreds of years. His *Tosa nikki* (Tosa diary), composed around 935, was one of the first and most accomplished poetic diaries in a long succession of works, a genealogy that leads to the travel accounts of the *haiku* poet Matsuo Bashō (1644–1694) and beyond. Tsurayuki's twenty entries represent about 10 percent of all those waka included.

The waka poet next best represented is Ōshikōchi no Mitsune (fl. 898–922), who was given seventeen entries. Mitsune, who was close to Tsurayuki, also served as co-compiler of the *Kokinshū*. A few selections by the other two compilers, Ki no Tomonori (?850–?904) and Mibu no Tadamine (fl. 898–920) are included as well. (Ki no Yoshimochi (d. 919), who wrote the influential Chinese-language preface to the *Kokinshū*, also is represented by one kanshi.)

On the basis of such evidence, it appears that Kintō was setting out to reinforce Japanese poetic values that had been established some or more hundred years previously. Rather than striking off in a new direction, he seemed to aim at establishing permanent standards on the basis of which the poets of his and successive generations should proceed. This anthology is therefore primarily one of hindsight.

A surprising number of the poems in Japanese selected for the *Collection* had already become famous in their own right through their inclusion in earlier anthologies. Out of a total of 216 poems in Japanese, twelve were selected from the *Man'yōshū*, more than fifty from the *Kokinshū* (that is, roughly a quarter of the total), and some from the *Shūishū*, Kintō's later anthology mentioned earlier. Some twenty-odd poems were also later included in the famed *Shinko-*

kinshū (New collection of poems ancient and modern), compiled in the early thirteenth century, a fact that reminds us again of Kintō's felicitous, if conservative, choices. In addition, the stature of the waka poets and their poems that have been included suggests, as Konishi points out, that the best examples of Japanese poetry were compared with poems composed in Chinese in order to show the accomplishments possible in the Japanese language. Many, if not all, of the waka—and indeed, the kanshi—would have been familiar to those who first used the *Collection*, as it was to the lines by Chinese writers that the Japanese continued to turn.

In chapter 1, Jonathan Chaves describes the practice of taking two, sometimes four, lines out of the context of a longer Chinese poem. Also, Kintō did not hesitate to pluck a short sequence of lines from longer kanshi by the Japanese poets. There are many reasons for this unusual aesthetic, but one of them has to do with the fact, as the title of the *Collection* indicates, that these lines were meant to be *sung* or, at the least (in modern terms), to be chanted or musically recited in some formal and communal fashion. Stephen Addiss addresses this complex matter in chapter 4, but in short, there appear to have been two traditions. One was created by Minamoto no Masanobu (920–993) with the help of the kanshi poet Sugawara no Funtoki, mentioned earlier, during the reign of Emperor Enyū (969–984), several generations before Kintō compiled his anthology. Those scholars who have examined the sparse and confusing evidence available believe that the verses in Chinese were first performed by chanting their *on* readings (the Japanese pronunciations assigned to the Chinese characters), which were then repeated in their *kun* readings (the appropriate word in Japanese represented by each character).

By Fujiwara no Kintō's generation, this practice of singing poetry for recreation seems to have become common in court circles. In the *Pillow Book*, for example, Sei Shōnagon remarks:

> There had been a large number of senior courtiers next to the first door of the long corridor of the Palace, but one by one they had slipped away, and now no one remained but the Captain First Secretary, Tadanobu, Captain Nobutaka of the Minamotos, and a certain Chamberlain of the Sixth Rank. They spoke about all sorts of things, chanted passages from the sutras, and recited Japanese poems.[10]

Similar comments can be found in the *Tale of Genji* and other monogatari of that period. The fact that such musical performance was widespread, on both informal and formal occasions, provides additional reasons that Kintō's selections were relatively conservative. Some of those who consulted the *Collection* were surely looking for works they already knew and wanted to perform. In that sense, the book functioned as a kind of libretto, or book of lyrics. Just as in similar collections of lyrics published in the United States in our century, some new texts are often included, but the most space is given to old favorites. In our case, these may be the lyrics to songs by Steven Foster or Cole Porter, whereas the Heian courtiers sought Michizane and Tsurayuki.

To assist those for whom the *Collection* was intended, the poems are divided into convenient categories. The book has two main divisions, the upper volume, which deals with the seasons, and the lower volume, which covers a wide variety of more than forty topics, ranging from wind and clouds to prime ministers and singing girls. These categories in turn set the parameters within which poetic decorum was possible for Kintō's generation.

There has been considerable speculation about how Kintō decided on these categories. In the case of court poetry, the *Kokinshū*—which did so much to set the design for all that followed—also contains categories in which poems by various poets might be grouped. These twenty divisions, encompassing some eleven hundred poems, were fairly broad. The first six covered the seasons, with subsequent categories of travel, parting, wordplays, love (five books all together), grief, miscellaneous (two books), miscellaneous poetic forms other than waka, and, finally court poems. In the case of the *Collection*, however, a smaller corpus of 803 poems was divided into much more specific groupings, as the translated text makes clear.

Some scholars have pointed out the importation into Japan by Kintō's time of a number of Chinese compendiums of general knowledge referred to as *leishu* (classified books), including works by such famous T'ang dynasty figures as Ou-yang Hsün (557–641) and Hsü Chien (659–727). Whatever the ultimate sources for these received categories in the *Collection*, it is clear that they have become much more precise. They may well represent a compiled list, and presumably as exhaustive a list as possible, of topics considered suitable for the public recitation of poetry in the Chinese or Japanese language. In this regard, the *Collection* may also reflect cultural aspects of the ceremonies and entertainments prevalent in the Heian court.

As Donald Keene observed, Kintō did not match Chinese poems with the waka they may have directly inspired, preferring instead to "group together *kanshi* and *waka* with similar echoes or 'perfumes,' anticipating the method of 'linking' in *renga* poetry."[11] A close examination of the text reveals that many of these poems were not originally written to fit the categories that Kintō chose.

As a random example, Kintō placed a waka by Fujiwara no Okikaze, the forty-ninth entry in the *Collection*, in the category "Late Spring." In the earlier *Kokinshū*, however, the poem is number 351 in a section entitled "Felicitation." This point is of some importance, since it suggests that at least some of these poems were originally conceived in terms that Kintō later reconceived.

Of course, we will never know for sure the precise genesis and inspiration of any particular work in the *Collection*. It is difficult for us, as modern readers, to understand the implications of the fact that Japanese court poetry was so often a communal art, one in which the mixture of public and private was very different from that in the history of our own tradition, certainly that after the Romantic period of the nineteenth century when the role of acceptable public poetry declined precipitously. That is, we may still be able to read with some pleasure an ode by Alexander Pope, but we can no longer take seriously the verse of John Masefield, that famous poet laureate of England. And it is almost impossible for us to distinguish between the public and the private in the case of the Heian court.

Even the use to which certain poems were put seems difficult for us to understand. For example, research by modern Japanese scholars has shown that many of the poems by Japanese contributors were originally composed to be written out on squares of paper that were then pasted onto screens in order to "textualize" the scene created by the artist. To a modern reader, for example, the poem by Ki no Tsurayuki (number 136 in the *Collection*) may seem to refer to the artist's response to viewing pine and wisteria growing together. The scholarly evidence suggests that the verse was written in response to a painted scene and so does not constitute a direct observation of nature itself.

Such a technique—in which art seems to be inspired by art rather than by the poet's encounter with reality—consequently seems distanced from our Western perspective, in which examples of art usually are specifically identified. Thus, when Keats describes his beloved Grecian urn, we believe that he actually saw it with his own eyes. When Baudelaire writes about artists in his famous poem "Les Phares" (Beacons), each verse begins with the name of an artist: "Rubens, fleuve d'oubli, jardin de la paresse. . ." (Rubens—river of oblivion, garden of languor. . .); "Rembrandt, triste hôpital tout rempli de murmures. . ." (Rembrandt—sad hospital filled with murmurs. . .); the work of art or artist is named; and the connection between poet and the object of his reflection is explicitly stated. In the case of the Heian aesthetic, however, both painter and poet evoke a vision of nature that, though refracted and abstracted, nevertheless remains evocative and beautiful.[12]

The possibility of this kind of abstracted beauty, as Ann Yonemura points out in chapter 5, was surely one reason for the choice by many generations of Japanese calligraphers of texts from the *Collection* to use in the practice of their art. Calligraphy, that most abstract and prized of East Asian artistic ideals, is one form of expression that, as the modern Japanese philosopher Watsuji Tetsurō observed, has been almost completely removed from the kind of mimesis seemingly required in the Western artistic tradition.[13] For many generations, these texts seemed to represent the ideal materials that calligraphers could use to create something of abstract and refined beauty.

The *Collection* thus served for many centuries not only as a source of beauty itself but also as a handbook of the arts, supplying poets and dramatists with lofty language, artists with subject matter, musicians with lyrics, and calligraphers with revered texts to copy. Much as been made of the synthetic nature of the traditional Japanese arts, with each category of creativity reinforcing another. Reading through a work like the *Collection* sustains and develops that contention in a remarkably striking way. It is no wonder that the text was popular for so long.

In the medieval period, before the arts of printing had developed in Japan (or in Europe), manuscripts had to be copied by hand and circulated. The *Collection* was widely reproduced, and copies of it were exceedingly valuable, as the following incident in the famous *Tsurezuregusa* (Essays in idleness) by the medieval priest and aesthete Yoshida Kenkō (1283–1352) makes clear:

> A certain man owned a copy of the *Wakan Rōei Shū*, which, he claimed, was in the hand of Ono no Tōfū [a celebrated calligrapher who lived from 986 to 996]. Another man commented, "I am sure that there must be a good reason for the attribution, sir, but does it not seem an anachronism that Tōfū should have written the manuscript of a work compiled by Fujiwara no Kintō, a man born after his death? It seems rather strange." The owner replied, "That's precisely what makes this manuscript so unusual." He treasured it more than ever.[14]

In 1600, the famous Jesuit Mission Press established in Kyushu during the so-called Christian Century produced an edition of the *Collection* set in movable type, one of the few Japanese classics deemed worthy of wide reproduction, along with the medieval war chronicle the *Heike monogatari* (Tales of the Heike) and, as a sample of European writing for the Japanese, *Aesop's Fables*.

With the coming of the Tokugawa period and the spread of printing later in the 1600s, the *Collection* became more widely available in printed editions and thus more studied and imitated than ever before. For commoners and towns-people, this elegant text became one of the indispensable links to the earlier accomplishments of aristocratic Japanese culture. Lines from poems were quoted in the poetry of the time and also in Saikaku's comic novels. The following haiku by the great poet and painter Yosa Buson (1716–1783) suggests something of readers' respect and affection for the *Collection*.

A maple leaf
As a bookmark
In the *Rōei shū*.

When reading this venerable text now, even in translation, it seems clear why this fluent combination of poetic texts produced "perfumes" well able to keep their fragrance for nearly a millennium.

1
Chinese Poets in the *Wakan rōei shū*

Jonathan Chaves

From the very beginning of the history of Japanese literature, the Japanese were fascinated by the literary heritage of China. Some of the Chinese classics were brought to Japan by early visitors, such as Korean Buddhist monks who did not limit themselves to purely Buddhist literature. The Japanese quickly took to writing in Chinese as well as in the vernacular, in much the same manner as writers in England, Italy, or Spain in the fourteenth century and afterward wrote both in Latin (or even Greek) as well as in English, Italian, or Spanish. Thus there developed two literatures in Japan, one in Japanese and one in Chinese. By the time that Fujiwara no Kintō compiled the *Wakan rōei shū*, sometime around 1013, Japanese taste in Chinese poetry, as well as in other genres of Chinese literature, had become quite sophisticated.[1]

Kintō was thus able to include in each section of the *Wakan rōei shū* three types of poetry: Chinese poems or poetic couplets written by Chinese writers of the past; Chinese-language poems written by Japanese courtiers; and *waka*, or Japanese-language poems.

Here we will limit ourselves to an examination of Japanese knowledge of Chinese literature during the Heian period and what might be described as Japanese taste in Chinese poets as reflected in the *Wakan rōei shū* and other writings of that era.

How did the Japanese get books of Chinese literature? Besides the agency of Korean monks, who brought with them a variety of Chinese texts, there was on the part of the Japanese what George Sansom characterizes as a "desire for knowledge, religious, philosophical, and, in a lesser degree, technical." He describes a "special trade mission to China" in 874–75 sent under official court auspices. This and other missions purchased various goods, including incense, perfumes, medicines—and books. Upon returning to Japan, they would first arrive at a point of entry in Kyūshū, where "the desire for Chinese goods and curiosities, including books, was so great that the officials were helpless [to prevent private citizens, including nobles, from buying items before the arrival of the officials who had a technical legal prerogative to make the first purchases]. The chief objects of trade were scrolls (of sutras or classical Chinese works), Buddhist images and paintings, temple furnishings, books of verse and prose, drugs, incense, and perfume."[2]

Our primary source for precise information about which Chinese books were available in Heian Japan is an extraordinary catalog of such books, entitled *Nihonkoku genzaisho mokuroku* (A catalog of [Chinese] books presently existing in the land of Japan) and compiled by Fujiwara no Sukeyo (847–897) sometime around 891. Although the Japanese scholar Kobase Keikichi demonstrated many years ago that a considerable number of Chinese books not listed in this work are recorded in other writings of the period as having been present in Japan, the *Nihonkoku genzaisho mokuroku* must nevertheless be considered a remarkably full register of Chinese works available to Heian courtiers, including, of course, Fujiwara no Kintō.[3]

Sukeyo arranges the 1,579 titles under forty categories derived from Chinese bibliographical categories. He starts with the Confucian classics and commentaries on those classics, including the *Shih ching* (Book of songs), the earliest anthology of poetry in East Asia and a foundation stone of all later Chinese poetry. He then lists the official dynastic histories, other histories, texts on administrative titles and structures, laws and punishments, philosophical works—including a remarkably high percentage of Taoist books, both classical philosophical works such as the *Chuang tzu* and books of alchemical practice aimed at attaining longevity or immortality—military manuals, works on calendrical studies and medicine, and finally, *pieh-chi* (separate [that is, individual] anthologies) of the writings of the poets and *tsung-chi* (mixed anthologies), which join more than one writer.[4] Included are anthologies of poetry by the following poets represented in the *Wakan rōei shū* (listed here in the order in which they appear in the *Nihonkoku genzaisho mokuroku*): Hsieh Yen, Sung Chih-wen, Ho-lan Sui, Wang Wei, Wei Ch'eng-ch'ing, Chang Cho (his novelette, *Yu hsien k'u*), Po Chü-i, Yüan Chen, Liu Yü-hsi.[5]

It is instructive to compare Sukeyo's catalog with the *I-wen chih* (Monographs on bibliography) of the Chinese dynastic histories, which list all the works produced during that particular dynasty using essentially the categories adopted by Sukeyo for his book or, perhaps more usefully, with the catalog of a good private library of the Sung dynasty. Fortunately, the catalog of one of the best of these has survived, the *Sui-ch'u-t'ang shu-mu* (Catalog of books in the hall of pursuing the origin), compiled by the owner of the library, which was considered one of the best in the Sung dynasty, Yu Mao (1124–1193). Yu, an important poet and bibliophile of the twelfth century, lists 608 separate anthologies of works by individual poets.[6] In comparison, Sukeyo's approximately 150 titles may seem meager, but more than three hundred of Yu's titles are by Sung dynasty writers, who of course would not have been available to Sukeyo in the late ninth century (the Sung dynasty extended from 960 to 1279). Thus we realize that Japanese readers of the early Heian period may have had access to about one-half the titles in Chinese poetry that might have been found in the finest private libraries in China itself.

From the point of view of our current conception of Chinese literary history, even a cursory reading of Sukeyo's list is surprising. Because Po Chü-i (772–846) was by far the favorite Chinese writer of the Japanese, two of his books of writings are included, adding up to a total of ninety-nine chapters, plus a collection of poems by Po's great friend Yüan Chen (779–831) and a small book of poems exchanged between Po and another poet-friend, Liu Yü-hsi (772–842). But the most famous T'ang poets, the great masters of the High T'ang (mid-eighth century) period, are barely represented. Sukeyo's list contains a twenty-chapter collection of poems by Wang Wei (701–761), merely three chapters of the poetry of the great Li Po (701–762), and, incredibly, no works at all by Tu Fu (712–770), generally considered today to be, in the words of the title of William Hung's classic book on him, "China's Greatest Poet,"[7] and as described by David Lattimore, "one of the great geniuses of world literature."[8] It is no wonder, then, that in the *Wakan rōei shū*, Wang Wei is represented by only one couplet, and Li Po and Tu Fu do not appear even once.

Are we to conclude that the Japanese simply did not like Tu Fu? Such a conclusion would be ahistorical because it would leave out of consideration the crucial fact that in China itself by the late T'ang–Five Dynasties–early Sung period (late ninth to tenth centuries), Tu's collected works had fallen into a fragmentary state. It was only in 1039—fully twenty-six years after the likely date of the *Wakan rōei shū*—that the scholar Wang Chu (997–1057) succeeded in issuing the first comprehensive, well-edited collection of Tu's complete poetry, the first edition that achieved widespread circulation and, in fact, formed the basis for all later editions of Tu's poetry. In their study of all the editions of Tu's poetry, Cheng Ch'ing-tu and his colleagues write:

The *Monograph on Bibliography* of the *New History of the T'ang Dynasty* records a "Collected Works of Tu Fu, sixty chapters, with a minicollection, six chapters," but this sixty-chapter edition of Tu's works disappeared during the chaotic conditions of the late T'ang and Five Dynasties periods and was no longer available by the early Sung. Although there were at the time several versions of Tu's collection, they all were mere fragments, and in addition, all were kept in private households, so that it was extremely difficult for the public to get to see them.[9]

Further light is shed on this sad situation by an associate of Wang's, the poet Su Shun-ch'in (1008–1048), who, in 1036, just three years before the publication of Wang's edition, attempted with less adequate resources to compile a serviceable edition of Tu's poetry. In a brief colophon to this book, Su writes:

> Tu Fu's biography [in the official dynastic history] says that there exists a sixty-chapter edition of his works, but only twenty of those chapters survive today, and they have not been edited and collated by a scholar, so that the ancient-style and regulated-style poems are all confusedly mixed together, and there is no order or sequence. For his works have not been esteemed by recent generations, and so more than half of them have been allowed to fall into obscurity. Alas! How lamentable![10]

If the leading scholars in China could not produce a reliable edition of Tu's works before 1039, it is no wonder that the Japanese did not have access to them in time for the compilation of the *Wakan rōei shū*.[11]

The Japanese preference for Po Chü-i, however, cannot be laid at the doorstep of mere accessibility. Rather, it is likely that Japanese envoys to China specifically requested the most complete available editions of his poetry and that is why the *Nihonkoku genzaisho mokuroku* was able to catalog no fewer than ninety-nine chapters of his writings. The matter is of great interest because Po's reputation in China itself was always somewhat equivocal, even though he always had admirers. A reading of the massive anthology of critical comments on Po's poetry compiled as part of the *Collectanea of Materials for the Study of Classical Literature*, published by Chung-hua shu-chü in the 1960s, reveals the frequency of negative or even mocking judgments of Po's style. Typical, and important because of its early date, is the following comment by Ou-yang Hsiu (1007–1072), a leading Neo-Confucian scholar and poet of the Northern Sung dynasty:

During the reign of [Emperor] Jen-tsung (1022–1063), there were several high officials who were famous as poets and, as a rule, admired the style of Po Lo-t'ien [Po Chü-i]. For this reason their diction is mostly of the easy type. One of them once wrote a couplet that went

> I have a salary to enrich my wife,
> yet no benevolence to reach the clerks and citizens.

A man mocked the poet, saying, "Yesterday I was passing through the streets, and I encountered a cart that was very heavily laden, with a skinny ox desperately struggling to pull it: could the passenger possibly have been that 'enriched wife' of yours?" Those who heard this passed it on as a good joke.[12]

This is the typical criticism of Po: his diction is too easy, or vulgar, inadequately subtle or allusive to be considered refined. And indeed, in at least some of his poems, Po strove quite consciously to achieve a readily comprehensible diction. In the important preface to his great series of fifty social-comment poems, the *Hsin yüeh-fu* (New music bureau ballads), Po wrote, "The diction is plain and direct, as I wish those who read them to understand them easily; the wording is straightforward and incisive, as I wish those who hear them to absorb deeply their admonitions."[13]

Characteristically, the *Hsin yüeh-fu*, although clearly one of the great achievements in the history of Chinese literature, are generally given a wide berth by later critics in China. In fact, they have never received their full due as a peak in Chinese cultural history. Either Po succeeded all too well in creating a diction that was simply too blunt and therefore vulgar for orthodox critics—who tended to prefer a denser, less colloquial diction peppered with obscure allusions—or some of the topics of these poems became politically unacceptable at certain periods.

Nonetheless, Japanese courtiers of the Heian period loved these poems, as reflected in the fact that Kintō included passages from no fewer than eight of them in the *Wakan rōei shū*. In China, however, when the *T'ang-shih san-pai-shou* (Three hundred poems of the T'ang dynasty), the single most widely read anthology of T'ang poetry, was compiled centuries later in 1763 or 1764, not one of the *Hsin yüeh-fu* poems was included. Burton Watson points out that poems of social concern,

> introduced into the aristocratic society of Heian Japan, had a novelty and tone of moral and social seriousness that no doubt compelled the Japanese

to reexamine their concepts of the nature and function of poetry and inspired some of them, such as Michizane, to write poems of a similar nature on the common people of their own land.[14]

This novelty would have been particularly intense given what Brower and Miner describe as "a distaste for the political that marks the Japanese [*waka*] poems."[15]

The most frequently advanced theory of why the Japanese so loved Po Chü-i is that the relative easiness of his diction made his poems comprehensible to them, with their presumably shaky command of classical Chinese. This might in turn have been another factor leading to their interest in the *Hsin yüeh-fu*, in which, as we have seen, Po was particularly striving for comprehensibility.

But the idea that the Heian Japanese had an inadequate command of Chinese must probably yield to a greater appreciation of the sophistication of their knowledge of both the language and the literature of China. In addition, it is patronizing to assume that the Japanese were drawn to a particular poet merely because he was "easy." Instead, we may have here one of many examples of how the Japanese exercised their own particular taste in Chinese writers and artists (painters, calligraphers), often giving deserved recognition to figures—or to bodies of work—unjustly denigrated or ignored in China itself.

Lady Murasaki, author of the *Tale of Genji*, informs us in her diary (as translated by Richard Bowring) that "Her Majesty asked me to read to her here and there from the Collected Works of Po Chü-i, and . . . I read with her the two books of Po Chü-i's New Ballads [that is, the *Hsin yüeh-fu*] in secret."[16]

Perhaps even more remarkably, in her court chronicle of the mid-eleventh century, *Eiga monogatari* (Tale of flowering fortunes), Lady Akazome Emon records how in 1022, after a special service for the dead, a group of court women "began a boisterous celebration, with the robes [which they had worn for the celebration] hanging casually from their shoulders. A number of them were chanting snatches of a ballad from the *Collected Works*, their voices mingling to splendid effect."[17] Here they chant three separate passages from "Liaoling—In Consideration of the Labors of the Women Weavers," from Po's *Hsin yüeh-fu*.[18] It is extraordinary that this poem, a poignant protest against the sufferings of the poor women who slave to weave fine silk robes for dancing girls who wear them once and then discard them, is here pressed unexpectedly into humorous service. Perhaps the fact that it could be used in such a manner without implying any disrespect or misunderstanding of its original purpose bespeaks by itself a high degree of familiarity with the text. That this may be the case is also indicated by the use of the simple phrase *Collected Works* with no further qualification, which is understood immediately here—as it is elsewhere in Heian literature—as referring to the works of Po Chü-i.

The ritualized or ceremonialized poetry contests that played such an important role in Heian social life at court might also refer specifically to Po's poetry. Ōe no Masafusa (1041–1111) writes about a contest in which two groups of courtiers are expected to debate the relative merits of the poems in the second and sixth chapters of Po's collected works.[19] The side briefed to defend the second chapter makes the mistake of first citing a poem dealing with a Buddhist temple (a couplet from this, number 102, appears in the *Wakan rōei shū*), upon which a member of the opposing team ridicules them on the implied grounds that temples are associated with death and it is bad luck to open with such a subject!

It would, however, be a mistake to assume that in embracing Po Chü-i, the Japanese were being entirely idiosyncratic. The contemporaneous poetic scene in China was quite complex, and at least three major schools of poetry were discerned by the late Sung–early Yüan dynasty critic Fang Hui (1227–1306). In an important essay on early Sung poetry, Fang identifies the three schools as (1) the Po [Chü-i] school, (2) the [Hsi]-k'un school, and (3) the "Late T'ang" school.[20] The style of the second of these schools, based on emulation of the late T'ang poet Li Shang-yin (813?–858), is the virtual opposite of Po Chü-i's style, as it is characterized by some of the densest, most impenetrable diction and obliquity of expression in all of Chinese literature, coupled with a rich, even decadent atmosphere and frequently obscure or hermetic allusiveness. No poetry of this precise type is found in either the *Wakan rōei shū* or any other Japanese book.

But the other two early Sung schools identified by Fang Hui are very much in evidence in the *Wakan rōei shū*. Despite the mainstream, orthodox disapprobation of Po Chü-i's "vulgarity," Fang Hui reminds us that some early Sung poets emulated Po Chü-i, modeling their works on his style. Foremost among these was Wang Yü-ch'eng (954–1001). In fact, so great was Wang's admiration for Po—as well as for Yüan Chen, Po's closest friend—that he burned as sacrificial offerings to their spirits some poems he had written in their style.[21] Wang's own poetry, of a very high caliber, owes much to Po's work, including his *New yüeh-fu*. "I am one who follows after Lo-t'ien [Po Chü-i]," Wang tells us, yielding nothing to Po's Japanese admirers in his veneration for the great poet.

The leading Japanese emulator of Po Chü-i was, of course, Sugawara no Michizane (845–903).[22] It is no coincidence that he is the most often represented Japanese author of *kanshi* (Chinese-language poetry) in the *Wakan rōei shū*. Interestingly enough, the one quality of Po's writing that some scholars felt Michizane's poems lacked was their ease of comprehension. Ōe no Masafusa is on record as asking (as translated by Marian Ury), "Why is it that Michizane's writings are hard to comprehend, while Po Chü-i's collection is accessible to all?" In answer to this, an interlocutor responds, "Everything depends on the poet's heart. . . . Michizane especially possessed the Way of mystery and depth [*yūgen*]."[23]

This passage, more than any other in Heian literature, conveys to us what may be the right explanation of Po's appeal to the Japanese while at the same time cautions us that the Japanese would never be content with merely imitating Po. By implication, the aesthetic qualities of Po's writing are associated in this quotation with *yūgen*, one of the highest terms of praise in Japanese aesthetic theory. This term was later elevated to the highest possible status in the writings of the great nō playwright Zeami (1364–1443), but here it is seen to have played a role already in Heian aesthetics. Michizane, of course, is understood as having derived his style in kanshi from Po Chü-i, but he is claimed by Ōe's colleague to have reached greater depths than did Po himself.

Some idea of the artistic use to which a major Japanese writer could put a single couplet by Po Chü-i—one that is found in the *Wakan rōei shū* (number 345)—can be seen in the great "Yūgao" chapter of Lady Murasaki's *Tale of Genji*. In one of the novel's most brilliantly constructed scenes, Genji and Yūgao are lying in bed together on the night of the mid-autumn moon (the fifteenth night of the eighth lunar month).[24] They hear various noises from outside the house, including two of the sounds most often associated in antiquity with the season of autumn in poetry: the pounding of fullers' mallets on their blocks, and the cry of wild geese. As Waley translates the passage, "The whole air seemed to be full of crashings and bangings. Now from one side, now from another, came too the faint thud of the bleacher's mallet, and the scream of wild geese passing overhead. It was all too distracting." It was distracting and disturbing especially to Yūgao, "so shrinking and delicate in her ways." Lady Murasaki is subtly preparing the climactic scene in which the "living spirit" of the jealous Lady Rokujō takes possession of the fragile Yūgao and destroys her. Later, after this tragic event, "To Genji even the din of the cloth-beaters' mallets had become dear through recollection, and as he lay in bed he repeated those verses of Po Chü-i. '*In the eighth month and ninth month when the nights are growing long/A thousand times, ten thousand times the fuller's stick beats.*'"[25] Still later, "in the autumn came a time of quiet meditation and reflection. Again the sound of the cloth-beaters' mallets reached his ears, tormenting him with memories and longings."[26] The motif of this haunting sound—as mediated through poetic lines—runs through the novel with the poignant evocativeness of M. Vinteuil's violin sonata in *A la recherche du temps perdu*, though Lady Murasaki anticipated by nearly a millennium Proust's poetic use of imagery to conjure up memory.

The couplet used so superbly by Lady Murasaki comes from a poem by Po Chü-i entitled "Hearing the Fulling Blocks at Night,"[27] translated here in full with the key couplet in italics:

In whose house, this brooding woman,
  in autumn fulling clothes?
The moonlight bitter, breezes cold,
  block and mallet sad!
In the eighth month, in the ninth month,
  just when nights are long,
a thousand poundings, ten thousand poundings,
  it never has an end.
She'll surely work 'til crack of dawn,
  her hair all turned to white:
with every stroke, another strand—
  a thread of whitest silk.

In all likelihood, Lady Murasaki's knowledge of this couplet derived from the *Wakan rōei shū*, in which it is the opening passage in the section "Fulling Clothes" and the subsection "Autumn." Although the date of *Genji*'s composition is disputed, it is generally believed that Murasaki wrote it in the first decade of the eleventh century. If she died as early as 1014,[28] she probably would not have seen the completed *Wakan rōei shū*. But she may have had access to earlier versions of the book, and she certainly had opportunities to meet Kintō himself. In one passage of her diary (the diary itself being dated 1009–10), she describes how she composed a Japanese waka poem in the presence of Kintō, who was considered at the time to be the preeminent arbiter of taste in both Chinese and Japanese poetry. "We were all telling ourselves how very careful one had to be not only with the words but with the delivery when composing in the presence of the Shijō Major Counselor Kintō."[29] More revealing of a personal relationship between them is another passage in which Kintō "poked his head in. 'Excuse me,' he said. 'Would our little Murasaki be in attendance by any chance?' 'I cannot see the likes of Genji here, so how could she be present?' I [Murasaki] replied."[30] This passage is thought to explain the origin of Lady Murasaki's nickname, which was derived from the name of a character in her novel. In any case, if she and Kintō were on such intimate terms, he may have shared with her early drafts of the *Wakan rōei shū*.

But if we consider Murasaki's use of the couplet by Po Chü-i from an entirely different point of view, the fact that she could extract such artistic treasure from a conventional image, used by Chinese poets for centuries, is a salutary reminder of a point made most compellingly by G. K. Chesterton in his wonderful book on Robert Browning: the paradox that conventions in literature can evoke deep feeling. "Convention means only a coming together, an agreement," writes Chesterton,

> [and] a poet must, by the nature of things, be conventional. Unless he is describing an emotion which others share with him, his labours will be utterly in vain. . . . Poetry deals with primal and conventional things—the hunger for bread, the love of woman, the love of children, the desire for immortal life.[31]

Thus Lady Murasaki and, for that matter, all traditonal Chinese and Japanese writers were able to create seemingly limitless variations on certain "conventional" images like the sound of the fullers' mallets in autumn, while maintaining their freshness and evocativeness.

These various references to Heian literature demonstrate the absolute dominance of Po Chü-i in the taste of the time. In the *Wakan rōei shū*, he is clearly the leading Chinese writer represented, and such poets as Yüan Chen and Liu Yü-hsi are included primarily because of their relationship with him (although both of them are superb poets in their own right). The other Chinese poets in the *Wakan rōei shū* are mostly minor figures but include several who wrote in what Fang Hui calls, in his survey of early Sung poetic schools, the "Late T'ang" style. Hsü Hun (791–854), with no fewer than ten couplets, and Tu Hsün-ho (846–907), with four, happen to be two of the key poets that inspired the early Sung writers of this school.

It is necessary to clarify the meaning in the eleventh century of the term "Late T'ang," because it has been used historically in a number of different ways. In 1965 when A. C. Graham published his important book *Poems of the Late T'ang*, he was using the phrase to refer to the densely textured, nearly metaphysical poetry of the late Tu Fu and such poets as Li Shang-yin. This type of late T'ang poetry is reflected in the Hsi-k'un style of the early eleventh century described by Fang Hui in his analysis of early Sung poetry but had no apparent influence in Japan.

When Fang Hui speaks of a "Late T'ang" school, however, he is referring stylistically to poems in which exquisitely observed vignettes of nature are presented in perfectly crafted parallel couplets, deceptively simple in diction but actually requiring intensive attention to detail. A good sense of this type of poetry is provided by the Ming dynasty scholar Yang Shen (1488–1559), who further divides "Late T'ang" into two separate lineages and traces both back to the T'ang dynasty itself. "They hated to use allusions," he says of one, "which they called 'conjuring up ghosts,' but only sought the actual scenes before their eyes, and then thought about them intensely. This is what is meant by the couplet [by Hsü Hun], 'While writing a line of five-character verse/I twist off several hairs of my beard.' "[32] A perfect example of this style is the couplet (number 182) by Hsü Hun himself, one of the ten by him in the *Wakan rōei shū* (which makes Hsü the third most quoted Chinese poet in the book, after Po Chü-i and Yüan Chen—who has eleven entries):

A single song of the mountain bird
 beyond the clouds of dawn;
ten thousand water fireflies,
 points in autumnal grass.

This couplet comes from a poem by Hsü called "Rising at Dawn, Taking a Boat from the Leng-chia Temple; Feelings Along the Way,"[33] a title characteristically showing the grounding of this type of poetry in the poet's own experience of nature. Stylistically, such poetry is quite close to Po Chü-i's poetry of personal experience. Both may have appealed to the Japanese because of a certain tendency in Japanese aesthetics toward simplicity and understatement combined with an appreciation of the most intimate details of nature. The perfection of this couplet's syntactic and imagistic parallelism is more fully revealed if the Chinese text is presented word by word:

i	*sheng*	*shan*	*shu*	*niao*	*yün*	*wai*
one	sound	mountain	dawn	bird	cloud	—beyond
wan	*tien*	*shui*	*ying*	*ch'iu*	*ts'ao*	*chung*
ten thousand	points	water	firefly	autumn	grass	—within

The paradoxical ability to convey simple naturalness through what is in fact elaborately careful word choice clearly appealed to the sophisticated Japanese aesthetic sensibility, and it also helps explain why poetry of this type played such an important role in the *Wakan rōei shū*.

We may summarize by stating that the taste revealed by the selections in the *Wakan rōei shū* indicates that of the three contemporaneous schools of poetry in China (the Po Chü-i, the Late T'ang, and the Hsi-k'un), the Japanese, as represented by Kintō, paralleled in their taste the first two and showed no interest in the stylistic characteristics of the third. There is no indication that the Japanese were aware of the existence of these schools as such; rather, they seem to have been naturally drawn to certain tendencies in Chinese poetry but not to others.

Another question that we need to address is the role of couplets in the *Wakan rōei shū*. The Chinese poems that are presented are, for the most part, classical *shih* poems (the relatively few prose poems, or *fu*, and prose works will be discussed later) with the same number of characters per line (usually five or seven; in the *Wakan rōei shū*, the seven-character meter is preferred). But aside from some complete quatrains (either presented as entries by themselves or divided into two couplets and split between two sequential entries), only freestanding couplets are included. The same is true of the kanshi written by Japanese authors. Did Kintō feel that the relatively short couplets would make better pendants to the five-line waka than the relatively long complete poems would? Did the Japanese actually have an aesthetic preference for the couplet?

Any analysis of this matter must consider that in the extensive *shih-hua* (comments on poetry) literature forming an important portion of the extensive corpus of Chinese literary criticism, couplets are frequently quoted to support the author's argument—much more frequently, in fact, than complete poems are. Often an author simply praises a poet to whom he wishes to call attention and then cites a long string of (often parallel) couplets by that poet to demonstrate the quality of his work, simply leaving the reader to relish their beauty. Most of shih-hua writings postdate the *Wakan rōei shū*. They are often said to begin with the *Liu-i shih-hua* (One-of-Six comments on poetry) by Ou-yang Hsiu (1007–1072) and then to flourish in the Sung and later dynasties.

Various forerunners of the full-fledged shih-hua date back to the T'ang dynasty and beyond, of which one of the most important is the *Shih-shih* (Rules for poetry) by the Buddhist monk Chiao-jan (730–799). In attempting to characterize a number of stylistic modes, he often uses couplets, as well as longer excerpts. For example, illustrating what Chiao-jan calls the "startling and common" (*hai-su*) mode is a couplet from the *Poems of the Wandering Immortals* by Kuo P'u (276–324):

Ch'ang-o [the moon goddess] lofts wondrous tones;
Hung Yai [a famous immortal] wags his chin![34]

This couplet demonstrates aspects of the parallelism so often found in couplets quoted in the shih-hua literature and also throughout the *Wakan rōei shū*, for example, in the way the names of two mythological figures are paralleled and the paralleling of *tone[s]* and *chin*. (In Chinese, the word *his* [*ch'i*] functions as an adjective and is therefore also syntactically parallel with *wondrous*.)

Chinese literary criticism and theory were first brought to Japan by the great Kūkai (774–835), in his *Bunkyō hifuron* (Secret treasure house of the mirrors of poetry), described by Richard Wainwright Bodman as "a unique collection of Chinese writings on poetics and prosody."[35] It is impossible to say whether the Japanese originally got from the shih-hua texts the idea of quoting couplets independently of their original poems or simply began doing it on their own, something that would not be that remarkable, given the general tendency in Chinese poetry toward self-contained couplets (in a typical "regulated verse" of eight lines, the "inner couplets"—lines 3 and 4, 5 and 6—must be parallel) and indeed toward end-stopped lines. In either case, the *Wakan rōei shū*, *Senzai kaku*, and other books like them show that the Japanese had developed a particular taste for the beauty of freestanding couplets of Chinese verse.

It remains to be pointed out that not all the excerpts from Chinese writers are shih poetry. Some are outright prose, including some of the pieces by Po Chü-i, and are usually written in the "parallel" or "four–six" prose, which sometimes seems almost like poetry. In one extraordinary example, number 587, the editor appears to have transformed two parallel lines of ordinary prose from the important Buddhist treatise *Mo-ho chih-kuan* (The great cessation and contemplation, by the monk Chih-i [538–597]) into a form of poetry by adding twice the character *hsi*, "ah!" a meaningless exclamation characteristic of the *Ch'u tz'u*, the ancient poetry of the southern state of Ch'u.[36] The passages appear to have been selected partly on the basis of whether they could be effectively sung to *rōei* music (see chapter 4, by Stephen Addiss, for more on this aspect of the book), because in some cases, prose could be set to music as well.

The majority of the non-shih passages are *fu*, or "prose poems" (also translated as "rhyme prose" or "rhapsody").[37] Although this form reached its peak of development in the Han dynasty (206 B.C.–220), with the exception of the third-century *Wen fu* (Prose poem on literature), all the examples in the *Wakan rōei shū* are by obscure T'ang poets. The fu did undergo a revival of sorts in the T'ang, but none of the works represented here can be considered major representatives of the genre, nor are any of them found in the huge *Ch'üan T'ang wen* (Complete prose of the T'ang dynasty, completed in 1814 and containing both fu and true prose). Remarkably enough, the taste represented by these fu is almost diametrically opposed to that implied by the majority of the shih selections in the *Ch'üan T'ang wen*. These fu are often oblique in diction, heavily allusive, rhetorically high toned, and self-consciously artificial in the manner of court poetry in the usual sense of the phrase.

It is, in fact, an indication of the richness and complexity of Heian taste in Chinese literature that the *Wakan rōei shū* could combine texts of the parallel prose and fu types with shih poetry largely of the Po Chü-i and "Late T'ang" types. This complexity should caution us about overgeneralizing on the subject of Japanese views of Chinese literature even as early as the Heian period.

2

The Translation: The *Wakan rōei shū*

Please note that Chinese poems by Chinese authors are set as follows: the willows have no energy; Chinese poems by Japanese authors as follows: they follow the breeze and secretly bud; and Japanese poems as follows: *Spring has already come.*

UPPER VOLUME

Spring

Establishment of Spring

1. They follow the breeze and secretly bud,
    not waiting for the time of fragrant flowers;
    welcoming spring, they suddenly transform,
    hoping for the grace of rain and dew.

    KI NO YOSHIMOCHI

    PROSEPOEM, ON THE DAY OF ESTABLISHMENT OF SPRING,
    AT THE INNER GARDEN PRESENTING FLOWERS
    The passage describes plum blossoms.

2. The pond's ice to the east is thawed by the passing breeze;
    the window's plum to the north is sealed in cold by snow.

    FUJIWARA NO ATSUMOCHI

3. *Spring has already come*
    Within the old year:

Should we say that
This is still the year before,
Or is this the new year now?

ARIWARA NO MOTOKATA

WRITTEN WHEN THE FIRST DAY OF SPRING ARRIVED
BEFORE THE OLD YEAR WAS OVER

4.   The willows have no energy,
          their branches start to move;
      the pond shows patterns, little waves,
          its ice completely thawed.

PO CHÜ-I

5.   Today—by whose well-timed plan, I wonder?—
      the spring breeze and spring waters
          arrived at the same time.

PO CHÜ-I

6.   As night dies with the final watch,
          cold chimes fade to silence;
      spring is born in incense fumes
          as the dawn brazier burns.

KORENAGA NO HARUMICHI

7.   *Will the warm winds*
      On this first day of spring
      Melt that frozen water
      I once scooped to cool my hands?

KI NO TSURAYUKI

8.   *It is said that spring has come;*
      Yet this morning,
      Can the mists be seen
      On the mountains of Yoshino?

MIBU NO TADAMINE

Early Spring

9. Ice is melting in the fields;
        the reeds' sharp points are short.
    Spring is entering every branch;
        the willow-eyes hang low.

    YÜAN CHEN

10. First it sends a gentle breeze
        to announce the news;
    next it orders twittering birds
        to explain the reason.

    PO CHÜ-I

11. Willows of the eastern shore, the western shore—
    slowly, quickly, not the same;
    plum blossoms on the southern branches, northern branches—
    opening, falling, there's a difference.

    YOSHISHIGE NO YASUTANE

    SPRING IS BORN FOLLOWING THE FORM OF THE EARTH

        Based on lines from poems by Po Chü-i.

12. The purple-dusted, tender bracken—
        men's hands making fists;
    the emerald-jade, chilly reeds—
        awls poking through a bag.

    ONO NO TAKAMURA

13. The weather clears, breezes comb
        the hair of the young willows;
    the ice is melting, wavelets wash
        the whiskers of old bog moss.

    MIYAKO NO YOSHIKA

14.   The garden takes on added beauty—
    sand in clear sky shades green;
    the woods are charged with vibrancy—
    leftover snow glows red.

KI NO HASEO

15.   *Near the icicles*
Dripping from the rocks
The bracken is sprouting—
The long-awaited spring has come!

SHIKI NO MIKO

16.   *The ice, melting in the mountain valleys,*
Spurts in waves from each crevice—
Are these not the first flowers of spring?

MINAMOTO NO MASAZUMI

17.   *As I look out,*
The snow is melting
On the high peaks of Hira.
The fields are filled with young shoots
That must be picked!

TAIRA NO KANEMORI

Spring Inspirations

18.   Beneath the flowers, forgetting to return,
    because of the lovely scene;
    facing my wine cup, urging me to drink,
    none other than spring wind!

PO CHÜ-I

19.   The wild flowers, full of fragrance,
    carpeting the ground in red;

the wandering catkins, in crazy patterns,
   netting the sky with emerald.

LIU YÜ-HSI

20. Songs and wine in every household,
       flowers everywhere!
     Please don't let it pass you by,
       springtime in Shang-yang!

PO CHÜ-I

21. Mountain peach bloom, peach bloom in the wilds:
     sheets of red broidery airing in the sun!
     Gateway willows, willows on the shore:
     strands of yellow "malt dust" twirling in the breeze!

KI NO TADANA

       Based on lines by Po Chü-i.

22. Adorning the wilds, they unfurl and spread
       their red-patterned embroidery;
     touching the sky, they weave and set adrift
       their emerald netting of silk.

ONO NO TAKAMURA

23. In the forest, the flower embroidery
       now blossoms and now falls;
     beyond the sky, the wandering catkins
       sometimes show, sometimes disappear.

SHIMADA NO TADAOMI

24. Mouth organs, songs — this moonlit night,
       love thoughts in every home!
     Poetry, wine — in the spring wind,
       feelings everywhere!

SUGAWARA NO FUNTOKI

25.   *Those who live in the luxuriant palace*
       Have leisure indeed—
       Sticking sprays of cherry in their hair,
       They have passed this day.

       YAMABE NO AKAHITO

26.   *I have come to know*
       The true meaning of spring:
       When the blooms are bursting,
       There are none with quiet hearts!

       MIBU NO TADAMINE

Spring Nights

27.   Backs to the candle, together we cherish
           the moon late in the night;
       treading on petals, we share lamentation
           for the springtime of our youth.

       PO CHÜ-I

28.   *The darkness of this spring night*
       Seems futile,
       For though the plum blossoms
       Cannot be seen,
       Can their odor yet be hidden?

       OSHIKOCHI NO MITSUNE

The First "Rat" Day

The First "Rat" Day refers to the first such day of the new year; it was the custom to have picnics out of doors, touch pine trees to obtain health and longevity, and eat specially concocted broths of "young greens" to harmonize the body.

29.   We recline on pine trees, rubbing waists against them,
      to absorb their immunity to encroaching wind and frost.
      We concoct vegetable broth and sip it with our mouths,
      in hopes our inner humors will be well tempered now.

      SUGAWARA NO MICHIZANE

30.   We recline on pine trees, their roots rubbing our waists;
      the blue-green of a thousand years now fills our hands.
      We pluck plum blossoms and stick them in our hair;
      these "snowflakes" in the second month will fall on our robes.

      TACHIBANA NO ARITSURA (OR ZAIRETSU)

            Aritsura became a Buddhist monk in 944.

31.   *On this day of the rat,*
      If we find no young pine shoots in the field,
      What can we take
      As a sign of long life?

      MIBU NO TADAMINE

32.   *This pine,*
      Pledged to live a thousand years,
      From today on,
      Taking virtue from Your Majesty,
      will live a thousand years.

      ONAKATOMI NO YOSHINOBU

33.   *Do not pull up the darling little pine*
      That grows on the spot
      In the field we choose
      On the day of the rat—
      I wait to be in its shade
      In a thousand years.

      FUJIWARA NO KIYOTADA

Young Greens

34. In the wilds gathering greens:
     in the world they delegate this to those of "orchid hearts."
     In the brazier concocting broth:
     it is the custom to entrust this to those with "soft-shoot fingers."

     SUGAWARA NO MICHIZANE

          These tasks are customarily entrusted to women.

35. *On the morrow*
     We can pick the young shoots:
     The reed fields at Kataoka
     Will have been burned clean today.

     KAKINOMOTO NO HITOMARO

36. *Thinking that spring has come,*
     We thought to pluck the young shoots
     In the fields we have marked off,
     But yesterday, and today as well
     The snow still falls.

     YAMABE NO AKAHITO

37. *So that those*
     Who do not come to see
     Can take pleasure,
     I have brought back
     From the spring fields
     A basket filled with plucked young shoots.

     KI NO TSURAYUKI

Third Day of the Third Month

38. When spring arrives, everywhere are peach blossom waters;
     no longer can one distinguish the route to the immortal source.

     WANG WEI

39.   In the last month of spring, that month's third day, Heaven being intoxicated with flowers—the height of the peach and the plum—such was our sovereign's beneficence for that day that in the leisure time after ten thousand calculations and although the winding stream was far and the residual traces cut off, we were to inscribe a "figure 8" following the lay of the land, to recall Emperor Wen of the Wei dynasty while giving play to an elegant mood, for such is the direction taken by our poetic intentions. Respectfully do I submit this little preface.

SUGAWARA NO MICHIZANE

> This is a prose preface describing a reenactment of the ancient Chinese practice of celebrating the Spring Purification Festival by floating wine cups in a winding stream and writing poems. The most famous example of this tradition took place in 353 when the great calligrapher Wang Hsi-chih gathered forty-two scholars at the Orchid Pavilion. Wang's preface written on this occasion is considered a masterpiece. The custom was initiated during the reign of Emperor Wen of the Wei dynasty (r. 220–226), although antecedents in the ancient Chou dynasty may have existed.

40.   Mist and cloudbanks, far and near,
         equally intoxicated!
      Peach and plum blossoms, pale or dark,
         urge on cups of wine!

SUGAWARA NO MICHIZANE

41.   The stream winds into a "figure 8,"
         on this the first Third Day;
      the source goes back to the years of Chou,
         how many seasons of frost?

FUJIWARA ATSUMOCHI

42.   Blocked by rocks, they come on slow—
         we secretly await them!

tugged by the current, they rush right past—
    hands reach out to stop them first!

SUGAWARA NO GAKI

> This poem describes the poets as they sit along the winding stream
> awaiting the arrival of the floating wine cups. In one version of the
> game, each poet is expected to complete a poem before the wine cup
> has gone by and then to take the cup and drink the wine.

43.   Night rain has secretly moistened them,
      their eyes like doubled wavelets newly coquettish.
      Dawn wind softly blows on them,
      their mouths, not speaking yet, first give a smile.

KI NO HASEO

PROSEPOEM ON THE FIRST FLOWERING OF THE
PEACH BLOSSOMS

44.   *This peach, which provides its fruit*
      Once in three thousand years,
      Now blooms in this happy spring
      I encounter for the first time.

ANONYMOUS

> According to legend, peaches of immortality, which bloom only once
> every three thousand years, grow in the gardens of the goddess "Queen
> Mother of the West."

Late Spring

45.   Brushing water, willow blossoms,
          tens of thousands, catkins;
      passing pavilions, oriole voices,
          only two, three sounds.

YÜAN CHEN

46. Lowering wings, sand gulls,
    tides start to ebb, it's dawn;
 scattering threads, "field horses,"
    the grasses deep this spring.

SUGAWARA NO MICHIZANE

> "Field horses" are *kagerō*, or shimmering heated air; will-o'-the-wisp.

47. Man will never return to youth—
    time must be cherished!
 years do not bring perpetual spring—
    let not your wine cup run dry!

ONO NO TAKAMURA

48. If Liu and Po had only known
    the fineness of this day,
 they surely would have written "here"
    and never written "where"!

MINAMOTO NO SHITAGŌ

> This is a clever allusion to a set of twenty poems entitled "Deep in
> Springtime" and exchanged between Po Chü-i and Liu Yü-hsi (Yüan
> Chen also produced a set). The opening line of the first poem in each
> set reads, "*Where* is it fine, deep in springtime?" Shitagō states that if
> the Chinese poets had been present at the late spring literary gather-
> ing that he is attending, their line would have read, "*Here* is it fine,
> deep in springtime." The passage demonstrates the extent to which
> Heian courtiers saw the great Chinese poets as exemplars of elegant
> taste. For Po Chü-i's set of poems, see *hou*, 9/7b ff.

49. *Many are the days and months*
 I pass in idleness;
 Yet the spring days
 Spent in flower viewing
 Are few indeed.

FUJIWARA NO OKIKAZE

The End of the Third Month

50. Try holding spring, spring will not stay;
      spring departs, and we are desolate.
      Regret the wind, the wind won't stop;
      the wind blows, and the flowers are forlorn.

      PO CHÜ-I

51. In the bamboo courtyard, you are at leisure,
          whiling away the entire day;
      in the flower pavilion, I am intoxicated,
          saying farewell to departing spring.

      PO CHÜ-I

52. I'm devastated that spring departs
          and cannot be retained;
      beneath the purple wisteria bloom,
          slowly, it is dusk.

      PO CHÜ-I

53. To see off spring, no need to put carts or boats in motion;
      farewell is said with fading birdsongs and with falling flowers.

      SUGAWARA NO MICHIZANE

54. If spring's vernal radiance were of one mind with me,
      it would break journey here tonight, in this poet's home.

      SUGAWARA NO MICHIZANE

55. For holding spring, a castle's walls
          would be no use at all:
      the flowers would still fall, and all the birds
          would fly into the clouds.

      TACHIBANA NO ARITSURA

56. *Even if I did not think*
     This were the last day of spring
     Could it be an easy thing
     To leave behind
     The shade of the blossoms?

     ŌSHIKŌCHI NO MITSUNE

57. *The flowers all have fallen now*
     Where I live; so for the departing spring,
     This a place once lived in,
     Now deserted.

     KI NO TSURAYUKI

58. *The spring will come again,*
     I think; yet
     As my own state seems so uncertain,
     This season has come to seem
     Sad indeed.

     KI NO TSURAYUKI

The Intercalary Third Month

59. This year's "intercalary" comes after spring's third month:
     we're able to view another month of flowers in Chin-ling!

     ATTENDANT CENSOR LU[?]

     > Lu is an unidentified poet, presumably of the T'ang dynasty but not
     > represented in the original *Ch'üan T'ang shih* (Complete poetry of
     > the T'ang dynasty).

60. Singing warblers, headed home to their valleys,
     linger still along the routes of solitary clouds;
     dancing butterflies, departing from the forests,
     flitter and flutter yet among a whole month's worth of flowers.

     MINAMOTO NO SHITAGŌ

61.   The flowers may regret returning to the ground,
          but it's useless to regret;
      the birds may plan to return to their valleys,
          but would certainly put off the date.

   "TŌJI TŌ"

          Not identified; possibly the poet Kiyohara no Shigefuji, about whom
          very little is known.

62.   *Cherry blossoms*
      Lasting even through this longer spring:
      Still, in our hearts,
      Could we ever weary of you?

   LADY ISE

                                               The Warbler

   The word *warbler* in Chinese poetry is often translated as "oriole" and refers to
   a Chinese variety of this bird. The editors of the book translated it into Japanese
   as *uguisu*, "Japanese nightingale," "bush warbler." For the sake of consistency,
   in this section it is always translated as "warbler."

63.   The cock has crowed, ah! such the loyal minister
          paying court at dawn.
      The warbler not yet emerged, ah! such the exiled worthy
          hidden in the valley.

   WRONGLY ATTRIBUTED TO CHIA TAO, ACTUALLY BY
   CHIA SUNG, A LITTLE-KNOWN LATE T'ANG POET

   PROSEPOEM, THE PHOENIX IS THE MONARCH

64.   Whose house is it where emerald trees
      have warblers singing though silken curtains still hang?
      And where the painted hall

awakened from dreams though pearl-sewn blinds
    have not yet been rolled up?

ATTRIBUTED TO HSIEH KUAN, AN OBSCURE T'ANG POET.

PROSEPOEM ON THE DAWN

65.   Choking on the fog, mountain warblers
      still make little music;
   piercing the sand, the shoots of reeds
      barely put forth leaves.

YÜAN CHEN

66.   Upon the terrace there is wine—
      warblers call the guests!
   the water's surface has no dust—
      breezes wash the pond!

PO CHÜ-I

67.   The warblers' songs seduce me into walking beneath the flowers;
   the grasses' colors hold me sitting by the riverside.

PO CHÜ-I

68.   Moved by the same kind, they'll seek each other out:
   "Swan Separated" and "Departing Goose" harmonize
      with spring warblings!
   Joining disparate energies so that they finally merge as one:
   "dragon chants" and "fishes leaping" accompany
      dawn twitterings!

SUGAWARA NO FUNTOKI

69.   The sleeves of dancing girls from Yen stop moving:
   they sense confusion mixed with the old rhythm.

The hat pins of "Young Chous" bob up and down
as they glance toward warblings among the new plum blossoms.

SUGAWARA NO FUNTOKI

> Numbers 68 and 69 both come from a poem by Funtoki on a musical
> performance at the palace. In paraphrase, "The musical composi-
> tions, 'Swan Separated' and 'Departing Goose'—because they imitate
> the sounds of birds—attract the warblers, who sing along. The music
> of the transverse flute has been compared to the chanting of dragons,
> and it is said that the music of the *ch'in* plucked-string zither inspires
> fish to leap. Dragons and fish are of different 'energies' from birds, and
> yet these, too, mingle with the songs of the warblers. But when the
> dancing girls (as beautiful as a famous Chinese courtesan of Yen in
> northeastern China) hear the birdsongs, they stop dancing because
> the familiar rhythm of the piece has become confused. Courtiers with
> an ear for music like that of the famous connoisseur Chou Yü (Young
> Chou) nod in the direction of the birdsongs, as Chou Yü is said to
> have done whenever he discerned an error in the performance."

70. Its new path at the present season
         penetrates old snow;
     its old nest from this time forth
         belongs to springtime clouds.

SUGAWARA NO MICHIZANE

71. At the western pavilion, as the moon sets,
         its song among the flowers!
     In the central palace, while lamps die out,
         its notes within bamboo!

SUGAWARA NO FUNTOKI

72. *On that very morning*
     When the verdant year turns
     What we await
     Is the first sound of the warbler's voice.

SOSEI

73. *There is no one*
     Who does not await
     the first sound of the nightingale
     In the pale verdant sky
     Of the rising spring.

     REIKEIDEN NO NYŌGO

74. *If the voice of the nightingale*
     Did not sound
     How could I know
     That spring has come
     To this mountain village of unmelted snow?

     NAKATSUKASA

Tinted Clouds

75. The clouds' radiance after dawn
        is redder than a fire;
     the grasses' color as skies clear
        is softer than any mist.

     PO CHÜ-I

76. Grasses, drilling through the sand,
        just three inches tall;
     clouds, straddling forests,
        only half a foot or so.

     SUGAWARA NO MICHIZANE

77. *The old year*
     Ended only yesterday;
     Yet the spring mists
     Are already rising
     On Mount Kasuga.

     ANONYMOUS

78. *Where is it*
    That the mists of spring are rising?
    Here in the mountains of beautiful Yoshino
    the snow continues to fall.

ANONYMOUS

79. *Here and there*
    The snow has melted
    On the peaks, and
    Bathed in morning sunlight,
    The haze of spring floats up.

TAIRA NO KANEMORI

Rain

80. Sometimes they hang beneath the flowers,
    secretly adding to the grief of Mo Tzu.
    Or at times they dance among the temple hairs,
    silently moving the thoughts of Master P'an.

PROSEPOEM ON THE FINE RAINS SCATTERING
THEIR THREADS

> Mo Tzu, one of the major philosophers of ancient China, wept as he
> watched white threads being dyed black. P'an Yüeh (d. 300), a poet
> famous for his laments on the death of his wife, was also known for his
> good looks. He is said to have grieved when he looked into a mirror
> and saw white hairs appearing on his head.

81. At Eternal Joy Palace, the sounds of bells
        die beyond the flowers;
    at Dragon Pond, the willow colors
        deepen with the rain.

"LI CHIAO" (ACTUALLY CH'IEN CH'I)

82. In nurturing, of course, it is the father and mother of flowers;

it moistens them all: how could it discriminate
between "sovereign" and "subject" herbs?

KI NO HASEO

The ancient Chinese pharmacopeia *The Classic of Basic Herbs* dis-
tinguishes three levels of *materia medica*: "sovereign," "minister"
(translated here as "subject"), and "assistant."

83. On days when flowers are newly opened,
     the dawn sun is moist with it;
when birds are aged and ready to go home,
     the evening sunset is darkened.

SUGAWARA NO FUNTOKI

This couplet makes the point that spring begins and ends with rain.

84. Its slanting footsteps, in places where
     warm breezes start to waft;
its hidden sounds, along the way
     where dawn sun's not yet cleared.

YOSHISHIGE NO YASUTANE

85. *Seeking out the cherries*
The rain began to fall;
Yet as I came to hunt those flowers
Now I would take shelter
In their shade.

ANONYMOUS

86. *Spring rain,*
Dropping from the branches
Of the fresh willows:
They appear as pearls
Pierced through with a thread.

LADY ISE

87.   White slivers, falling plum petals
        float on gully waters;
     yellow tips, the new-grown willows
        emerge above city walls.

PO CHÜ-I

88.   Plum blossoms, touched with snowflakes,
        fly onto our lutes;
     willow colors, blended with mist,
        enter our wine cups.

CHANG HSIAO-PIAO

89.   Slowly perfumed beneath the new seal of winter snow;
     stealthily budding even before springtime winds have wafted.

EMPEROR MURAKAMI

90.   Green threads weave the willows
        in front of T'ao Ch'ien's gate;
     white jade is fashioned
        into the plum on the Ridge of Yü.

ŌE NO ASATSUNA

> T'ao Ch'ien (365–427), one of China's greatest poets, wrote an auto-
> biographical sketch entitled "Mr. Five Willows." The Ridge of (the
> Greater) Yü is one of five in China's Kuang-chou (Canton) Province
> famous for the beauty of their plum blossoms.

91.   On Five Ridges, rich in greenery, clouds come and go;
     still we only love the ten thousand plum trees
        of the Ridge of the Greater Yü.

UNATTRIBUTED

92. Who says spring colors come from the east?
     Exposed to warmth, the southern branches are first
        to open blossoms.

SUGAWARA NO FUNTOKI

93. *Our young spring sapling*
     We dug and moved last year
     Has burst forth in bloom

ABE NO HIRONIWA

94. *I thought to show to you,*
     My beloved,
     The flowering plum,
     But it cannot be seen,
     As the snow is falling.

YAMABE NO AKAHITO

95. *Plum blossoms:*
     I went to check their fragrance—
     No one has broken their branches
     Yet, I know not why,
     You mists that are hiding them—
     Dissolve and go away!

ŌSHIKŌCHI NO MITSUNE

Red Plum

96. The plum holds "chicken tongue,"
        perfume with reddish vapor;
     the river displays its jeweled blossoms,
        waves showing emerald patterns.

YÜAN CHEN

     "Chicken tongue" is a variety of incense.

97. The pale red, so freshly elegant
    that "vermilion snow," prescription of immortals,
    is embarrassed at its color;
    the rich perfume so fragrantly wafting
    that smoke from courtesans' braziers
    must yield in aroma.

    TACHIBANA NO MASAMICHI

98. Possessing color, they're easily discerned beneath remaining snow;
    those lacking feeling will find it hard
        to distinguish them in setting sunlight.

    PRINCE KANEAKIRA

99. In the mortar of the immortals, wind wafts them up,
        trying in vain to winnow this snow;
    in the wilds, braziers, their fires glowing,
        yet never raising smoke.

    KI NO TADANA

    > This is a complex parallel couplet, in which the first line evokes white
    > plum blossoms and the second calls forth the red variety. The imagery
    > of the first line appears to conflate two metaphors: the white blossoms
    > are compared to snowflakes (a conventional comparison in Chinese
    > poetry) and, at the same time, to the white powder that appears in the
    > alchemist's alembic or brazier as he attempts to concoct a particular
    > type of elixir.

100. *Show this plum blossom*
     To someone other than yourself:
     Is there another who can grasp
     Its color and its perfume?

     KI NO TOMONORI

101. *I do not dwell on the color, the perfume*

Of the plum blossoms, but compare them
To the transience of this world.

EMPEROR KAZAN

Willows

102. The forest warblers, where are they singing
      like bridges on a zither?
      The wall-topping willows, at whose house do they expose
      their yellow "dust of malt?"

PO CHÜ-I

103. They've grown to the point that they can brush
      those horseback-riding guests,
      but still don't really hide from view
      the men who climb the tower.

PO CHÜ-I

104. The flowers at the shrine of the goddess of Wu—
      redder than her rouge;
      the willows at the village of Wang Chao-chün—
      greener than her eye shadow.

PO CHÜ-I

105. Now, indeed, I realize as I've gotten older,
      my inspiration has slackened:
      facing all of this, no matter how I try,
      I can't write a line of poetry!

PO CHÜ-I

   "All of this" refers to the beautiful scene described in the previous
   couplet (number 104). Of course, the statement is playfully self-con-
   tradicting, as it actually forms part of a poem! Numbers 104 and 105
   together constitute a complete quatrain.

106. The plum blossoms at the Ridge of Greater Yü
        have already fallen;
     who comes to ask of their powdered makeup?
     And the apricot blossoms of K'uang-Lu Mountain
        have not yet opened;
     why should anyone hasten to their red elegance?

ŌE NO KORETOKI

> The connection of this passage with the theme of willows is implied
> by a process of elimination: since the plums are gone and the apricot
> not yet arrived, the willows are the only thing of beauty to be seen.

107. Clouds propping up a mirror of red—
        the sun from the Fu-sang Tree!
     Springtime twirling strands of yellow pearls—
        breezes through young willows!

SHIMADA NO TADAOMI

> In ancient Chinese belief, "Fu-sang Tree" refers to a tree in the Far
> East from whose branches the dawn sun arises. As it appears in the
> morning, the sun reminds the poet of a round, bronze mirror.

108. At Hsi K'ang's house, they greet clear skies—
        courtyard moonlight darkens;
     Along Lu's pond, with every day,
        the water mist is thicker.

PRINCE TOMOHIRA

> The couplet refers to two famous men of the Six Dynasties period in
> China. Hsi K'ang (223–262) was one of the so-called Seven Sages of
> the Bamboo Grove and a poet and musician known for his mastery of
> the *ch'in* (Chinese zither). "Lu" refers to Lu Hui-hsiao, an official of
> the Southern Ch'i dynasty (479–501), known for his perspicacity. In
> the official Chinese histories, willows are said to have grown at the res-
> idences of both men. The meaning of the first line is that the willows
> have flourished to the point that they block the moonlight even on an
> unclouded night.

109. At the heart of the pond, the moon is floating—

they interweave with cassia branches!
Along the shore, the breeze is blowing—
they mingle with duckweed leaves!

SUGAWARA NO FUNTOKI

This couplet describes how the willow branches dip into the pond, or
are reflected in the pond, where either the branches themselves or
their reflections (or both) seem to cross the branches of the cassia tree
traditionally said to grow in the moon, here reflected in the water.

110. *It is the moment in spring*
When the strands of the green willow
Twist and twine together,
Just as the flowers in great profusion
Burst into bloom.

KI NO TSURAYUKI

111. *With the coming of spring*
Just as the threads of the willow tangle
So are the thoughts of my absent lover.

ANONYMOUS

112. *Like threads once wrapped in a cocoon,*
The strands of the spring willow
Now surpass themselves with deepening color.

FUJIWARA NO KANESUKE

Flowers—with Falling Flowers

113.   Flowers shine in the Imperial Garden;
swift carriages race in the dust of the nine avenues.
Gibbons cry on the deserted mountain;
slanting moonlight glitters on the paths to a thousand cliffs.

ATTRIBUTED TO CHANG TU, AN UNKNOWN CHINESE POET
OF THE T'ANG DYNASTY

PROSEPOEM ON LEISURE

114.   The pool's colors radiate—indigo dyes the water;
        the flowers' brilliance scintillates—fire scorches spring.

PO CHÜ-I

115.   If from far, I see a house with flowers,
            I just go in;
        I don't worry about whether they're high or low,
            acquaintances or not!

PO CHÜ-I

116.   Glittering in sunlight, glittering in the breeze:
        high and low, a thousand kernels, ten thousand kernels of jade!
        Dyeing the branches, dyeing the ripples:
        surface and lining, once steeped, twice steeped, in rouge!

SUGAWARA NO FUNTOKI

FLOWERS' RADIANCE FLOATING ON THE WATER

117.   Who says the water lacks a heart?
        When rich loveliness overhangs, ah! the waves change color!
        And who says flowers cannot speak?
        When light ripples float them, ah! reflected, they move their lips!

SUGAWARA NO FUNTOKI

> Numbers 116 and 117 both come from the same source: "Flowers'
> Radiance Floating on the Water." The title as given is an abbreviated
> version of the full title: "Preface to My Poem on the Theme 'Flowers'
> Radiance Floating on the Water' Which All Were to Compose While
> in Attendance at a Banquet in Late Spring at the Pool Pavilion of the
> Cold Spring Courtyard."

118.   Would you call this water?
        But it is the mirror, pure and glittering,
            used by the women of Han to put on makeup!
        Would you call these flowers?

But it is brocade, dazzlingly lovely,
  its patterning washed by the people of Shu!

MINAMOTO NO SHITAGŌ

SAME THEME AS ABOVE

119. What threads are they woven from?
    —it's only evening rain.
  They're cut from no fixed pattern,
    just by the springtime breeze.

SUGAWARA NO FUNTOKI

120. The flowers fly like broidery—
    how many layers of makeup?
  The weaver is the springtime breeze;
    they've not been folded in boxes!

MINAMOTO NO FUSAAKIRA

    These "boxes" would ordinarily be used to store the fine, carefully
    folded, embroideries, but these, woven of blossoms by the wind, are
    freely floating on the breeze.

121. Now I realize the spring wind's skill
    on the weaver's loom:
  not only does it weave in colors,
    but fragrances as well!

MINAMOTO NO FUSAAKIRA

    Numbers 120 and 121 come from the same poem.

122. My eyes have grown poor in viewing broideries
    left over from the weaving in Shu Province;
  my ears had grown weary of hearing zither tunes
    —now done playing—from Ch'in City.

MINAMOTO NO SUKENORI

The first line of this couplet refers to flowers as embroideries produced in Szechwan, China, a place famous for fine weaving. Now, however, the blossoms have largely scattered. The second line uses the music of the Chinese zither—particularly excellent in the ancient northwestern state of Ch'in—to characterize the singing of the warbler that now, as spring draws to a close, is no longer to be heard.

123. *If there were no cherry blossoms whatsoever*
      In this world,
      Then how tranquil our hearts might be
      In spring!

ARIWARA NO NARIHIRA

124. *Those who come to visit*
      The flowers in my garden:
      How I shall miss them,
      Now that the petals have fallen.

ŌSHIKŌCHI NO MITSUNE

125. *Are we alone to see*
      These mountain cherries?
      To show the others,
      Shall we break off branches
      To carry back as gifts?

SOSEI

Falling Flowers

126. The falling flowers without a word
            simply leave the branch;
      the flowing water has no heart,
            by nature it enters the pond.

PO CHÜ-I

127. At dawn we tread the fallen flowers
          as we go out together;
      with evening we follow the flying birds,
          returning in time with them.

PO CHÜ-I

128. The spring blossoms, one by one,
      crash the party where all are happily drunk;
      late-season warblers, note by note,
      participate in the symposium where poetry is recited.

ŌE NO ASATSUNA

129. The fallen petals lie scattered in confusion
          since the wind went wild;
      the singing birds have lapsed into silence
          now that the rain has battered them.

ŌE NO ASATSUNA

130. They flit from the pavilion—phoenix wings!—
          pirouetting down balustrades;
      they descend the tower—dancing girls' sleeves!—
          twirling against the stairs.

SUGAWARA NO FUNTOKI

131. *The wind blowing beneath the trees*
      Where the petals fall
      Does not feel cold at all;
      Snow, unacknowledged by the sky,
      Is falling.

KI NO TSURAYUKI

132. *You servants who keep the palace clean!*

If you have any feelings
Appropriate to this spring day,
Give up your sweeping!
[so that the beauty of the fallen leaves can be seen]

ANONYMOUS

Wisteria

133. I sadly yearn for Compassion Temple
          as the third month draws to a close,
      where purple wisteria blossoms fall,
          and birds sing harmoniously.

PO CHÜ-I

134. The purple wisteria, beneath the dew —
          remaining hues of petals;
      the blue-green bamboo, wrapped in mist,
          late-season songs of birds.

MINAMOTO NO SUKENORI

135. *At the Bay of Tako*
      The wisteria are at their height,
      Let us break off these sprays to decorate our hair
      To show those at home
      Who have not seen them.

NAWAMARO

136. *The pine retains its reputation*
      For changeless green,
      While the wisteria, clinging there,
      Blooms, then aimlessly fades away.

KI NO TSURAYUKI

Azaleas

137. Late-season stamens still in blossom—
       red azaleas!
     Autumn corollas now first forming—
       white hibiscus flowers!

PO CHÜ-I

138. Night wanderers will want to seek them out
         to use as torches;
     Cold Food Festival families
         must be surprised to pluck them!

MINAMOTO NO SHITAGŌ

> The azaleas are such a brilliant red that they resemble fire. Those who
> walk out of doors at night could use them to illuminate their way.
> They will come as a surprise at the Cold Food Festival (105 days after
> the winter solstice), during which fires are prohibited.

139. *My thoughts,*
     Like mountain azaleas
     Blooming on Tokiwa Mountain:
     Though I do not speak them,
     My love is strong.

ANONYMOUS

Yamabuki *(yellow rose)*

140. Daubing them with yellow ocher, Heaven is quite right:
     the "knock-on-winter" is wrong to bud in the late-spring breeze.

UNATTRIBUTED

> The flower known as "knock-on-winter" in China blooms in late win-
> ter, hence the name. But the Japanese flower apparently in question
> here appears in late spring. Heaven corrects the error implicit in their

name by coloring them yellow, "yellow ocher" being the substance used to correct errors in old books.

141. At my study window, there are volumes,
     neatly stacked together;
the official pages bear no text—
commands not yet received.

YOSHISHIGE NO YASUTANE

The yellow flowers are compared to books with yellow pages, used to record imperial commands. They have no writing on them, of course. (The yellow coloration of certain old books was caused by the dyeing of the paper with a special yellow substance to prevent insect damage.)

142. *Reflected in the waters*
At the Kamunabi River
Where the frogs sing,
Are the yellow mountain roses
In full bloom now?

ATSUMO NO ŌKIMI

143. *If only one*
Of these eightfold mountain roses in my garden
Might remain, unfallen,
As a souvenir of spring!

TAIRA NO KANEMORI

Summer

Changing Garments

144. Back to the wall, the guttering lamp
     has shone all through the night;

opening the box, I find robes and sash
    still fragrant after a year.

PO CHÜ-I

145. Light silk clothes—I'm waiting for our people
    to prepare them for me to wear;
vintage brew—I think I'll call the village elders
    for a drink.

SUGAWARA NO MICHIZANE

WRITTEN AT SANUKI

146. *How sad to change my garments*
Dyed in the colors of spring
On this day that is chosen
For summer clothing.

MINAMOTO NO SHIGEYUKI

The Start of Summer

147. The "bamboo leaf" wine stored in jars
    is ready after a whole spring;
the roses growing beneath the stairs
    now blossom as we enter summer.

PO CHÜ-I

148. Mosses grow upon the rocks,
    their light clothes worn short;
lotus blossoms emerge from the pond,
    their little canopies sparse.

MONONOBE NO YASUOKI

149. *I thought that the fence around my house*
Kept out the spring;

Now, seeing the white blossoms of the unohana
I know that summer has come.

MINAMOTO NO SHITAGŌ

Summer Nights

150.   The wind blows through the withered trees—
          rain beneath clear skies!
       The moon illuminates level sands—
          frost on a summer night!

PO CHÜ-I

151.   Nights when breezes blow from bamboo
          I sleep beside the window;
       times when the moon illuminates the pines,
          I walk out on the terrace.

PO CHÜ-I

152.   A moonless night sky, the window tranquil
          after fireflies have gone by;
       then, deep in the night, the porch all white
          as the bright moon rises.

"PO" [?]

153.   *Those poets of olden times*
       Who wrote that summer dawns would come
       Even before they slept—
       Were they never troubled
       By thoughts of love?

ANONYMOUS

154.   *The cry of the cuckoo,*
       Brief as a summer's night

As, lying alone,
Thoughts of my loved one come.

ANONYMOUS

155. No sooner to lie down
On a summer's night
Then, with the cry of a cuckoo,
The dawn comes faintly.

KI NO TSURAYUKI

The Tuan-wu Festival

156. At times he dangles precariously from the doorway's lintel;
he has no prospect of walking freely in his garden back home.

SUGARAWARA NO MICHIZANE

"ARTEMESIA MAN"

A human figure made of artemisia would be hung in the doorway to
ward off evil spirits on the occasion of the Tuan-wu Festival, which
occurs on the fifth day of the fifth lunar month, or nearly midway
through the summer. Michizane, who wrote this poem in exile, may
have been subtly hinting at his own situation, involving his fruitless
desire to return to the capital.

157. My colt,
Just like my iris today
And both too young—
They'll surely lose!

ŌNAKATOMI NO YORIMOTO

During the Tango Festival, held on the fifth day of the fifth month, iris
roots were suspended from the eaves of roofs to ward off evil influ-
ences. The longest roots were regarded as the best. Young horses were
also raced in competitions on those days.

158. *Until yesterday*
I felt no connection to the iris;
Now they bloom on the eaves of my house,
Dear as my own wife.

ŌNAKATOMI NO YOSHINOBU

> The poem contains a pun involving *tsuma* (wife) and *tsuma* (the edge of the eaves of a roof).

Enjoying Coolness

159.   Upon the ground of green moss dissolves remaining heat;
beneath the shade of verdant trees I pursue the evening coolness.

PO CHÜ-I

160.   The dew-moistened mat freshly glitters,
glossy as it welcomes night;
my breeze-swept lapels refreshingly flutter,
cool long before the fall.

PO CHÜ-I

161.   It's not that no heat ever comes to these chambers of Zen,
but when you can make the mind serene, the body will feel cool.

PO CHÜ-I

162. Imperial concubine Pan's fan of clustered snow?
—Replaced by wind along the shore, it is forever forgotten.
King Chao of Yen's "Coolness-Summoning Pearl"?
—In the moonlight glimmering on the sand, we've found one for ourselves.

ŌE NO MASAHIRA

> "Imperial concubine Pan" (Pan *chieh-yü*) of the Han dynasty is famous for a poem in which she compares herself to a round, snow white fan that is discarded once the summer is over and it is no longer needed to produce coolness.

163. Lying, I view the scenery—a newly painted screen
       of gazing at the water;
     walking, I chant poems from old collections that describe
       enjoying the coolness.

SUGAWARA NO MICHIZANE

164. The pool is chilly, the water has nothing of the dog days of summer;
     the pines are tall, the wind has a sound that conjures autumn.

MINAMOTO NO FUSAAKIRA

165. *I thought it might be cool,*
     Yet going through the clumps of grasses
     Those summer wild pinks blooming there
     Make it seem all the hotter!

ANONYMOUS

166. *The water which drips and flows*
     Seems to have come from autumn itself:
     How cool the water of the spring is
     In my hand!

NAKATSUKASA

167. *Each time I scoop the water*
     From the spring between the rocks,
     Shaded by the pines,
     It seems a year
     Without a summer!

EGYŌ

Late Summer

168. At the bamboo pavilion, shade congeals,
       perfectly suited to summer;

by the water-view balustrade, the breeze blows cool,
  no need to wait for autumn.

PO CHÜ-I

169. *Which first*
  Will be put upon the ground—
  The summer fan no longer needed,
  Or the autumn frost itself?

MIBU NO TADAMINE

170. *Even the fierce gods*
  Who never listen, each time we pray,
  Are surely pacified
  On this day of the Summer Ceremonies,
  So people say.

MINAMOTO NO SHITAGŌ

Orange Blossoms

171. The orange fruits hang heavy
    in the mountain rain;
  the palm-tree fronds waft coolness
    of breezes from the lake.

PO CHÜ-I

172. Branches have gold bells attached
    after the spring rain;
  blossoms waft a purple musk
    along the southern wind.

PRINCE TOMOHIRA

173. *Breathing the odor*
  From the orange blossoms
  That wait for the fifth month to bloom,

I inhale the fragrance of the sleeves
Of a love of long ago.

ANONYMOUS

174. *Cuckoo, you seek out*
The odor of the orange blossoms
As you sing:
Do you mourn a lost love?

ANONYMOUS

Lotus

175. Windblown lotus—the aging leaves
        still mournfully green;
    waterside smartweed—remaining blossoms
        desolately red.

PO CHÜ-I

> Although this is an autumn poem, it apparently is included here
> because of the reference to "windblown lotus leaves."

176. As leaves unfurl, their shadows turn
        in moonlight on the steps;
    the flowers open, their perfume wafts
        on breezes through the blinds.

PO CHÜ-I

177. The mist is parted by their fans of green,
        this morning of pure wind;
    the water floats their robes of red,
        this autumn of white dew.

HSÜ HUN

> Like number 175, this autumn poem is included here because it
> describes lotus.

178. Bamboo branches on the shore hang low—
     fit perch for birds;
     lotus leaves in the pond are moving—
     that must be fish swimming!

KI NO ARIMASA

179. What need is there to go off searching
     remote spots in the Wu Mountains?
     Here they are, flowers growing
     beneath our sovereign's throne!

EMPEROR DAIGO

> This poem was composed during the Engi period (901–923). It
> describes the screen painting "Thousand-Leaved Lotus at the Wu
> Mountains." The "sovereign" referred to is not Emperor Daigo him-
> self, but the cloistered emperor Uda (r. 887–897).

180. A sutra has been named for you,
     Buddha taken you for his eyes:
     We know that you among all flowers
     have planted the roots of goodness.

MINAMOTO NO TAMENORI

> This couplet uses Buddhist imagery to eulogize the lotus. The Lotus
> Sutra, one of Buddhism's most important sacred texts, was named
> after it, and in the Vimalakirti Sutra, Buddha's eyes are compared to
> lotus blossoms.

181. *The leaves of the lotus*
     Remain unsullied
     By the water's filth;
     Why then do the jewel-like drops of dew
     Deceive us?

BISHOP HENJŌ

Hototogisu *(Cuckoo)*

182. A single song of the mountain bird
        beyond the clouds of dawn;
ten thousand water-fireflies,
    points in autumnal grass.

H S Ü   H U N

183. *In the [rainy] darkness*
Of the fifth month,
The sound of the hototogisu
Grows more distant
In the dimness.

A S U K A   N O   M I K O

184. *I did not move ahead*
But stayed here on the mountain path,
For I wanted to hear again
The voice of the hotogisu.

F U J I W A R A   N O   K I N T A D A

185. *If I had never woken up*
This night, then I could only know
the voice of the hototogisu
By what the others
Might have told me!

M I B U   N O   T A D A M I

Fireflies

186. The fireflies' lights fly randomly—
        autumn's getting near;

the water star sinks early now—
nights begin to lengthen.

YÜAN CHEN

The "water star" is the planet Mercury.

187. When reed-grown water darkens,
     the fireflies know it's night;
     when wind in the willows blows briskly,
     geese will usher in the fall.

HSÜ HUN

188. Bright, bright, they're still here—
     who needs to seek moonlight up on the roof?
     Brilliant, brilliant, never melting—
     how did snowflakes pile up around my bed?

KI (NO HASEO)

PROSEPOEM ON AUTUMN FIREFLIES ILLUMINATING BOOKS

The passage is based on two allusions to poor scholars who could not afford to use lamps but were so eager to continue their reading at night that one of them climbed up on the roof to read by moonlight while the other read in bed by moonlight reflected off the snow outside his bedroom window.

189. Through the pages of the *Mountain Classic*—
     as if passing among peaks!
     Among the verses of the Ocean Prosepoem—
     they seem to live in the waves!

TACHIBANA NO NAOMOTO

SAME THEME AS ABOVE

This conceit is that as the fireflies flit through (presumably illustrated) copies of the *Mountain [and Ocean] Classic* and the *Ocean Prosepoem* (both actual Chinese works), they seem to be among real peaks and waves.

190. *The grass is thick, the house in ruin;*
     The wind never stopped the flickering light:
     It must have been a firefly!

ANONYMOUS

191. *Conceal them as I may,*
     My thoughts, like summer fireflies
     Reveal themselves:
     Thoughts of love, burning bright.

ANONYMOUS

Cicadas

192. Slowly, slowly, ah! spring sun,
     when jade tiles are warm, ah! hot springs drip.
     Gently, gently, ah! autumn wind,
     when mountain cicadas drone, ah! palace trees redden.

PO CHÜ-I

Whereas most of Po Chü-i's couplets in the *Wakan rōei shū* are taken from his *lü-shih*, or "regulated-verse" poems—usually consisting of eight lines with five (or seven; rarely six) characters per line throughout the poem—this couplet comes from the twenty-first of Po's important series of fifty poems of social commentary or protest, the *Hsin yüeh-fu* (New music bureau ballads), named after the Han dynasty institution that was said to have collected folk poems reflecting the people's various concerns. Po himself complained that his enormous popularity in China itself was based on what he considered his more frivolous works, whereas the *Hsin yüeh-fu*, which he was particularly proud of having written, were relatively unknown. In later centuries, too, of all Po's works, these tended to be the least known. It is interesting that the *Wakan rōei shū*'s editor demonstrates here a knowledge of these poems. "Li Palace Is Tall," the first of the fifty, starts by describing one of the emperor's "detached" palaces (Japanese emperors would emulate the Chinese example by building such residences for temporary stays or vacations, for example, the famed Katsura *rikyū*), indicating that the place is in a state of disrepair because the emperor has not gone there for years. Po then praises the emperor for his consideration in remaining at the central palace, because of His Majesty's realization that such an excursion would involve an enormous waste of manpower and resources. The poem is therefore a type of memorial in verse, expressing a policy suggestion through a eulogy of the emperor.

193.   Over a thousand peaks the bird paths
    are moistened by Plum Rain;
in the fifth month, cicadas' voices
    escort the Wheat-Crop Autumn.

LI CHIA-YU

"Plum Rain" and "Wheat-Crop Autumn" are calendrical terms, the first referring to the fourth or fifth month of the lunar calendar and the second to the fourth month, actually the first summer month but apparently considered to have an autumnal tinge because of the ripening of the wheat.

194.   Birds alight on green weeds—
    the garden of Ch'in, deserted.
Cicadas drone among yellow leaves—
    the palace of Han turns autumnal.

HSÜ HUN

195.   This year, even more than usual,
    my heart breaks at their sound:
it's not that the cicadas are so sad,
    but the traveler is sad.

SUGAWARA NO MICHIZANE

196.   The years come, and the years go,
    yet we hear them without change:
do not say that after fall

they simply disappear.

KI NO HASEO

197. *How high the tips of the branches*
      On the summer peaks;
      I seem to hear the voice of the cicada
      From the heights of heaven itself.

ANONYMOUS

198. *Just look—those who will not acknowledge love*
      For fear of reproof
      Show themselves to be no more
      Than the husk of a weeping cicada.

MINAMOTO NO SHIGEMITSU

Fans

199. It is unmelted snow at the height of summer,
      unlimited wind throughout the year.
      Summon autumn, it appears in your hand!
      Hide away the moon: just tuck it in your lapel!

PO CHÜ-I

200. No need to wait for the night water-clock
          to sound out the first watch;
      only play with it during the time
          before the autumn wind starts to blow.

SUGAWARA NO FUNTOKI

      The fan looks like the moon but can "come out" at any time, unlike
      the real moon that emerges only at night.

201. *The banks of the river of stars in heaven*
      Must surely be cool,

For this Festival of the Weaver;
Yet let me lend my fan to cool
Those celestial loves as well.

NAKATSUKASA

The Festival of the Weaver (Tanabata) occurs on the seventh day of
the seventh month.

202. The breeze from this fan
Will clear the mist
From the Milky Way,
And the bridge of stars
Will cross the clear sky.

KIYOWARA NO MOTOSUKE

SAME THEME AS ABOVE

203. Giving over to you this fan
That moves the winds of autumn,
The grasses will surely never fail
To be moved [by your virtue].

NAKATSUKA

The poem incorporates a reference to the Analects of Confucius
(XII, 19), which states, "The virtue of the gentleman is as the wind;
the virtue of the petty man is as the grass." This is thus a poem prais-
ing imperial virtue.

Autumn

Establishment of Autumn

204. Sighing, soughing, this cool wind
and my graying temple-hair:
who arranged it so that they would turn autumnal together?

PO CHÜ-I

205. As chickens gradually disappear,
         Autumn colors still few;
      where Li was wont to hasten by,
         the evening sound is faint.

YOSHISHIGE NO YASUTANE

> This couplet describes the courtyard of the residence of a recently
> deceased teacher. The chickens he used to feed no longer come. Be-
> cause it is still early autumn, the sounds of leaves falling from the trees
> is still faint. In a famous passage in the Confucian *Analects*, Li, the son
> of Confucius, describes how one day when he was hastening past the
> courtyard, his father questioned him as to his reading of the classics.

206. *Autumn has come:*
      The eye cannot sees nothing clearly,
      But the sound of the wind
      Brings a sudden awareness.

FUJIWARA NO TOSHIYUKI

207. *A sudden sense of sorrow:*
      I realize that the beginning of autumn,
      Has come
      With the falling of the leaves

ANONYMOUS

Early Autumn

208. We're simply pleased that summer's heat
         has left with the dog days,
      but unaware that autumn has brought
         a second color to our hair.

PO CHÜ-I

209. Rain through the locust blossoms
         moistens earth newly autumnal;

wind in the paulownia leaves
    cools sky on the brink of night.

PO CHÜ-I

210. Some flaming heat remains here yet—
    our clothes are still quite thick;
the morning cool comes secretly—
    first known by bamboo mats.

KI NO HASEO

> The second line of this couplet remarkably anticipates a famous pas-
> sage from a poem by the great Sung dynasty poet Su Shih (Su Tung-
> p'o, 1037–1101), "[On the Painting] 'Evening View Along the River in
> Spring' by Hui-ch'ung": "Beyond the bamboo, flowering peach, two
> or three branches;/along the spring river, the water is warming—the
> ducks are the first to know."

211. *Only a few days*
    Since the beginning of autumn,
    Yet, awakening in the morning,
    How cold are my sleeves.

SHIKI NO MIKO

The Seventh Night

The seventh night of the seventh month of the lunar calendar is associated with
the romantic legend of two stars, the Herd Boy (in Aquila) and the Weaving
Girl (Vega in Lyra). Although they are in love, they can meet only on this night,
when magpies form a bridge for them to pass over.

212. I remember how when I was young
    we always "Prayed for Skill";
hanging from the bamboo poles
    the votive threads were many!

"PO"

Young men and women would celebrate the seventh night by hang-
ing colored threads from poles and performing other ceremonies. The
men would pray to the two stars for success in literature, and the
women, for skill in embroidery and other womanly tasks.

213. The two stars together now
have still not told the entirety of the pain of parting;
the fifth watch, and soon the dawn—
they're often startled by the cool wind's sighing, sighing sound.

ONO NO YOSHIKI

214. The dew becomes their parting tears,
    pearls that fall in vain;
the clouds are fragments of her toilette,
    hairdo not yet formed.

SUGAWARA NO MICHIZANE

215. From last night, the sound of the wind
    has become much sadder;
and with the crack of dawn, the dew
    is tears innumerable.

NO ATTRIBUTION IN TEXT; ACTUALLY BY ŌE NO ASATSUNA

216. As she goes, her robe touches waves—
    these clouds must turn all moist;
the candle lighting their way dips in water—
    this moon will soon go out.

SUGAWARA NO FUNTOKI

    The two lovers must cross the Heavenly River (the Milky Way)
    to meet.

217. Although her vows she has entrusted
    to the gentle ripples,

her heart expects the crescent moon
   to be her go-between.

SUGAWARA NO SUKEAKIRA (THE SON OF SUGAWARA NO
FUNTOKI, AUTHOR OF THE PREVIOUS COUPLET)

218. *Crossing the Milky Way*
      Is not so far,
      And so it is I wait for you to cross
      The whole year long.

KAKINOMOTO NO HITOMARO

219. *Although their meeting can occur*
      Only one night a year,
      The star lovers can meet
      For endless autumns!

KI NO TSURAYUKI

220. *True, they can meet only*
      Once a year,
      Yet how few times
      The star lovers
      Have lain together!

ŌSHIKŌCHI NO MITSUNE

Autumn Inspirations

221. In the woods, we warm our wine
         burning the red leaves;
      on the rocks, we inscribe our poems,
         brushing off green moss.

PO CHÜ-I

222. Ch'u meditations everywhere,
         clouds and water chilly;

Shang tones sound, crisp and pure,
   winds and strings autumnal.

PO CHÜ-I

> "Ch'u" is the name of an ancient Chinese kingdom centering on the
> modern provinces of Hunan and Hupei, where Yellow Crane Terrace
> is located. The *Ch'u tz'u,* or "Songs of Ch'u," is an anthology of
> poems associated with the poet Ch'ü Yüan, who was exiled here in the
> fourth century B.C. The poems are filled with expressions of sadness
> and frustration. "*Shang*" is one of the notes of the Chinese pentatonic
> scale and is associated with the season of autumn.

223. In general, through all four seasons
     my heart is full of pain;
   but of them all, the one that breaks it
     is the time of autumn.

PO CHÜ-I

224. The forms of things quite naturally
     can wound the traveler's mood;
   we ought to take the character "grief"
     and write it as "fall heart."

ONO NO TAKAMURA

> The word *ch'ou,* or "grief," consists of an upper component, *ch'iu,* or
> "autumn," and a lower component, *hsin,* or "heart." The poet pro-
> poses dividing these components into two separate words.

225. It's always been in autumn-time that people have been moved;
   the reason is their hearts are tugged
     by that season's signs.

SHIMADA NO TADAOMI

226. And what place is the one that most profoundly
   moves men's hearts?

—Where wind through bamboo rustles leaves
  beneath the bright moonlight.

SHIMADA NO TADAOMI (ALSO BEARS AN ERRONEOUS
ATTRIBUTION TO PO CHÜ-I)

> Numbers 225 and 226 both come from the same poem by Shimada
> no Tadaomi.

227. Of Szechwan tea's floating froth-blossoms
  we've gradually forgotten the taste;
  of Ch'u silk's snow white colors being fulled
  the sound starts to be heard.

TAKAOKA NO SUKEYUKI

228. *The autumn bush clover blooming*
  In the deserted fields of Iware
  Where the young quail sings—
  Today I remember
  How I saw this with my beloved.

ANONYMOUS

229. *Autumn—so moving*
  In the dusk—
  The wind blows through the tips of the reeds,
  Their roots soaked with dew.

GENERAL FUJIWARA NO YOSHITAKA

Autumn Evenings

230. Thinking of him, at evening I ascend
  the pine-tree terrace and stand;
  cricket-thoughts, cicada-sounds—my ears are filled with autumn.

PO CHÜ-I

231. I gaze at the mountain—the hidden moon
    still conceals its image;
    I listen to the stairs—the splashing stream
    gradually increases its sound.

SUGAWARA NO FUNTOKI

232. *Autumn in nightfall:*
    The tips of the pampas grass,
    At the foot of Ogura Mountain,
    Dimly seen.

ANONYMOUS

Autumn Nights

233. Autumn nights so long,
    autumn nights she never sleeps, though sky never turns bright.
    Flickering in dying lamplight, her shadow on the wall behind.
    Soughing, soughing comes the sound of dark rain beating on the
        window.

PO CHÜ-I

> These lines come from another of Po's great series of protest poems,
> the *Hsin yüeh-fu* (see number 192 for the previous example). This one
> laments the sad fate of an imperial concubine doomed to languish in
> the Shang-yang Palace (one of several special palaces for concubines)
> from the age of sixteen to the age of sixty, not favored by the emperor
> because her youth was passed during his deep infatuation with the
> infamous Yang Kuei-fei.

234. Slow, slow, the water clock, as nights begin to lengthen;
    brilliant, brilliant, river of stars, the sky about to dawn.

PO CHÜ-I

> These lines come from Po's most famous poem, which tells the story of
> Emperor Ming-huang's doomed love for his concubine Yang Kuei-fei.

235. In Swallow Tower, nights of frosty moonlight:
as autumn comes, they lengthen for her alone.

PO CHÜ-I

> As Po relates in a preface to these poems, the tower was the residence
> for ten years of P'an-p'an, the concubine of a certain Secretary Chang.
> After Chang's death, she chose to reside there rather than serve a new
> master. (The couplet comes from the first of a set of three poems.)

236. On creeping vines, the dew thickens
where people have been put to sleep;
all night long, not one cloud,
only brilliant moonlight.

ONO NO TAKAMURA

237. Moored beside a reed-grown islet,
dreams in the solitary boat;
at the encampment among elms and willows,
hearts travel ten thousand miles.

KI NO TADANA

RAIN ON AN AUTUMN NIGHT

238. *On those long, long winter nights,*
Extending like the drooping tail
Of the mountain bird,
Must I then sleep alone?

ATTRIBUTED TO KAKINOMOTO NO HITOMARO

239. *Before I've finished talking to my love,*
The dawn has come—
What ever became of
Those autumn nights
Said to be so long?

ŌSHIKŌCHI NO MITSUNE

Night of the Fifteenth (with The Moon appended)

The fifteenth of the eighth month is the night of the Mid-Autumn Festival, considered to be the night of the most beautiful full moon of the year. On this night, moon-viewing gatherings are held, and poems are written about the moon.

240. A thousand or more miles of Ch'in domain:
crystal clear, the ice spreads out!
Thirty-six palaces of the house of Han:
sparkling, brilliant, the powdered makeup!

KUNG-CH'ENG I (*CHIN-SHIH* DEGREE, 871)

> These lines describe the effect of the moonlight on the night of the fifteenth, around the T'ang dynasty capital, Ch'ang-an.

241. On the loom where she weaves embroidery,
already can be discerned the words of love.
On the blocks where clothes are fulled,
suddenly are added sounds of sadness at parting.

KUNG-CH'ENG I

THE ABOVE [TWO ENTRIES] ARE FROM THE "PROSEPOEM
ON THE NIGHT OF THE FIFTEENTH"

> The first half of this passage alludes to the story of a woman, Su Jo-lan, whose husband was away on official duty. She wove the text of a poem—a palindrome—into her embroidery to express her grief at this enforced parting.

242. On the night of the third five,
colors of the newly risen moon;
two thousand miles away,
the heart of my friend.

PO CHÜ-I

> Yüan the Ninth (referred to in the title) is Po Chü-i's great friend Yüan Chen, also an important poet and represented in the *Wakan rōei shū*.

243. Mount Sung: outside and inside, a thousand layers of snow;
The River Lo: above and below, two individual pearls!

PO CHÜ-I

244. Throughout the twelve months,
no night surpasses this night's loveliness.
Over thousands of miles, tens of thousands of miles,
all strive to view the brilliance that shines on our home.

KI NO HASEO

245. Emerald ripples, golden waves, early fifteenth night:
the autumn wind has planned to make it just like sky above!

SUGAWARA NO ATSUSHIGE (WRONGLY ATTRIBUTED TO
PO CHÜ-I)

> Numbers 245 through 248 form a complete eight-line "regulated verse"
> by Atsushige, entitled "The Moon's Reflection Filling the Autumn
> Pond." Hence in line 1, it is the pond that looks "just like sky above."

246. We think that frost has glazed the lotus
early in the season;
you'd say a rainfall had swept over every blossoming reed!

SUGAWARA NO ATSUSHIGE (WRONGLY ATTRIBUTED TO
PO CHÜ-I)

247. The shore so white, we take the beams
for cranes perched in the pines;
the pond turned translucent, one can count
fish among waterweeds!

SUGAWARA NO ATSUSHIGE (WRONGLY ATTRIBUTED TO
PO CHÜ-I)

248. Compared to this, that "Jasper Pond"

is an ordinary name;
the brilliant luminosity of this night
is lovelier than jade.

SUGAWARA NO ATSUSHIGE (WRONGLY ATTRIBUTED TO
PO CHÜ-I)

"Jasper Pond" is the name of the legendary location where in antiquity,
the Queen Mother of the West sumptuously entertained Emperor Mu
of the Chou dynasty.

249. Gold oil, one drop—dew in autumn wind;
jade box, third watch—clouds in cold River Han.

SUGAWARA NO FUNTOKI

The "gold oil" is used to polish bronze mirrors; the moon is thus
obliquely compared to such a mirror. The "jade box" would be
used to store the mirror; at the "third watch" of the night (11 P.M.–1
A.M.), the box is formed of clouds in the sky (the "River Han," or
Milky Way).

250. Yang Kuei-fei returning
to the T'ang emperor's thoughts;
Lady Li departing—
the Han monarch's sorrow!

MINAMOTO NO SHITAGŌ

This couplet compares the poet's sadness at not being able to see the
moon because of rain to the grief of two famous Chinese emperors
after the deaths of their favorite concubines.

251. *Seeing the reflection of the waves*
Where the moon shines on the surface of the pond,
And counting the days, I know
We have reached the very midst of autumn.

ANONYMOUS

The Moon

252. Who's been stationed for so long
        out beyond Lung-chou?
      And where's a new parting taking place
        in the courtyard out front?

PO CHÜ-I

> As the complete text of the poem reveals, the two lines of this cou-
> plet describe examples of situations in which the moonlight exacer-
> bates sorrow:
>
> THE MID-AUTUMN MOON
>
> Over ten thousand miles, the pure brilliancy
>   is beyond imagination,
> adding to sadness, increasing sorrow
>   throughout the entire world!
> *Who's been stationed for so long*
>   *out beyond Lung-chou?*
> *And where's a new parting taking place*
>   *in the courtyard out front?*
> Night when the former concubine, favor lost,
>   returns to her quarters;
> hour when the old general, fallen to barbarians,
>   ascends the lookout tower.
> How many people, hearts now broken,
>   does it shine upon?
> —And the Jade Rabbit and Silver Toad
>   completely unaware!
>
> In Chinese mythology, the Jade Rabbit and Silver Toad are inhabi-
> tants of the moon.

253. The autumn waters swell and rise,
        speeding the boat on its way;
      the nighttime clouds all disappear,
        the moon advances slowly.

"YEH CHAN YING" (ERRONEOUS FOR YING CHAN, A
COMPLETELY UNKNOWN FIGURE)

> This single couplet is the only surviving specimen of his work.

254. If you don't get drunk out at Ch'ien-chung
        how can you bear to go?
     The moon above the Mo-wei Mountains
        will be at its very brightest.

PO CHÜ-I

255. Hard to tell what year this snow
        fell on Heavenly Mountain;
     easy to take it for the pearls
        once gathered at Ho-p'u Bay.

MIMUNE NO MASAHIRA

256. Would you have it cause harmonious ringing
        of the Feng-ling bells?
     But what about the fact that cranes
        from Hua-t'ing cry in alarm?

PRINCE KANEAKIRA

      The moonlight may appear to be frost, which, according to one
      old text, causes the bells of Feng-ling to sound, but it might actually
      be dew, which another old text claims causes cranes to cry out
      in warning.

257. Tears of homesickness, several rows—
        the soldier off on duty;
     boatman's song, a single tune—
        the venerable fisherman.

YOSHISHIGE NO YASUTANE

      Both lines assume the presence of the moon.

258. When I look far into the heavens,
     Is that not that moon
     The same that rises
     From Kasuga at Mount Mikasa?

ABE NO NAKAMARO

259. *The geese*
Fly side by side in the white clouds:
Their very numbers can be counted
Under the brilliance of the autumn moon.

ANONYMOUS

260. *One is not always pensive*
In this world,
Yet I looked upon the moon
So many, many times.

PRINCE TOMOHIRA

The Ninth Day (with Chrysanthemums appended)

The ninth day of the ninth month of the lunar calendar is set aside for climbing to high places and enjoying the view.

261. The swallows know the Tutelary Day—
    they fly off from their nests;
 chrysanthemums, since it's the Ninth Day now,
    brave the rain to blossom.

"LI TUAN" (ACTUALLY HUANG-FU JAN)

There are two "Tutelary Days," dedicated to the local earth deity, one in spring and one in autumn.

262. Adopting practices from the time of Emperor Wu of Han,
we place dogwood branches in the robes of courtiers;
seeking out the customs of Emperor Wen of Wei,
we use the yellow flowers to aid the arts of ancestor P'eng.

KI NO HASEO

The association of dogwood with the Ninth Day Festival goes back to the time of Emperor Wu of the Han dynasty in the second century B.C. Chrysanthemums were believed to be an ingredient in certain recipes for the elixir of longevity or immortality of the sort particularly popu-

lar during the reign of Emperor Wen of the Wei dynasty in the third
century A.D. Ancestor P'eng was the oldest man in antiquity.

263. Before the Three Latenesses, ah! we blow the blossoms,
like morning stars whirling in the Heavenly Han River!
We take full cups, ah! floating their colors,
and think they are autumn snowflakes swirling in the River Lo!

KI NO HASEO

> Those who arrive late at formal banquets (there are three degrees of
> lateness) are penalized by being compelled to drink several cups of
> wine. All the various metaphors in this passage refer to the appearance
> of chrysanthemum petals floating where they are placed to celebrate
> the season and also to increase health and longevity. The "heavenly
> Han River" is the Milky Way.

264. In Sweet Valley's waters we float the blossoms:
those who draw water downstream and achieve supreme longevity
    number more than thirty people.
The "terrain's pulse" is mixed with other flavors:
those who imbibe the "sun's essence" and halt the aging of their faces
    live five hundred years.

KI NO HASEO

> Numbers 262, 263, and 264 all come from the same poem by Ki no
> Haseo, in which he describes a celebration of the Ninth Day Festival
> during which the emperor conferred chrysanthemum petals on the
> courtiers. This passage is based on various technical terms drawn from
> the vocabulary of alchemical Taoism. Certain spots in China, such as
> "Sweet Valley," were believed to produce water with particular medi-
> cinal properties that might add to the years of those who drank them
> under the proper circumstances. "Terrain's pulse" and "sun's essence"
> (terms for water from underground springs and a variety of chrysan-
> themum, respectively) are, according to old Taoist books, ingredients
> in elixirs of immortality.

265. *The clear dew*
That falls [this festival day]

On the chrysanthemums of my abode,
Will it not collect, as the ages go by,
Into a pool of Sweet Valley water?

NAKATSUKASA

Chrysanthemums

266. Frosty tangle—my ancient temple-hair
        is three parts gray;
      dew-covered chrysanthemums—the new-grown blossoms
        are one-half yellow.

PO CHÜ-I

267. It's not that among flowers I especially love chrysanthemums
      but just that after this flower blossoms, there are no further flowers!

YÜAN CHEN

268. As mountain mists bring season's close,
        they accompany pine and cedar in fading late;
      as autumn sunlight dies early,
        they mock the orchid for withering so soon.

KI NO HASEO

REMAINING CHRYSANTHEMUMS

269. In Li County, every village neighborhood
        consists of wealthy households;
      In Master T'ao's home, the family sons
        are in no danger of "toppling from the hall"!

MIYOSHI NO KIYOYUKI

    This couplet is based on the conceit that the scattering chrysanthe-
    mum petals resemble gold coins. "Li County," the location of the
    Sweet Valley referred to in number 264, is famous for its chrysanthe-

mums, so everyone who lives there must be rich. Among the great Chinese poets, T'ao Ch'ien is best known for his love of chrysanthemums, as well as for his poetic complaints about the inadequacy of his offspring, but with so much family wealth at hand, they probably were not in danger of "toppling from the hall," that is, failing to maintain the family's reputation.

270. The orchid in its garden feels ashamed
    to be made of vulgar bones;
the morning glory on the hedge
    believes in no "long life."

YOSHISHIGE NO YASUTANE

Both orchids and morning glories are inferior to chrysanthemums, believed to be an ingredient in the elixir of immortality.

271. Orchid blossoms in the garden—
    after their purple has been crushed by storms,
in the caves of P'eng-lai, moonlight glitters
    on these among the frost.

SUGAWARA NO FUNTOKI

Chrysanthemums outlive orchids; they grow in P'eng-lai, the "isles of the immortals," remaining in bloom even in wintry weather.

272. *The chrysanthemums,*
Seen above the celestial clouds,
Might well be confused
With the very stars of heaven.

FUJIWARA NO TOSHIYUKI

273. *Even should you pluck one, you still must guess:*
These chrysanthemums seemingly white,
Concealed by the first frost.

ŌSHIKŌCHI NO MITSUNE

The End of the Ninth Month

274. Block it with the impregnability of Hsiao-Han Pass—
      hard to hold the soughing sound
         along the avenues of cloud!
      Set brave Meng Pen to run in pursuit—
      how could even he detain the clear pipings
         in the realms of wind?

MINAMOTO NO SHITAGŌ

> By alluding to one of China's most famous strategic locations and a renowned warrior of antiquity, this passage characterizes the impossibility of preventing the end of autumn. The "soughing sound" and "clear pipings" are the natural music produced by nature during the season of autumn.

275. Although with head and eyes I could accede to monks who beg,
      to make a donation of the autumn would be most difficult!

MINAMOTO NO SHITAGŌ

276. On the peak of literature, reining in its horse—
         fall sunlight, a white pony!
      Across the sea of poetry, setting sail—
         sounds of the red leaves!

ŌE NO MOCHITOKI

> Autumn is a particularly rich season for poetry, but now it is ending. The particular beauties of the season, including the clear, sunlit days and the red leaves, are now departing on a journey by sea or by land— both allegorically representing the realm of letters. The comparison of sunlight to a white pony superimposes another layer of metaphor derived from the Taoist philosopher Chuang Tzu, who used the image to convey the rapidity with which time passes.

277. *The mountain's desolation*
      Shows autumn is now past;

There is a morning frost
On every branch of the evergreens.

FUJIWARA NO YATSUKA

278. *A memento of departing autumn:*
Frost on the very cord with which
I bind up
My own white hair.

TAIRA NO KANEMORI

Lady Blossoms (patrinia scabiosaefolia *or* patrinia palmata)

279. This flower's color is that of steamed millet;
its popular name is "Lady Blossom."
When I hear this name, I would playfully ask her
        to accompany me in old age,
except that I fear she will despise this old man's frosty hair!

MINAMOTO NO SHITAGŌ

> Shitagō has apparently misread one detail in the Chinese source for
> the phrase "steamed millet." In the original text, a letter by Emperor
> Wen of the Wei dynasty (r. 220–226), the phrase is "steamed *chestnuts.*"
> The two characters for "millet" and "chestnut," in Chinese pro-
> nounced *su* (Jpse. *zoku/awa*) and *li* (Jpse. *ritsu/kuri*), respectively, are
> easily confused. *Su* (millet) consists of the element "west" over the
> element "grain" (a structure wittily exploited by the *haiku* poet Bashō
> in one passage of his travel diary, *Oku no hosomichi* [Narrow road to
> the deep north]), whereas *li* consists of "west" over "tree." "Grain" and
> "tree" differ by only two dots.

280. *Should I pass the night*
In a field of blooming maiden flowers,
Will I be branded, without logic,
A man who is flirtatious?

ONO NO YOSHIKI

281. *When I see the maiden flowers*
     My soul cannot be comforted,
     For how much they remind me
     Of my past affections through so many autumns.

FUJIWARA NO SANEYORI

> This poem is said to have been written after the death of Saneyori's
> mother.

Bush Clover (hagi)

282. In the dawn dew as deer cry, this flower first comes out;
     repeatedly I gather them, moved by seasonal feeling.

THIS POEM IS NOT ATTRIBUTED IN THE TEXT, BUT IT WAS
WRITTEN BY SUGAWARA NO MICHIZANE

283. *My heart seems bruised*
     Just as those broken branches
     The farmers use to bind up
     The autumn bush clover at the harvest.

ANONYMOUS

284. *Sad I was*
     That all had faded;
     Yet the white dew on
     The autumn bush clover
     Now glistens
     To bend its very branches.

LADY ISE

285. *How I would like to add*
     To the cry of the deer at my retreat
     This brocade of autumn-blooming bush clover!

KIYOWARA NO MOTOSUKE

Orchids

286. Before me are even sadder things:
aging chrysanthemums, fading orchids, two or three bunches of each.

PO CHÜ-I

287. Is it that the sun produces no light?
— Floating clouds obscure it, and it suddenly goes dark.
Is it that the clustered orchids are not fragrant?
— The autumn wind blows on them, and they fade away too early.

PRINCE KANEAKIRA

PROSEPOEM ON T'U-CH'IU

> In the title of the work from which this excerpt is taken, T'u-ch'iu is
> the name of a place in China where a great statesman of the past once
> went into exile; hence it is a reference to reclusion or retirement in
> general. The poet compares the emperor to the sun and a loyal min-
> ister (in this case, by implication, himself) to an orchid. Both can tem-
> porarily lose their brilliance or fragrance, respectively, when calum-
> niated or wronged in some manner by scheming courtiers (clouds and
> autumn wind).

288. Congealed like makeup applied to the face
    of the phoenix girl;
pooling like tears that drop in pearls
    from the eyes of the mermaids.

MIYAKO NO YOSHIKA

> This passage uses two allusions to describe the beauty of dewdrops on
> red orchids. The "phoenix girl" is Nung-yü (Playing-with-jade),
> famous in Chinese antiquity for her ability to imitate the cry of the
> phoenix when she played the flute. The "mermaids" are said to live
> beneath the sea, where they weave an exquisite variety of silk and
> weep tears of pearls.

289. The song startled the retainer of Ch'u,
        his autumn strings all fragrant;
     her dream cut off, the concubine Yen
        found perfume all about her pillow.

TACHIBANA NO NAOMOTO

> This passage uses two allusions to evoke the orchid's subtle fragrance.
> The "retainer of Ch'u" is Sung Yü (?mid-third century B.C.), a semi-
> legendary court poet of the ancient Chinese state of Ch'u. One of
> Sung's alleged compositions, set to the music of the *ch'in* lute, is a
> variation on "The Hidden Orchid," which came to him when he was
> housed in an "orchid chamber" at a palace. According to the *Tso-
> chuan* (Commentary of Master Tso), a Chinese historical text, a lowly
> concubine of Duke Wen of Cheng named Yen Chi dreamed that a
> heavenly messenger presented her with an orchid; afterward, she won
> the duke's favor and gave birth to the future Duke Mu, at which time
> she was named Orchid.

290. *The perfumed odor of a skillful hand unknown*
     Pervades these autumn fields.
     Who has taken them off and put them here,
     Those "purple trouser" flowers?

SOSEI

The Morning-Glory (asagao)

291. The pine tree lives a thousand years
        but in the end must fade;
     the morning glory lives one day,
        yet this is a time of splendor!

PO CHÜ-I

292. Coming but not staying—
     the banks of shallots have dew brushed away by dawn.
     Leaving and not returning—
     the hedges of morning glories have no blossoms

that last until the dusk.

PRINCE KANEAKIRA

VOTIVE ESSAY [WRITTEN IN HIS OWN HAND DONATING A
TEXT OF THE LOTUS SUTRA]

293. *How uncertain:*
Even through a rift in the morning mists,
I cannot see who it might be—
Flower of morning faces.

ANONYMOUS

294. *I have always looked upon*
The flower of morning faces
As a fleeting thing—
Yet are both the flower's life
And our own not the same?

FUJIWARA NO MICHINOBU

Gardening

295. I've seen many people who plant flowers to please the eye,
before each season cultivating, preparing for later enjoyment.

SUGAWARA NO FUNTOKI

296. But by myself, I live at leisure, and my boy servant is lazy:
spring trees in spring I plant, autumn flowers in autumn.

SUGAWARA NO FUNTOKI

Together with the previous entry, this poem forms Funtoki's "Quatrain
on Planting Autumn Flowers."

297. At leisure, I think the day I see your blossoms blooming red
will be the very day my temple hairs have turned all white.

YOSHISHIGE NO YASUTANE

298. While I was planting them, I was not thinking of Yüan-liang,
but that when these would bloom, I'd offer them to the World-
Honored One.

SUGAWARA NO MICHIZANE

> Yüan-liang is T'ao Ch'ien (365–427), one of China's greatest poets,
> famous for his love of chrysanthemums and often alluded to in poems
> about this flower or in inscriptions on paintings of it. "World-Honored
> One" is one of the sobriquets for Buddha.

299. *I never thought see*
A speck of dust on them
Since we planted these wild carnations,
Just like the bed in which my wife and I have always slept.

ŌSHIKOCHI NO MITSUNE

> This poem contains a pun on *tokonatsu* (wild carnation) and *toko*
> (bed).

300. *I worry*
Over these flowers I love,
For what will happen to them,
When they are covered with frost?

ANONYMOUS

Red Leaves

301. Unbearable! The place of red leaves and green moss
is also beneath a sky of cool wind and evening rain.

PO CHÜ-I

302. The forest dyed in mottled yellow, cold, displays its leaves;
the water made of azure crystal, calm, shows not a ripple.

PO CHÜ-I

303. Inside the cave, pure and shallow, is the crystal water;

in the garden, sparse and sere, are embroidered trees.

YOSHISHIGE NO YASUTANE

304. Other leaves—alone in sobriety,
        pine-needle colors in the gully;
    lingering ripples join their force—
        sounds of Embroidery River!

ŌE NO MOCHITOKI

> This rather hermetic couplet indirectly portrays the background against
> which red autumn leaves are seen: the forest, in which only the pine
> needles remain "sober"—that is, stay green rather than turning red—
> and the river in which the fallen leaves float, its ripples reminiscent of
> the Embroidery River in Szechwan, China, because of the embroidery-
> like effect of the leaves on its waters. The reference to sobriety is to a
> famous poem of the fourth century B.C., "The Fisherman," in which
> the poet, feeling wronged by his enemies at court, proclaims himself to
> be the "only sober" man in the kingdom.

305. *How the dew and the autumn rains*
    Have dripped through,
    Even to the lowest branches on Moru Mountain,
    Coloring them for autumn.

KI NO TSURAYUKI

306. *Like so many brocades rolled out,*
    These colored leaves of oak appear
    Through the gaps in the mist
    On Sao Mountain.

FUJIWARA NO KIYOTADA

Falling Leaves

307. Third autumn month and the palace water clock
        is dripping on and on—
    empty stairs where rain drops fall. . . .

Ten thousand miles away, and where is my hometown garden?
—Falling leaves in layers through the window....

ATTRIBUTED TO CHANG TU

PROSEPOEM ON SADNESS

308. City-wall willows, palace locusts—
     in vain they drop their leaves:
     the grief of autumn will not reach
     the hearts of high-placed men.

PO CHÜ-I

309. The autumn courtyard is unswept; bramble cane in hand
     I leisurely tread on paulownia—yellow leaves—as I stroll.

PO CHÜ-I

310. In the shadows of paulownia and catalpa—
     a sound of rain swishing emptily.
     Above the back of the oriole—
     several bits of red still hanging on.

MINAMOTO NO SHITAGŌ

> This sound may be that of falling leaves sounding like rain. The reference to the oriole is probably based on a detail of Chinese bestiary lore to the effect that when the oriole flies at night, it purposely uses the foliage of the trees as cover.

311. Woodcutting, grass gathering, I come and go,
     my cane stepping through the robe of Chu Mai-ch'en.
     Withdrawn in seclusion, I happily roam,
     my sandals treading the herbs of Ko Chih-hsien.

TAKAOKA NO SUKEYUKI

THE FALLEN LEAVES IN THE MOUNTAINS I TREAD

> Chu Mai-ch'en was a famous upright official of the Han dynasty. When he returned in glory to his hometown, the emperor is reported to have

said, "To return to one's hometown after reaching a high position is like wearing an embroidered robe and walking around at night." Ko Chih-hsien, or Ko Hung, was a famous alchemist of the third century. His book, *Pao P'u Tzu*, contains recipes for the elixir of immortality.

312. With every night, its light increases—
     moon of the Wu gardens;
   each morning, its sound is less and less—
     wind of the Shang-lin Park.

PRINCE TOMOHIRA

   The Wu gardens and Shang-lin Park are ancient imperial pleasure sites in China, made famous by early *fu* prose poems. As the leaves fall, the moonlight increases, and the sound of wind through the leaves fades away.

313. Following the wind, the falling blossoms
     carry soughing sounds;
   frothing against rocks, the plunging falls
     play their lovely lute.

MINAMOTO NO SHITAGŌ

314. *Maple leaves are floating*
   On the Asuka River;
   How the autumn winds must be blowing
   On the peaks at Kazuraki.

KAKINOMOTO NO HITOMARO

315. *In the Godless Month,*
   How the leaves rain down
   In the forest of Kaminabi,
   Along with the winter showers themselves.

ANONYMOUS

   The "Godless Month" is a poetic name given to the tenth month. Among the traditional explanations given for the term is that the

Shintō gods have retired to the Izumo Shrine on the Japan Sea, thus
departing from the Yamato area where the capital was located.

316. *Unseen by any,*
The colored leaves in the deep mountains
Fall in the night
Into a brilliant brocade.

KI NO TSURAYUKI

Wild Geese (with Returning Geese appended)

Although some of the verses do refer to "returning geese," there apparently is
no separately designated section for this theme.

317.   Ten thousand miles—exiled to the south
from whence geese fly north in the third month of spring.
I do not know what year it will be
when I will be able to return with you.

WEN HSÜAN (LITERARY ANTHOLOGY; ERRONEOUS FOR
WEI CH'ENG-CH'ING)

318.   The river colors at Hsün-yang, swelled now by the tide;
the autumn sounds above P'eng-i Lake, brought hither by the geese.

LIU YÜ-HSI

319.   Four or five clusters of mountains, colors
freshened by rain;
two or three lines of wild geese,
dotting the clouds of autumn.

TU HSÜN-HO

320. "The stretched bow will be hard to evade!"
—They haven't cast off doubts about the first-quarter moon
hanging above;

"That racing arrow will be easy to avoid!"
—They also make a mistake about the rushing torrent
   flowing below.

Ō E   N O   A S A T S U N A

   The geese, flying across the sky, are confused and frightened by the
   crescent moon—which they take for a bow about to shoot an arrow
   at them—and by the rushing torrent below—which they mistake for
   the arrow.

321. Geese fly across the azure void,
        writing calligraphy on the blue paper;
     a hawk attacks the frosted woods,
        scattering brocade threading from the loom.

SHIMADA NO TADAOMI (BENEATH THE CHINESE TEXT,
WRONGLY ATTRIBUTED TO SUGAWARA NO MICHIZANE)

322. Across the emerald-jade ornamented zither
        are arrayed the standing bridges;
     on paper compounded of blue-green moss
        are several lines of calligraphy.

S U G A W A R A   N O   M I C H I Z A N E

   These are two metaphors for the appearance of geese against the
   autumn sky. The "bridges" of line 1 are the individual wooden brackets
   supporting the strings of the plucked-string instrument known as the
   cheng in Chinese (similar to the Japanese *koto*). Each bridge is mov-
   able, thus allowing the performer to change the tuning of each string.

323. Cloud garments, presented on a journey to Fan Shu;
     windswept creaking of a scull, a boat
        riding the waves of the Hsiao and Hsiang.

P R I N C E   T O M O H I R A

   These are two elaborate metaphors for the clouds in the autumn sky
   flown through by the geese, and the sound of the geese honking,
   respectively. While minister of Ch'in, Fan Shu (or Fan Chü) was vis-

ited by an emissary of Wei, an old friend named Hsü Chia. When Fan appeared dressed in tattered garments, Hsü Chia in compassion presented him with a set of good clothes. The second line compares the honking of the geese to the creaking sound made by the scull of a boat riding out the wind. The Hsiao and Hsiang are the southern Chinese rivers famed for the beauty of their scenery.

324. *In the autumn wind*
I hear the cries
Of the first wild geese—
Whose message
Do they bring with them?

KI NO TOMONORI

325. At mountain's waist, returning geese—
a slantwise-tightened scarf;
on water's surface, forming a rainbow—
a cloth not yet unfurled.

MIYAKO NO ARINAKA

326. *As the spring mists float upward,*
The flying geese leave us behind—
Perhaps they are used to living
Only in villages without flowers.

LADY ISE

Insects

327. Chattering, chattering beneath the darkened window,
droning, droning deep within the grass—
on autumn days, grieving women's hearts,
through rainy nights, saddening the ears of men!

PO CHÜ-I

328. The frosted grass is soon to wither—
the insects' feelings turn anxious;

the windswept branches have yet to settle—
the birds find it hard to perch.

PO CHÜ-I

> We use the reading *chi* (anxious) from Po's collected works in prefer-
> ence to the reading *k'u* (embittered) found in the *Wakan rōei shū*. The
> "Meng-te" of the title is Po's good friend Liu Yü-hsi, himself a major
> T'ang poet represented in the *Wakan rōei shū* by a number of couplets.

329. I'm vexed by the shortness of the legs on my bed:
    the crickets' chirping is so much louder!
I hate my walls for being hollow inside:
    the rats poke holes through them!

ONO NO TAKAMURA

> This follows couplet 236 in a poem by Ono.

330. In a mountain inn, at times of rain,
    their chirping is faintly heard;
at a rustic pavilion, a place of wind,
    their weaving sounds feel quite cold.

TACHIBANA NO NAOMOTO

331. Beside the woods, grieved at distance,
    through wind so dimly heard;
beneath the wall, chanting poems of solitude,
    in moonlight colors, so cold!

MINAMOTO NO SHITAGŌ

> In each line, it is the poet who is "grieved" or "chanting poems" and
> the insects that are "dimly heard" by him or whose sounds feel "so
> cold" to him.

332. *Who was it who promised*
"Now I will come"?
I wait for the long autumn night to pass,
Weeping while the crickets cry.

ANONYMOUS

333. *Cicadas, do not call out*
      So sharply!
      In these long autumn nights,
      My own sorrows seem greater than yours.

FUJIWARA NO TADAFUSA

Deer

334. Green moss along the path, worn smooth—
         monks returning to the temple;
      red leaves, now making rustling sounds—
         deer are in the woods.

WEN T'ING-YÜN

335. Discreetly causing their bodies to turn color
         when they eat artemisia
      as they appear, following the wind of virtue
         that blows upon the grass.

KI NO HASEO

WHITE DEER

> In this couplet, from a poem inspired by the presentation at court of a
> white deer, the poet alludes to the tradition that the virtue of a good sov-
> ereign causes the appearance of the white deer as an omen. The *Shih
> ching* (Book of songs) contains a famous poem that describes deer eat-
> ing artemisia. The *Lun yü*, or Confucian *Analects*, describes the virtue
> of the sovereign as a wind that naturally causes the "virtue" (or influ-
> ence, power) of petty men to bend in submission. The poet has woven
> together these allusions in a complex compliment to the emperor.

336. *On Tokiwa Mountain*
      Where no maples grow,
      The deer who live there
      Must discover through their own cries
      That autumn has come.

ŌNAKATOMI NO YOSHINOBU

337. *As dusk approaches*
      At Ogura Mountain,
      In the very cries of the deer,
      Does autumn not seem to vanish away?

KI NO TSURAYUKI

Dew

338. How admirable! On this third night
          of the ninth month of the year
      the dew looks just like pearls, the moon
          appears to be a bow.

PO CHÜ-I

> The "ninth month" of this couplet refers, of course, to the lunar cal-
> endar, so that the scene described here must be imagined as taking
> place later than in September of the solar calendar.

339. Dew drips on orchid clusters, cold jade so white;
      wind swallows pine needles, elegant lute so clear!

MINAMOTO NO FUSAAKIRA

340. *On the bush clover,*
      In the field where a buck deer
      Stands in the early morning
      The white dewdrops glistens like jewels

ŌTOMO NO YAKAMOCHI

Fog

341. Fog in bamboo at dawn encages
          the moon that is swallowing the ridge;
      the wind in the duckweed slowly escorts
          the spring as it crosses the river.

PO CHÜ-I

342. Although we grieve that nighttime fog
        buries our pillows,
    we love the morning clouds
        as they emerge from horses' saddles.

    ŌE NO ASATSUNA

343. *Its foothills shrouded in mist*
    Rising from the river,
    The autumn mountain
    Seems to rise
    From the very heavens themselves

    KIYOWARA NO FUKAYABU

344. *For whose sake*
    Might this brocade be hidden?
    The autumn mists now rise to cover
    The slopes of Mount Sao.

    KI NO TOMONORI

Fulling Clothes

345. In the eighth month, in the ninth month,
        just when the nights are long,
    a thousand poundings, ten thousand poundings,
        it never has an end!

    PO CHÜ-I

    This couplet plays a crucial role in one of the greatest episodes of
    Lady Murasaki's masterpiece, *Tale of Genji*. This is the chapter enti-
    tled "Yūgao." As Genji and Yūgao lie in bed in autumn, they hear var-
    ious sounds from the street outside, including the echoing of the
    fulling blocks as clothes are being prepared for the colder weather.
    Later, after Yūgao's tragic death, when Genji hears this sound again,
    he recalls the Po Chü-i couplet, which now takes on a deeper mean-
    ing for him as it conjures up memories of Yūgao. Lady Murasaki's use
    of this couplet bears witness to the important function of the *Wakan*

rōei shū as a transmitter of Chinese poetry to Heian courtiers, whose knowledge of this poetry often derived not from the separate collected works of the poets but, rather, from the *Wakan rōei shū*.

346. Across the stars of the Northern Dipper
      fly the wild geese;
beneath the moon of the southern tower
they full cold-weather clothes.

LIU YÜAN-SHU

347. Where clothes are fulled, at dawn they grieve
      the boudoir moon is chilly;
they cut and sew, and send them this autumn
where frontier clouds are cold.

FUJIWARA NO ATSUMOCHI

348. As they cut and sew, they are unsure
      of proper length and size;
with frontier grief, no longer former waists
to fit around!

TACHIBANA NO NAOMOTO

> This is a rare example of *kanshi* (Chinese-language poetry) in which the Japanese author appears to make a mistake in Chinese syntax, or at least to write clumsily. The second portion of the second line reads literally, "certainly will not former-waist-encircle." Although there are various forms of inversion after a negative in Chinese poetic diction, this gives too much work to the negative, *pu*. The poet probably had in mind the final couplet from the poem "Fulling Clothes" by Hsieh Hui-lien (397–433), anthologized in the *Wen Hsüan* (Literary anthology), a book with enormous influence in Japan. The couplet may be translated as "The waists they tailor after the old pattern,/but no one knows if today they still will fit."

349. Beneath the breeze, their perfume wafts
      as paired sleeves are lifted high;

before the moon, their mallets sound aggrieved
while their eyebrows are cast down.

PRINCE TOMOHIRA

350. Year after year, yearning in separation,
    they are startled by autumn geese;
night after night, the muffled sound
    reaches the cocks of dawn.

PRINCE TOMOHIRA

     This and number 349 are from the same poem.

351. *Its foothills shrouded in mist*
    Rising from the river,
    The autumn mountain
    Seems to rise
    From the very heavens themselves.

KIYOWARA NO FUKAYABU

Winter

Early Winter

352. In the tenth month in Chiang-nan the weather is superb;
    how wonderful, that the winter scene
        should seem like springtime glory!

PO CHÜ-I

353. The four seasons, in desolation, reduced now by three-fourths;
    the ten thousand creatures, stumbling along,
        have wilted by more than half.

EMPEROR DAIGO

354. From my bed, I roll away and store the green-bamboo mat;
from the storage box, I take out and open the white cotton clothes.

SUGAWARA NO MICHIZANE

355. *In the Godless Month*
The showers fall, then cease,
In an uncertain sky,
Bringing winter.

ANONYMOUS

Winter Nights

356. A single cold lamp, this night above the clouds;
several cups of warm brew, a springtime in the snow!

PO CHÜ-I

357. The year's luster naturally dies before our lamps;
the traveler's thoughts now are born only from his pillow.

TACHIBANA NO ARITSURA

358. *My passion too strong,*
I hasten to my beloved,
But the wind from the river
Is cold,
And the plover cries.

KI NO TSURAYUKI

Year's End

359. The chilly flow carries the moon, clear as in a mirror;
the nighttime breeze mingles with frost, sharp as the blade of a sword.

PO CHÜ-I

360. The wind and clouds easily bring year's end before men's eyes;
     the years and months are hard to recapture from beneath old age.

KORENAGA NO HARUMICHI

361. *The departing year*
     Leaves regrets behind as well:
     Even my image in the clear mirror
     Seems to darken and to age.

KI NO TSURAYUKI

Brazier Fires

362. The yellow thick and the green clear—
     wines are ready to greet the winter;
     behind vermilion curtains, red brazier flames
     flare up with the night.

PO CHÜ-I

363. To see, there are no will-o'-the-wisps,
     to hear, no orioles:
     this winter month, for pleasant warmth
     we turn to the fire's welcome.

SUGAWARA NO FUNTOKI

364. This fire must have been obtained
     by boring flowering trees:
     as we face it, all through the night
     we have a sense of spring.

SUGAWARA NO FUNTOKI

    This and number 363 are from the same source. The fire in the bra-
    zier must be the first fire ever lit, obtained by boring into the wood of
    trees with primitive drills.

365. At other times, although we drink
          among orioles and flowers,
     these days we are not willing to part
          from beside the beast-shaped charcoals!

SUGAWARA NO SUKEAKIRA

> According to the *Chin shu*—the official history of the Chin dynasty
> (265–419)—a certain Yang Hsiu had, for his brazier, charcoals shaped
> into the forms of animals.

366. *More painful still*
     Than the banked fires
     Of emotion suppressed
     Is the enmity earned
     By expressing them.

ATTRIBUTED TO ARIWARA NO NARIHIRA

Frost

367. Of the ten thousand things, it is autumn frost
          that is able to fade colors;
     of the four seasons, it's winter's sun
          that most erodes the years.

PO CHÜ-I

368. Autumn's third month—snow on the banks, the flowers
          first blossom white;
     a whole night of frost in the forest—
          the leaves have turned all red.

WEN T'ING-YÜN

> Following an early gloss, the editors see the first line in this couplet as
> referring metaphorically to the white blossoms of reeds along the
> riverside, possibly because they think it unlikely that a poem set in
> autumn (and not winter) would refer to snow. But this would result in

the metaphorical snow being paralleled by the actual frost, which would be unlikely in regulated-verse poetics. Then, however, we are left with the *imaginary* blossoming of the flowers paralleling the *actual* reddening of the leaves, but that seems less disruptive of the couplet's general realism.

369. The boudoir cold, she's startled awake from a dream:
    some has formed on this lonely wife's fulling block.
    The mountain deep, they're moved within their hearts:
    it first invades the Four Old Whiteheads' temple hairs.

KI NO HASEO

THE DARK LADY IN CHARGE OF FROST

It is *frost* that has formed on the block used by the wife to full winter clothes for her husband, away at the frontier, and that has invaded the hair of the famous recluses, the Four Old Whiteheads, who went into seclusion to protest the depredations of the first emperor of the Ch'in dynasty in 221 B.C. According to the *Huai-nan Tzu*, an important philosophical text of the second century B.C., "When the third month of autumn arrives, the dark lady emerges and proceeds to bring down the frost and snow."

370. The "superior man," deep in the night,
    raises no warning at the sound;
    the old venerable, late in life, is startled
    when it appears on temple hairs.

SUGAWARA NO MICHIZANE

Again, in accordance with a basic principle of Chinese poetics, because this is a so-called *yung-wu* poem (singing of things, that is, a poem devoted to characterizing a single object either natural or man-ufactured), the "thing" in question—in this case, frost—is not actually named but is evoked through imagery and allusion. The "superior man," or crane, which is sometimes alluded to in this fashion, does cry out when dew appears, according to certain old texts, but not for the frost, which it apparently dislikes so much that it falls mute

when the frost appears (see the next couplet for another reference to
this idea).

371. Its every cry has now been stifled,
the crane of Hua-t'ing;
with each step, he's startled afresh,
the man wearing sandals of fiber.

SUGAWARA NO MICHIZANE

Hua-t'ing, already referred to in number 256, is a place associated with
the third-century poet Lu Chi. While in exile, he "longed to hear the
cries of the cranes at Hua-t'ing." The "sandals of fiber" are suitable for
the summertime. Again, both lines refer obliquely or allusively to the
presence of frost.

372. At dawn it's formed between the roof tiles—
ducks have changed their color!
At night, it settles on the ornamented gate,
as cranes swallow their cries.

KI NO ARIMASA

The "(mandarin) ducks" are the roof tiles themselves. Either the tiles
are actually formed into the paired male and female ducks—symbols
of marital fidelity—or one type of tile (round or perhaps convex) is
considered male, and the other (flat or concave) is seen as female. The
"ornamental gate" alludes to the story of Ting Ling-wei of the Han
dynasty, who is said in the *Sou shen hou chi* (Latter collection of
accounts of seeking strange things) to have turned into a crane after
death and, in this form, to have returned to his hometown and perched
on an ornamented gate.

373. *The night is cold;*
Awake, I hear the cries
Of the mandarin duck,
The frost on its wings,
Which cannot be brushed away.

ANONYMOUS

Snow

374. At dawn we enter the gardens of the king of Liang:
      snow covers the myriad hills!
      At night, we climb the tower of Master Yü:
      the moon shines bright for a thousand miles!

ATTRIBUTED TO HSIEH KUAN

PROSEPOEM ON WHITENESS

375. Sands from the Silver River, extending
         for three thousand miles,
      flowers from Plum Blossom Ridge
         displayed in ten thousand trees!

PO CHÜ-I

> These are two metaphors for the appearance of the snow. The "Silver
> River" is the Milky Way.

376. The snow seems like the feathers of geese,
         blown about in confusion;
      the men are wearing crane-feather robes
         as they stand or pace.

PO CHÜ-I

377. Sometimes it follows the wind, not returning,
      as if someone were shaking the feathers of many cranes.
      Or sometimes it remains even in a clearing sky,
      seemingly woven of a myriad foxes' foreleg hairs!

KI NO HASEO

PROSEPOEM ON SPRING SNOW

378. Its wings seem like a flock of cranes
         perched around a pond;

my heart feels like that of the man, inspired,
who rowed a boat along.

EMPEROR MURAKAMI

> The second line of this couplet employs one of the best-known allu-
> sions in all of Chinese literature. According to the *Shih-shuo hsin-yü*,
> a fifth-century compilation of anecdotes about the elegant scholar
> officials and recluses of the day, Wang Hui-chih rowed a boat one
> snowy night to visit his friend Tai K'uei. But upon arriving at Tai's
> front door, Wang abruptly turned around and went back home. When
> questioned about his strange behavior, Wang replied, "I went there
> riding the inspiration of the moment; when the inspiration ended, I
> returned. What need was there actually to see Tai K'uei?" For gener-
> ations, this story has exemplified the spontaneous, Taoistic freedom of
> action characteristic of the sages of the Six Dynasties period.

379. I stand in the courtyard, and my head becomes a crane!
I sit beside the brazier, so no tortoise-wrinkles form on my skin.

SUGAWARA NO MICHIZANE

380. The color of the autumn fan
   in the boudoir of concubine Chieh;
The sound of the nighttime lute
   on the terrace of the king of Ch'u.

TACHIBANA NO ARITSURA

> The appearance and sound of the snow blowing in the wind remind
> the poet of the white silk fan discarded in autumn (because it is no
> longer needed) to which concubine Pan compares herself in a famous
> poem and to the music that presumably accompanied the nighttime
> revels of an ancient king of Ch'u in south-central China. More pre-
> cisely, they remind the poet of earlier poems that made these com-
> parisons. As so often is found in the *Wakan rōei shū*, the couplet is a
> fabric woven of literary allusions or recastings of earlier material.

381. *Here in the capital,*
How wondrous, this first snow—

Yet in the mountains of Yoshino,
It must have fallen long since.

ANONYMOUS

382. The white snow
Must already be piled high
On Mount Yoshino —
For here in the old capital,
It is already bitterly cold.

SAKANOUE NO KORENORI

  The old capital refers to the city of Nara.

383. As the snow falls,
Flowers seem to appear on every tree;
Yet which of those branches may I pluck
To choose a blossom of plum?

KI NO TOMONORI

Ice (with Spring Ice appended)

384. Ice has sealed the water's surface —
  there are no waves to hear;
  snow has dotted the tips of forests —
  now there are flowers to see!

SUGAWARA NO MICHIZANE

385. The frost prevents the crying of the crane —
  it's too cold now for dew;
  the water causes the fox to be suspicious —
  still too thin, the ice!

TAKAOKA NO SUKEYUKI

  Foxes were believed to be able to hear faint movements of water below
  thin ice; so only when a fox was willing to cross a frozen expanse of ice
  would horsemen consider it safe to ride over.

386. *The moonlight in the vast sky*
 Is so cold
 That the water catching its reflection
 Has frozen first.

 ANONYMOUS

387. As ice melted, we saw more water
     than we could see land;
 when snow cleared, we watched as mountains
     drew closer to the pavilion!

 PO CHÜ-I

> As the title of this couplet reveals (although one could draw the same
> conclusion from the content of the couplet itself), this is a passage
> from a poem on early spring rather than winter. It is included here
> because of its theme of ice and in fact belongs to the "appended" sec-
> tion on "Spring Ice." It is apparent that sometimes when such an
> appended section is announced, there may be no separate heading
> demarcating the subsection, although in other parts of the book, such
> a heading is duly provided. The phrase "long lines" in the title refers
> to the fact that the poem is written in the seven-character meter; that
> is, there are seven monosyllabic words per line throughout the poem,
> as opposed to the "short" line of five words per line. Most *kanshi* are
> in either the five- or the seven-word meter, although six-word-per-line
> poems do occur, as well as four-word-per-line archaizing poems rem-
> iniscent of the classic *Shih ching* (Book of songs).

388. As the ice melts, the ruler of Han
     must feel suspicious of Pa;
 as snow melts away, the prince of Liang
     will no longer summon Mei.

 TACHIBANA NO ARITSURA

> These are two allusions to incidents from the Chinese past. While
> leading advance troops, Wang Pa, a minister of Emperor Kuang-wu of
> Han, arrived at a river. He sent back a message stating that the ice was
> solid and that the river could be crossed, so as to encourage the
> emperor's troops to continue their advance, even though in fact the

river surface had not yet completely frozen. But when the emperor arrived, the ice had frozen solid, and it was possible to cross. The prince of Liang summoned his court poet, Mei Sheng, to view the snow together with him.

389. At the barbarian frontier, who was it
          that was able to uphold the integrity of his mission?
      At Hu-t'o River, one was afraid of failing
          in a subject's loyalty.

MINAMOTO NO SUKENORI

> The answer to the question is Su Wu, a Han emissary to the barbarian Hsiung-nu who was imprisoned and starved by the Han in the hope of forcing him to submit. But Su Wu staunchly refused and kept himself alive by eating snow and bits of felt. The "Hu-t'o River" is the river where Wang Pa falsely reported that the ice was solid (see the previous passage), albeit with good intentions.

390. *The waters between the banks of the mountain rivers*
      Are rising;
      With the spring breezes,
      The ice in the valleys
      Will surely melt today.

ANONYMOUS

Hail

391. The roebuck's teeth, rice grains in a sieve,
          every sound so crisp;
      from dragons' jaws, pearls are tossed,
          every kernel cold.

SUGAWARA NO MICHIZANE

> The hailstones are compared to roebuck's teeth, themselves often compared to grains of white rice and to pearls, said to be guarded by dragons, who keep them in their jaws.

392. *In the deep mountains*
Hail must now be falling;
Here on the hills,
The trailing vines
Are tinged with color now.

ANONYMOUS

The Festival of the Names of the Buddhas

During the twelfth month of the lunar calendar, the Sutra of the Names of the Buddhas is recited, and the Names are venerated as an act of penitence for the evil deeds of the year.

393. A brazierful of incense, and a single oil lamp:
with white hairs, late at night
he venerates the Sutra of Buddha Names!

PO CHÜ-I

394. The incense comes from his heart of Zen,
no need for any fire;
flowers blossom in his joined palms,
not because of spring.

SUGAWARA NO MICHIZANE

395. *As this year*
Draws to an end,
May all the sins we have committed
Vanish without a trace.

ATTRIBUTED TO TAIRA NO KANEMORI

396. *When I think on*
[The sins] that have piled on me
Through the days and months,

How can I best prepare
For what will follow in the new year?

ANONYMOUS

LOWER   VOLUME

Wind

397. Spring wind stealthily prunes the courtyard trees;
night rain secretly penetrates the rock-top moss.

FU WEN

> There is no known writer of this name; he is presumably Chinese,
> given the form of the name, but the Chinese records—including the
> original edition of the massive anthology of all known T'ang dynasty
> poems, the *Ch'üan T'ang shih*—do not record him.

398. "*Entering the Pines*," it easily turns wild;
it would agitate the soul of Wang Chao-chün!
The "*Flowing Stream*" will not flow back;
it surely escorts Master Lieh as he rides away.

KI NO HASEO

PROSEPOEM ON THE *CH'IN* LUTE HEARD IN THE WIND

> "[*Wind*] *Entering the Pines*" and "*Flowing Stream*" are two famous
> compositions for the *ch'in*, or Chinese "lute" (actually a plucked-
> string instrument consisting of seven silken strings stretched over a
> hollow wooden sound-board, pressed down by the fingers of one hand
> and plucked by the fingers of the other hand). Wang Chao-chün is the
> Han dynasty princess who was married off to the khan of the Hsiung-
> nu barbarians. As she rode unhappily into foreign territory, she com-
> posed a piece expressive of her grief and played it on the *p'i-p'a*,
> another plucked-string musical instrument related to the Middle
> Eastern *oud* and the Western lute. "*Flowing Stream*" is a composition
> by Po Ya, a *ch'in* master of legendary repute. "Master Lieh," or Lieh
> Tzu, is the famous Taoist philosopher said to be able to ride the wind.

399. In the hands of the ruler of Han,
    it blows without ceasing;
above the grave of Master Hsü,
    it fans what hangs there still.

FUJIWARA NO YUKIFUJI

> The first emperor of the Han held a "three-foot sword" in his hand
> with which he boasted of having conquered the empire; the wind is
> compared to it in sharpness. From a tree "above the grave of Master
> Hsü," his lifelong friend Chi Cha hung his sword, which Master Hsü
> had admired while he was alive. Note that in the first line the wind *is*
> the sword and that in the second it "fans" the actual sword that is
> hanging from the tree.

400. Concubine Pan crafted her fan; now she may boast of it!
Master Lieh has hung up his carriage;
    no longer may he go to and fro.

YOSHISHIGE NO YASUTANE

> Regarding "concubine Pan," see number 162; she herself made the fan
> to which she compares herself; now that the wind has stopped, she
> will be able to boast of its usefulness. Master Lieh (see number 398)
> no longer has any wind to act as his carriage.

401. *Even though the winds of autumn blow*
    You do not arrive;
    The only sound that comes
    Is from the stalks of the reeds.
    Are filled with sound.

NAKATSUKASA

402. *Faintly,*
    In the dim moonlight rays of dawn
    The maple leaves cascade
    As the wind blows down the mountain.

MINAMOTO SANEAKIRA

Clouds

403. The bamboo mottled along the banks of the Hsiang,
clouds congeal above the traces of the playing of the zither.
The phoenixes departed from the terrace of Ch'in,
the moon grows old at this spot where flutes once played.

ATTRIBUTED TO CHANG TU

PROSEPOEM ON SADNESS

> The daughters of the ancient sage-emperor Shun wept so bitterly that
> their tears mottled the bamboo along the Hsiang River. They are also
> said to have played the zither after becoming the goddesses of the
> Hsiang. Hsiao Shih was a master of the flute. He taught his wife,
> Nung-yü, how to play, and their rendition in duet of the cry of the
> phoenix was so poignant that real phoenixes actually came to listen.
> Duke Mu of Ch'in, Nung-yü's father, built the Phoenix Terrace for
> them to live in. One day, the musical couple mounted a pair of
> phoenixes and together ascended from the terrace into the sky.

404. The mountains remote—clouds bury the tracks
    of travelers passing through;
the pine trees are cold—wind blows to fragments
    the dreams of wanderers.

ATTRIBUTION UNCERTAIN

405. All day long I gaze at the clouds, mind unattached to them;
at times I see the moon break through, at night, completely serene.

YÜAN CHEN

LIVING IN SOLITUDE

406. On the morning when the Han Whiteheads fled from Ch'in,
their view of the moon above the solitary peak was blocked;
on the evening that Fan Li withdrew from Yüeh,
his eyes were fogged by mists on the Five Lakes.

ŌE NO MOCHITOKI

PROSEPOEM ON THE THEME "SEEING CLOUDS, YOU CAN
TELL THE PRESENCE OF HERMITS"

The Four Whiteheads and Fan Li are famous recluses who withdrew
from the world, in the case of Fan Li, after having brilliantly served
his lord. In both cases, clouds (or mist) are signs of the presence of
admirable men. Note that this is a use of clouds as an *auspicious* sym-
bol; in other cases, they can represent evil-minded ministers obscur-
ing the judgment of the sovereign, in the same way that clouds
obscure the sun or moon.

407. For moments, they borrow the cragginess of peaks,
      yet do not carry stones;
    in the void, they steal the forms of mountain heights,
      yet when have they grown pines?

MIYAKO NO ARINAKA

408. Confused, we cannot find the place
      of the Han emperor's dragon visage;
    the chickens of the prince of Huai
      have lost their residence.

ŌE NO MOCHITOKI

This poem anticipates the next subject heading by describing
through oblique allusions an autumn sky from which the clouds
have disappeared. During a period of reclusion undertaken by
Emperor Kao-tsu of the Han dynasty, his wife, Empress Lü, was able
to track him down by observing the clouds above the mountains
where he was in residence. The prince of Huai compounded an
elixir of immortality, and when some of it was left behind after he
ascended to heaven, his dogs and chickens licked it up and joined
him in the clouds.

409. *Shall I think of you*
    As someone altogether separate from me?
    Just like the white clouds

On the highest peaks
Of Mount Katsuragi?

ANONYMOUS

Clear Skies

410. As mist dissolves outside the gate,
     the green mountains draw nearer;
as dew weighs down before the window,
     verdant bamboo hangs low.

CHENG SHIH-JAN

    Nothing is known about this poet.

411. On purple-canopied ridges, the mists are sparse;
clouds withdraw beyond seven hundred miles.
In hanging sheets of waterfalls, the foam is cold;
the moon shows pure in more than forty feet of height!

FUJIWARA NO KORESHIGE

AS MOUNTAIN SKIES CLEAR, AUTUMN VISTAS ARE MANY

412. Clouds dissolve in the azure void—
     the sky's skin is peeling!
Breezes move transparent ripples—
     the water's face grows wrinkles!

MIYAKO NO YOSHIKA

413. Paired cranes emerge from the marsh,
     dancing, clothed in fog;
a single sail merges with water,
     disappearing into clouds.

SUGAWARA NO FUNTOKI

    As the modern editors point out, the text wrongly gives the charac-
ter *shuang*, "frost," as the first word in the couplet. The correct read-

ing is *shuang*, "paired," as determined by the necessary parallelism with the first word of the second line, *ku*, "single." Such scribal errors are quite common in China, because of the language's extremely high number of homonyms. Both the words are pronounced exactly the same—*shuang*, first tone—and therefore easily confused in the mind of a copyist who is writing quickly and perhaps without complete attention. One would think, however, that for a Japanese poet writing in Chinese, as in this case, this particular type of error would be unlikely, as the written characters would not necessarily correspond to familiar sounds. Of course, both the words in question are also pronounced the same in their Japanese *on* readings (*sō*). It is conceivable, therefore, that however unrelated the Chinese language may be to spoken Japanese, a *kanshi* poet like Funtoki would in time develop a specifically aural relationship with the words, which might eventually lead to precisely the same sort of sound-based errors as in Chinese poems copied out by native speakers of Chinese.

414. Returning to Mount Sung, cranes dance,
    the sun appears on high;
drinking River Wei, dragons ascend,
    no clouds left behind.

ŌE NO MOCHITOKI

> Mount Sung in Honan Province is the central sacred peak in the system of five directions (north, south, east, west, and center). A certain Prince Ch'iao, having become an immortal, is said to have come to this mountain riding on a crane. A black dragon is said to have drunk up the River Wei, leaving a mountain range in its dried-out riverbed. Clouds "follow dragons," as wind "follows tigers," according to the *I ching* (Book of changes).

415. *The mists have cleared,*
The deep blue of the sky
Shows calm, and the very air itself
Seems somehow ashimmer.

ANONYMOUS

Dawn

416.   The beauty finishes adorning herself at her morning toilet;
the bell resounds in the palace of Wei.
The wanderer still travels beneath a fading moon;
at Han-ku Pass, cocks crow.

ATTRIBUTED TO CHIA SUNG

PROSEPOEM ON THE DAWN

417.   Several rows of south-flying geese,
a sliver of west-leaning moon;
a man traveling alone, taking to the long road...
The wayside inn is still closed.
Weeping in the lonely city, troops that have fought a hundred battles—
the barbarian flutes have not ceased.

ATTRIBUTED TO HSIEH KUAN

PROSEPOEM ON THE DAWN

418.   In magnificent, golden rooms
the dark moth-brows are being drawn;
they've finished banqueting on jeweled mats—
alone, red candles flicker on.

ATTRIBUTED TO HSIEH KUAN

This also is from "Prosepoem on the Dawn." Numbers 416, 417, and 418 all come from poems of this name, although two different poems are involved, one by Chia Sung (number 416) and one by Hsieh Kuan (numbers 417 and 418).

419.   Five sounds from the palace water-clock,
after the first light;
a single point, the window lamp, now about to fade.

PO CHÜ-I

These are the final two lines of a superb four-line *chüeh-chü* (quatrain):

My mind—ten thousand threads of thought,
    a letter—just two sheets;
I try to seal it, but read again,
    as if wanting to linger!
Five sounds from the palace water-clock,
    after the first light;
a single point, the window lamp, now about to fade.

This is one of the many poems that bear poignant witness to Po's great
friendship with Yüan Chen, the "Yuan the Ninth" of the title.

420. *If there were no daybreak*
    Then there might be rising,
    No regretful partings
    With the clear dew!

KI NO TSURAYUKI

Pine Trees

421. There are only the two pine trees at the bottom of the stairs;
not another thing at all to penetrate my mind.

PO CHÜ-I

422. When green mountains carry snow,
    we learn the true nature of pines;
when azure void lacks even one cloud,
    it pleases the hearts of the cranes.

HSÜ HUN

423. A thousand feet high, piercing the snow—
they might be a metaphor for the stature of Hsi K'ang!
From a hundred feet away, they scatter in the breeze—
are any left to be struck by Yang Yu's arrows?

KI NO HASEO

PROSEPOEM ON WILLOWS CHANGING INTO PINES

The pines are a metaphor for Hsi K'ang, the eccentric poet and musician of the third century, in the *Shih-shuo hsin-yü*. According to a passage in the *Shih chi* (Records of the historian) of Ssu-ma Ch'ien (second century B.C.), Yang Yu-chi (also Yang Yu) was such a great archer that on every try, he could hit willow catkins floating in the wind from a hundred paces away.

424. At the height of ninefold summer, moonlight in the heat—
bamboo holds the breezes that waft to and fro.
Deep in the winter, cold morning of white snow—
pine trees emblem forth the virtue of the gentleman.

MINAMOTO NO SHITAGŌ

PROSEPOEM ON THE KAWARA RETREAT-PALACE

425. The glory of the Duke Eighteen—
revealed after the frost!
the colors of a thousand years
deepen in the snow.

MINAMOTO NO SHITAGŌ

The first line of this couplet defies translation, as it is based on the actual form of the Chinese character (*kanji*) for "pine tree." This character can be analyzed in such a manner as to yield the three words, "ten-eight (that is, eighteen) duke," following a Chinese story of a man who dreamed of a pine tree growing from his stomach. An interpreter suggested that this meant that the man would become a duke in eighteen years, basing his interpretation on an analysis of the character *sung* (pine tree). But this is a false—or, more precisely, a folk—etymology, and yet such analyses of written characters were an extremely popular form of prognostication.

426. Holding rain-sounds, the pines on the ridge—
and yet the sky is clear;

burning with fire, leaves of the autumn forest—
but these flames are cold.

ŌE NO ASATSUNA

> The first line of this couplet refers to the sound of the wind in the pines, an aural image appearing in Chinese and Japanese poetry nearly as frequently as that of autumn leaves.

427. *Even the unchanging green of the pine,*
When spring comes,
Shows an ever deeper hue.

MINAMOTO NO MUNEYUKI

428. *It has been so long since I first saw*
You charming pines
At the shore of Sumiyoshi;
The passing of how many ages
Have you witnessed
On that spot?

ANONYMOUS

429. *How venerable these pines at Sumiyoshi!*
Growing together through all time
Since the god, manifested in human form,
First came down to earth.

ANBŌ HŌSHI

Bamboo

430. Misty leaves all vague, unclear,
    invaded by colors of night;
windswept branches sighing, soughing,
    almost autumn sounds.

PO CHÜ-I

431.   On the site of Juan Chi's whistling,
       someone steps through moonlight;
       at the place where Tzu-yu gazed,
       birds perch upon the mist.

CHANG HSIAO-PIAO

This couplet contains two allusions to famous scholar-wits of the Six
Dynasties period in China. Juan Chi was one of the so-called Seven
Sages of the Bamboo Grove. He was known for his piercing *hsiao*
(whistling), a sound produced at beautiful locations in nature as an
act of communion with the Tao. Wang Hui-chih, or Tzu-yu, was the
son of the great calligrapher Wang Hsi-chih. Wang Hui-chih loved
bamboo so much that he planted nothing else around his house.
When a friend asked him why, he replied, "How can I live a single day
without This Gentleman!" This passage from Wang's biography in
the *Chin shu*, or the official history of the Chin dynasty, forms the
basis for a famous passage in Sei Shōnagon's *Pillow Book*. When a
group of courtiers challenged her and her fellow court women by
thrusting a branch of bamboo into their chambers, she immediately
responded by exclaiming, "Ah! So it is This Gentleman!" to the aston-
ishment and admiration of all present. Sei Shōnagon in all probabil-
ity learned the allusion from its use in the *Wakan rōei shū*, especially
the following entry, in which it figures explicitly. (Note that Wang
Hui-chih also figures in an allusion underlying number 378.)

432.   In Chin times, Administrator for Cavalry Wang Tzu-yu
       planted it and called it "This Gentleman."
       In T'ang times, Adviser to the Heir Apparent Po Lo-t'ien
       loved it as being "my friend."

FUJIWARA NO ATSUMOCHI

For the Wang Tzu-yu allusion, see the previous entry. Po Chü-i (Lo-
t'ien) has a poem, "Written Beneath the Bamboo Beside the Pond"
(*hou*, 6/9a), that contains the following couplet:

The water here can show calmness of nature —
    it is my friend!
the bamboo is able to grasp voidness of mind —
    it serves as my teacher!

The poet appears to have confused the two lines, perhaps on purpose.

433. Burgeoning shoots have not yet produced
    singing-phoenix flutes;
  spreading roots have just displayed
    reclining-dragon patterns.

PRINCE KANEAKIRA

434. *I hear the sound*
  Of the falling winter rains;
  Yet the knotted bamboo,
  Unlike the other grasses of this world,
  Never changes color.

ANONYMOUS

Wild Grasses

435. Along the sands, rain now dyes the mottling of the grass;
  across water's surface, breezes drive the swishing of the waves.

PO CHÜ-I

> "Wei-chih" in the title is Po's great friend Yüan Chen, author of the
> poem from which the next entry is taken.

436. Hsi Shih's complexion—today, where is it found?
  It must be here, on the hundred grasses, waving in spring wind.

YÜAN CHEN

> Hsi Shih was a famous beauty of antiquity.

437. His gourd and rice dish are often empty,
  and grasses flourish in the lane where Yen Hui lives.
  He resides deep among the weeds and brambles,
  and rain moistens the doorposts of Yüan Hsien's hut!

TACHIBANA NO NAOMOTO

> These are allusions to two men famous for maintaining their moral
> integrity despite living in poverty. Interestingly, Naomoto has paral-
> leled a Confucian with a Taoist figure, although the Taoist is in fact a

Confucian worthy turned into a spokesman for Taoist ideas, a favorite
humorous device of the great Taoist philosopher Chuang Tzu. In the
Confucian *Analects* (*Lun yü*) VI/9, Confucius praises his favorite dis-
ciple, Yen Hui (in the translation of James Legge): "Admirable indeed
was the virtue of Hui! With a single bamboo dish of rice, a single
gourd dish of drink, and living in his mean narrow lane, while others
could not have endured the distress, he did not allow his joy to be
affected by it."

Yüan Hsien was also a disciple of Confucius, employed by Chuang
Tzu (fourth century B.C.) as an exemplar of Taoist serenity. As trans-
lated by Burton Watson, "Yüan Hsien lived in the state of Lu, in a tiny
house that was hardly more than four walls. It was thatched with grow-
ing weeds, had a broken door made of woven brambles and branches
of mulberry for the doorposts. . . . Yüan Hsien said, 'I am poor, but I
am not in distress.'"

The poet here compares his genteel poverty with that of these two
figures from the past, using a frequently employed rhetorical device to
speak of himself as if he were they.

438. The colors of the grasses as snow clears
    begin to spread around;
the songs of birds as dew is warmed
    gradually warble forth.

ŌE NO ASATSUNA

439. Mount Hua has them, but horses' hooves are still exposed;
the wilds of Fu still lack them, yet in human pathways
    they start to show.

YOSHISHIGE NO YASUTANI

"The wilds of Fu" are where a certain Fu Yüeh was residing when
King Wu-ting of the Yin dynasty dreamed that he should seek him out
and make him prime minister.

440. *You who cuts the grass*
On the hill—
Do not cut so cleanly,

Leave it as it is,
So that when my lord comes,
There will be fodder for his horses!

ANONYMOUS

441. *When the grasses sprouting under the trees*
      In Ōraki Forest grow old,
      Colts will no more graze with pleasure,
      And none will come to cut them short.

ONO NO KOMACHI

442. *Even without a [spring] burning,*
      The [young] grasses seem to push upward;
      Only the sun needs shine on them
      In the fields of Kasuga.

MIBU NO TADAMI

> This poem contains a number of complex wordplays, among them
> the fact that the characters for Kasuga mean here "spring sun."

Cranes

443. We despise the small man who climbs to high position:
      witness the crane who once rode in a carriage.
      We hate the sharp mouth that overthrows families:
      the sparrow that can pierce the roof!

WRONGLY ATTRIBUTED TO CHIA TAO; ACTUALLY BY
CHIA SUNG

PROSEPOEM, THE PHOENIX IS KING

> This passage combines no fewer than three allusions. The first refers
> to Duke I of Wei who is said in the *Tso chuan* (Commentary of Master
> Tso) to have loved his pet crane so much that he presented it with a
> carriage to ride in. The citizens of Wei were so demoralized by this
> unfair favoritism that they refused to go to battle, and the state of Wei
> ultimately was defeated. The poet's use here of the crane to symbol-

ize the "small man" is highly unusual; ordinarily, the crane is presented as a noble bird, even as a Taoist symbol of longevity or immortality, or as a companion to hermits and retired gentlemen.

In the *Analects* (XVII/18), Confucius says, "I hate those who with their sharp mouths overthrow kingdoms and families." This is conflated here with a metaphor from poem 17 in the *Shih ching* (Book of songs). In this poem, a woman states that she refuses to marry a man to whom she has apparently been betrothed against her will. At one point she says (in the translation by Arthur Waley, who numbers it as poem 68 in his *Book of Songs*),

> Who can say that the sparrow has no beak?
> How else could it have pierced my roof?
> Who can say that you have no family?
> How else could you bring this suit?

Here, the sparrow piercing the roof clearly represents the influence of the man's family, which has, from the woman's point of view, interfered with her own family. Chia Sung uses the metaphor more generally, probably wishing to take advantage of its bird imagery.

444. Just like Li Ling when he entered barbarian territory:
he only saw members of a different race!
Or similar to Ch'ü Yüan exiled in Ch'u:
everybody else was drunk!

ATTRIBUTED TO HUANG-FU TSENG

PROSEPOEM, THE CRANE IN THE MIDST OF A FLOCK
OF CHICKENS

Li Ling was the Han dynasty general who led the Han forces against the invading Hsiung-nu nomads. He was taken prisoner by them after a major defeat in battle. Ch'ü Yüan, a fourth-century B.C. poet, was sent into exile in the southern state of Ch'u after his enemies at court slandered him to the king. In his famous poem "Yü fu" (The fisherman), he describes his encounter with an old fisherman. Ch'ü (who appears as a character in his own poem) complains that the whole world is drunk while he alone remains sober. The fisherman cautions him to be less arrogant. Ch'ü Yüan eventually, however, drowns himself in a river.

445. Sounds come to us on our pillows—
thousand-year-old cranes!
Reflections fall into our wine cups—
the peaks of the Five Elders!

PO CHÜ-I

> "Five Elders" is the name of a group of peaks in the Mount Lu mountain range in Kiangsi Province.

446. Clear screams—scattered sounds of cranes
beneath the pines;
cold light—one dot, a lamp in the bamboo grove.

PO CHÜ-I

> In this wonderful poem, "At Home Leaving Home," Po describes how, even though he is living at home, he "leaves home," using the phrase that signifies becoming a Buddhist monk. The complete poem reads,

> Clothing, food all paid for,
>   kids all married off:
> from this time on, I'll not take on
>   any family matters!
> At night I sleep—my body is
>   a bird roosting in the wood;
> morning, I eat—my heart like that
>   of a monk who begs for alms.
> *Clear screams—scattered sounds of cranes*
>   *beneath the pines;*
> *cold light—one dot, a lamp in the bamboo grove.*
> At midnight I enter *samadhi*, seated
>   cross-legged:
> the girl calls me, my wife summons me,
>   I pay no heed to them!

> The compiler may have noticed that both this and the previous poem employ related rhyme-categories, so that entries 445 and 446 actually rhyme (*feng*, "peak," rhymes with *teng*, "lamp," in the original Chinese texts). Technically, they belong to different categories, but some flexibility is allowed in mixing closely related rhymes.

447. In pairs they dance out in the courtyard
          where the flowers fall;
       several cries beside the pond
          as the moon comes out.

LIU YÜ[-HSI]

448. The crane returned to his hometown:
       Ting Ling-wei's words could be heard by all.
       A dragon met him with new regalia:
       T'ao An-kung's equipage then appeared to all.

MIYAKO NO YOSHIKA

PRESENTATION TEXT ON THE IMMORTALS

   In regard to Ting Ling-wei, the immortal who turned into a crane and
   then flew back to his hometown (at which time Ting's voice could be
   heard speaking to the astonished multitudes), see number 372. T'ao
   Kung-an is an alchemist whose labors were so successful that a dragon
   carriage descended to carry him up to heaven, again in full view of the
   people below.

449. The hungry squirrel, agitated by nature,
          anxiously suckles its young;
       the old crane, serene at heart,
          tranquilly lies asleep.

MIYAKO NO YOSHIKA

450. It cries at the Milky Way, startling from afar
          the solitary sleeper on his pillow;
       mingling with the wind, its cries wildly merge
          into the plucking of five strings.

MINAMOTO NO SHITAGŌ

451. When the tide rises high
       At Wakanoura,
       The waves roll onto the beach,
       And the cranes cry out,
       Heading for the reed-girt shore.

YAMABE NO AKAHITO

452. *The cranes*
   Flying in a flock in the vast sky,
   Look as though their very hearts were filled
   With propitious blessings.

   LADY ISE

   These "blessings" are for the long life of the senior palace attendant
   Fujiwara Michiko, for whom the poem was written in 913.

453. *The cranes*
   In the Bay of Fukei where the winds of heaven
   Blow [their blessings] —
   Why do they not return
   Above the clouds?

   FUJIWARA NO KIYOTADA

   Kiyotada wrote this poem when he was raised in rank and appointed
   governor of Kii Province, in order to express both his gratitude and his
   desire to return later to court. The Bay of Fukei is located in present-
   day Osaka Prefecture.

   Gibbons

454. At Jasper Terrace, covered with frost—
   a single cry of the dark crane pierces heaven!
   Down the gorges of Szechwan, deep with autumn—
   at the fifth watch of night, the grieving gibbon
      screams at the moon!

   HSIEH KUAN

   PROSEPOEM ON PURITY

455. As the Yangtze River flows through the Pa gorges
      it starts to form the word;
   gibbons, once you're past Wu-yang,
      really break your heart!

   PO CHÜ-I

   As the Yangtze flows through the gorges, it is said to form the charac-
   ter Pa, which is also an alternative name for part of Szechwan

Province. Gibbons are known for their plaintive cries, said to arose feelings of homesickness in the traveler. See Robert Van Gulik's excellent book, *The Gibbon in China: An Essay in Chinese Animal Lore* (1967), and the appended recording of gibbon cries made from Van Gulik's own family of pet gibbons.

456. After three cries of the gibbon, my tears
   of homesickness start to fall;
inside this single leaf of a boat, my body,
   all sick, is carried.

PO CHÜ-I

457. The barbarian goose gives one honk—
in autumn, bursting the wandering merchant's dream.
The gibbons of Pa sing out three cries—
at dawn, moisture appears on the traveler's sleeve.

ŌE NO ASATSUNA (ACTUALLY BY HIS SON, SUMIAKIRA)

The notion that three cries of the gibbon cause homesickness (see also the previous passage) is found in an old folk song.

458. One thread of smoke from someone's house—
   the autumn village, remote;
three sounds of crying from the gibbons—
   the gorge at dawn so deep.

KI NO HASEO

459. The gorge at dawn—deep among the vines,
   one cry from a gibbon;
the woods at dusk—as flowers fall
   the birds begin to sing.

ŌE NO ASATSUNA

460. The valley is quiet—we hear only
   the voices of mountain birds;

the plank road is precarious—we step steeply
　through the cries of gibbons in the gorge!

ŌE NO ASATSUNA

461. You monkeys in the mountain gorges,
　Do not cry so pitifully—
　For is today not a time
　Of special merit?

OSHIKŌCHI NO MITSUNE

　　Here "merit" refers to the fact that on the occasion of his pilgrimage
　　to the Western River near Kyoto, the retired emperor Uda (r. 887–897)
　　ordered poems to be written on the theme, inspired by Chinese
　　poetry, of monkeys crying in the mountain ravines.

Pipes and Strings

462. One note from the phoenix pipes,
　in autumn startling the clouds from Ch'in Ridge;
　several movements of "Rainbow Robe,"
　at dawn escorting the moon over Mount Kou.

KUNG-CH'ENG I

PROSEPOEM ON LIEN-CH'ANG PALACE

463. The first, the second strings sing and sigh:
　Autumn wind brushing pines, sparse tones fading!
　The third, the fourth strings peal and ring:
　at night, the crane, recalling its offspring,
　　crying from the cage!
　And the fifth string's sound, most poignant, stifled moaning:
　Lung River's waters, frozen, choking, unable to flow at all.

PO CHÜ-I

THE FIVE-STRING PLAYS

　　Po Chü-i is arguably the greatest describer of music in Chinese poetry
　　and one of the greatest in world literature. In this, one of his magnifi-

cent series of fifty protest poems, he is lamenting the fact that the brilliant "five-string" instrument has supplanted the classic *ch'in* zither — which in turn becomes a virtual symbol of Confucian civilization — but in characteristic fashion, before revealing his polemical point, he empathetically describes the five-string's seductive beauty.

464. As the mood leads, I please myself
    with music of pipes and strings;
somehow or other, of my poems,
    some have become known to people.

PO CHÜ-I

465. At once it causes the wife, mending clothes
    beneath the lamp,
to stitch in error a petal from the "shared heart" plum!

CHANG HSIAO-PIAO

    "Shared heart" is a variety of plum blossom. The commentators also refer to a flute tune entitled "Plum Blossoms Falling"; perhaps that is the piece she hears when she works at night.

466. Her gauze dress becoming a heavy robe,
she resents the heartlessness of the woman who wove it!
The pipes and strings playing a lengthy tune,
she's angry with the musicians for never ending!

SUGAWARA NO MICHIZANE

THE SINGING GIRL GROWS LISTLESS IN SPRING

467. "Falling Plum-Petals" — the tune is old, his lips now blow
    the snowflakes;
"Plucking Willows" — the sound is new, his hands now grasp
    the mist!

SUGAWARA NO MICHIZANE (SAME AS THE PREVIOUS)

    This elegant couplet describes the playing of two musical compositions. As he listens to the first, the poet imagines that the lips of the flutist who plays this classical flute piece are actually blowing the falling plum blossoms, which in turn are compared with falling snowflakes. The second piece, a new composition for the plucked-string zither, makes the poet imagine that the hands of the musician are holding branches of willow, which were traditionally offered in parting to symbolize "clinging" feelings of attachment, these branches with their catkins in turn being compared to mist. The metaphors of snowflakes for plum blossoms and willow branches (when seen from a distance, as in Impressionist paintings) for mist are conventional but are put to brilliantly innovative use in this remarkable couplet. Note also that the use of visual and tactile images to convey the effect of sound constitutes synaesthesia, the mixing or crossing of sense impressions, something with which the Symbolist poets of nineteenth-century France and their contemporaries, the pre-Raphaelites of England (for example, Dante Gabriel Rossetti), were fascinated but that East Asian poets had already mastered centuries ago.

468. Hsiang-ju once used it to flirt
     with Cho Wen-chün—and got her!
   So don't let the one within the curtains
     listen too closely to its sounds!

PRINCE KORETAKA

"The Ch'in Zither." The great Han dynasty poet of the second century B.C., Ssu-ma Hsiang-ju, did indeed win the heart of his wife-to-be in this manner, according to his official biography in the *Shih chi* (Records of the historian) of Ssu-ma Ch'ien.

469. *At the sound of the koto,*
     The pine breezes from the mountain peaks
     Begin to sound;
     From which string, which summit
     Do these echoes begin?

ANONYMOUS

Letters (with Bequeathed Letters appended)

470. Submerged phrases stifle their joys,
     like swimming fish with hooks in mouths

emerging from the bottom of a deep abyss;
floating elegances flutter in formation
like high-flying birds entangled in harpoon-arrows,
tumbling from the heights of layered clouds!

LU CHI

PROSEPOEM ON LETTERS

The *Wen fu*, or "Prosepoem on Letters," by Lu Chi (261–303), is one of the masterpieces of Chinese literary criticism, a poem-on-poetry exploring the creative process and the essential nature of literature itself in brilliant (and often quite abstruse) phrases and images. The best of the several English translations available is by Achilles Fang, first published in the *Harvard Journal of Asiatic Studies* 14 (1951): 527–566, and reprinted in John L. Bishop, ed., *Studies in Chinese Literature* (Cambridge, MA: Harvard University Press, 1965), pp. 3–42. The American poet Archibald MacLeish was a colleague of Fang's at Harvard and from him learned about the *Wen fu* and used several concepts from it in his own book on the art of poetry, *Poetry and Experience* (Cambridge, MA: Riverside Press, 1960). Although neither the Chinese nor the Japanese ever produced a truly systematic treatise on the art of literature, like Aristotle's *Poetics*, such works as the *Wen fu* are among the most sophisticated explorations of the subject in world literature.

471. Your bequeathed writings, thirty scrolls in all,
scroll after scroll filled with sounds of gongs and jade stones!
The earth on the plains of Dragon Gate
may have buried your bones but will never bury your name.

PO CHÜ-I

INSCRIBED AFTER THE COLLECTED WORKS OF
VICE GOVERNOR YÜAN, TWO POEMS

This is the entire second poem of the pair.

472. Your diction so skillful, you've stolen
the parrot's tongue!
Literary ornaments that partake
of the feathers of the phoenix!

YÜAN CHEN

Hsüeh T'ao, to whom the poem from which this passage comes was addressed, was one of the leading women poets of the day. The reference to the parrot is probably intended as a true compliment; the emphasis is indeed on the parrot's ability to speak rather than on its imitative character. In a poem by Yüan's friend Po Chü-i, a red cockatoo in a cage is used as a metaphor for a brilliant man of letters restrained by official duties.

473. A tapestried curtain opening at dawn
      on a mica-inlaid hall;
   white pearls dropping in autumn
      on a crystal plate!

CHANG HSIAO-PIAO

These are images for the beauties of a writer's work.

474. "Yesterday there was a tree on the mountain":
   its talent is comparable to mine!
   Today, there is a flower in the courtyard:
   it makes me ashamed of my writing!

FUJIWARA NO ATSUMOCHI

The first line alludes to chapter 20 of the *Chuang Tzu*, "The Mountain Tree." Chuang Tzu points out (in Watson's translation), "Because of its worthlessness, the tree is able to live out the years Heaven gave it." But soon afterward, his disciples questioned him about this matter, beginning their inquiry in this manner: "Yesterday there was a tree in the mountain. . . " (Watson, *The Complete Works of Chuang Tzu* [New York: Columbia University Press, 1968], p. 209).

475. Young Wang's eighth-generation descendant
   gathered the old writings of household supervisor Hsü.
   The lifelong friend of Chiang Yen
   collected the bequeathed works of administrative aide Fan.

MINAMOTO NO SHITAGŌ

PREFACE TO THE COLLECTED WRITINGS OF MASTER KYŌ

The author here presents two examples of men of the past who collected and published the works of their predecessors. In the second case, it would also be grammatically possible to consider "friend" and "Fan" as being in apposition, which would yield "[He was] the life-long friend of Chiang Yen:/[they] collected the bequeathed works of administrative aide Fan."

476. Ch'en K'ung-chang's words merely cured a headache;
Ssu-ma Hsiang-ju's prosepoem only transported beyond the clouds.

TACHIBANA NO ARITSURA

The poet praises the writings of a contemporary by implying that they are superior to those of two great masters of the past, Ch'en Lin (K'ung-chang) of the Six Dynasties period, and Ssu-ma Hsiang-ju, the master of the prosepoem (*fu*). Both men wrote pieces said to have cured the headache of one emperor and to have transported another above the clouds. (One wonders where the reader of Lieutenant General Minamoto, who is being praised here, would be transported!)

477. The recent benevolence of conferred position
is inscribed, an epigraph in rock!
The collected writings after "unicorn's capture"
are how the world knows this "Confucius"!

ŌE NO MOCHITOKI

THE SHRINE OF SUGAWARA [NO MICHIZANE]

This is an elaborate conflation of allusions intended to eulogize the great Sugawara no Michizane (845–903). The poet Ōe no Mochitoki lived from 955 to 1010. In 993, the emperor conferred high posthumous official rank on Michizane, who had been sent into undeserved exile. Shrines were erected to Michizane, as he had already attained the status of a deity in the Shintō religion (Confucianism, too, had a tradition of apotheosizing great men). The first line of the couplet explicitly refers to this event. The second line alludes to Confucius's alleged authorship of the *Spring and Autumn Annals*, a chronicle of the history of the state of Lu. According to China's great historian Ssu-ma Ch'ien, writing in the second century B.C., Duke Ai of Lu captured a creature while hunting which Confucius recognized as a unicorn. "Alas," he lamented, "my road has run out!" and he proceeded to write *Spring and Autumn Annals*, "putting aside his brush" after recording the capture of the unicorn. The Confucian philosopher Mencius, in the fourth century B.C., presents a statement by Confucius to the effect that the world would probably remember him because of the *Spring and Autumn Annals*. Mochitoki appears to be comparing Michizane's notorious exile with the "ending of the road" for Confucius (probably referring to the end of his chances at obtaining an official position)—symbolized by the capture of the unicorn—and Michizane's "later collected works" with the *Spring and Autumn Annals*. Michizane's post-texile writings are, without question, his most poignant.

478. *If this were not a world*
Filled with untruths,
How happy I would be to receive
Words of love from another!

ANONYMOUS

Wine

479. The colors of the Hsin-feng wine
glow fresh and pure in the parrot-nautilus cup!
The sounds of Eternal Joy Palace music
murmur softly in the phoenix-flutes.

KUNG-CH'ENG I

PROSEPOEM ON SEEING OFF A FRIEND AS HE RETURNS TO
TA-LIANG

The chambered nautilus is called a "parrot shell" because of its resemblance to the head and beak of a parrot. In this case, such a shell has been made into a wine cup. (It is unclear whether this is fanciful or whether such cups actually existed.)

480. Liu Po-lun, general-who-establishes-power in the Chin dynasty, loved wine; he wrote the *Ode in Praise of Wine* which was transmitted to the world. Po Lo-t'ien, adviser to the heir apparent of the T'ang dynasty, also loves wine; he has written the *Eulogy of Wine* to continue his work.

PO CHÜ-I

This is a passage in "parallel prose" from the preface to the eulogy. Liu Ling (d. after 265) was one of history's famous wine drinkers. His *Ode in Praise of Wine* is his only surviving work. Liu is said to have instructed a man servant to follow him everywhere with a shovel so that if Liu dropped dead, he could be buried on the spot without any fuss.

481. The tree leaning into the wind late in autumn,
the man facing wine in his later years:
his drunken visage is like its frosty leaves—
both are red, but not because of spring.

PO CHÜ-I

482. Your livelihood has been cast off—now poetry
is your profession!
Your hometown garden has been forgotten—
now wine is your native land!

PO CHÜ-I

483. Tea can dissipate depression, but its efficacy is slight;
the daylily's said to cause forgetting of sadness,
but its power is quite faint.

PO CHÜ-I

Both tea and daylilies are inferior to wine.

484. If Jung Ch'i-ch'i had understood as well
how to get drunk,
he surely would have mentioned "four"
instead of just "three joys"!

PO CHÜ-I

Jung Ch'i-ch'i appears in the Taoist classic *Lieh Tzu*. When Confucius and his disciples meet this old, impoverished recluse, they ask him the cause of his apparent happiness. He says he has "three joys": that he was born a human being, that he was born a man (and not a woman), and that he has reached the age of ninety.

485. The country of the Clan of Intoxication Land
alone throughout four seasons can boast of mild,

harmonious weather;
the citizens of the County of Wine Springs
never for even a single moment experience frozen,
darkened land.

ŌE NO MASAHIRA

WARMTH OR COLD DEPENDS ON WHETHER YOU
DRINK WINE

> Although the "country of the Clan of Intoxication Land" is an imagi-
> nary place, invented by T'ang writer Wang Chi, there actually is a
> County of Wine Springs in Kansu Province, China.

486. The fruits are tribute from Shang-lin Park;
put them in your mouth and they melt!
The wine has been sent from Hsia-jo village;
poured out, it is quite exquisite!

ŌE NO ASATSUNA

> Shang-lin Park was the legendary hunting park of Emperor Wu of the
> Han dynasty, immortalized by his court poet, Ssu-ma Hsiang-ju, in
> the "Prosepoem on the Shang-lin Park." A complete translation can
> be found in Burton Watson's *Chinese Rhyme-Prose: Poems in the Fu
> Form from the Han and Six Dynasties Periods* (New York: Columbia
> University Press, 1971). Hsia-jo village was famous for the quality of its
> wines, derived from the superb water of its natural springs (in general,
> the quality of East Asian rice–based wines was thought to derive pri-
> marily from the flavor of the water used to brew them).

487. First we encounter Juan Chi, who becomes our guide;
then we meet Liu Ling, and ask about the local customs.

TACHIBANA NO HIROMI

ENTERING THE LAND OF INTOXICATION

> The attribution is considered erroneous, and the actual author is not
> known. That is unfortunate, because he has negotiated here a delight-
> ful witticism: on entering the land of intoxication, we encounter two
> famous Chinese drinkers, Juan Chi, one of the seven sages of the
> Bamboo Grove, and Liu Ling, the author of the "Ode in Praise of
> Wine," both of them from the Six Dynasties period.

488. This township borders on the Land of Virtue Established,
        yet you never walk over there;
   its territory touches Never-Never Land—
        just sit, and all's forgotten!

PRINCE TOMOHIRA

SAME THEME AS ABOVE

> Both the Land of Virtue Established and Never-Never Land are imaginary places described by the Taoist philosopher Chuang Tzu. For example, he tells us (in the words of "The Master from South of the Market"), "In Nan-yüeh there is a city and its name is The Land of Virtue Established. Its people are foolish and naive, few in thoughts of self, scant in desires." See Burton Watson, trans., *The Complete Works of Chuang Tzu*, p. 211. In other words, this is one of the many versions of the Taoist paradise. Tomohira's point is that in the Land of Intoxication, one is already *in* paradise, so there is no need to go there.

489. These clouds from Wang Chi's land
        go twirling down the stream, so delicate!
   This snow from Hsi K'ang's mountain
        follows the ripples, and flies!

YOSHISHIGE NO YASUTANE

> Wang Chi wrote *An Account of the Land of Intoxication*. Hsi K'ang is said to have resembled a "jade mountain collapsing" when he was drunk. The "clouds" and "snow" are petals fallen into a stream and seen while the poet is intoxicated.

490. *I feel as though I might see*
   The moon at dawn!
   Reflected together in my sake cup
   Are both the sun
   And the ceremonial vines of abstinence.

ŌNAKATOMI NO YOSHINOBU

> The vines are hung drown from a headband as a sign of abstinence in important Shintō ceremonies, such as the Great Thanksgiving

Festival (Daijōsai), an autumn ceremony carried out on the occasion of a new emperor's enthronement. The pun on "moon" (*tsuki*) and "sake cup" (*sakatsuki*) gives rise to the double reflection mentioned in the first two lines of the poem.

Mountains

491. Dark colors, eye shadow from afar
     overlooking the azure ocean;
   sounds of waterfalls, from a distance
     falling from the white clouds.

HO-LAN SUI (? AN UNKNOWN CHINESE POET; ALSO APPEARS AS HO-LAN HSIEN)

THOUSANDS-FEET-HIGH MOUNTAIN

492. Beautiful places basically have no established owners:
   in general, mountains belong to the people who love mountains.

PO CHÜ-I

493. The crane at night, startled from sleep,
     cries bitterly at the pine-tree moon;
   The flying squirrel at dawn comes spiraling down
     through the coldness of mist in the gorge.

MIYAKO NO YOSHIKA (ALSO WRONGLY ATTRIBUTED TO MIYAKO NO ARINAKA)

494. The white-silk fan thrown to the ground,
     her blue-dark brows appear;
   the curtain of gauze now rolled away,
     the blue-green screen shines bright.

PRINCE TOMOHIRA

This is a truly brilliant couplet, wittily employing two of the most conventional images for distant mountain ranges to depict a double scene. We can picture a palace lady's boudoir or a mountain landscape or, better yet (following William Empson's classic *Seven Types of Ambiguity* [London: New Directions, 1947, reprint of 1930 publication]), both simultaneously. A mountain range seen from a distance is often compared to the curving line of a woman's eyebrows, carefully penciled in. The reverse comparison has poets praising a lady's beauty by comparing her eyebrows to the mountains. Screen paintings, needless to say, often showed mountain landscapes, and so actual mountains are frequently said to resemble painted screens! Tomohira takes advantage of this "pictorialism" to present the revelation of the hidden screen as either (or both) the discovery of a work of art in a boudoir (such screens often serving as decorations for beds) and/or the appearance of mountains previously hidden behind a veil of mist.

495. The myriad pipings arise at dawn,
　　　then fade at tips of trees;
　　clustered waterfalls ring out at evening,
　　　chilly at the valley's heart.

ŌE NO MOCHITOKI

496. *The mountain*
Is a bamboo hat
In name only!—
Perhaps it gained that name
Because the sun shines there
Morning and evening!

ANONYMOUS

The reference is to Mount Mikasa, which can be read as "bamboo hat mountain," located in present-day Nara Prefecture.

497. *The White Mountain of Koshi*
Where the clouds hover
Must be ancient indeed,
Since snow has been piling there
For many a year.

ATTRIBUTED TO MIBU NO TADAMI

White Mountain is located in present-day Fukui Prefecture.

498. *As I look abroad*
     The pine branches of Mount Yoshino
     Are filled with snow—
     For how many generations
     Has it been piling up there?

TAIRA NO KANEMORI

Mountains and Waters

499. Mount T'ai yields not the least territory
     and so can reach its full height;
     the Yellow River and the sea reject not the thinnest stream
     and thus can reach their depth.

"HAN SHU"

> This passage in parallel prose comes from a memorial presented, by
> his minister Li Ssu, to the then king of Ch'in, later to become the first
> emperor of Ch'in in 221 B.C. It is actually found in the biography of Li
> Ssu in the *Shih chih* of Ssu-ma Ch'ien (ca. 145–ca. 85 B.C.). As prime
> minister of the Ch'in dynasty, Li was one of the key architects of early
> Chinese history. The passage in question, in which Li is apparently
> urging the ruler to accept the tribute of even the smallest powers,
> draws on a passage in the writings of the eclectic philosopher Kuan
> Tzu. For more on Li Ssu and his policies, see Derk Bodde, *China's
> First Unifier* (Hong Kong: Hong Kong University Press, 1967).

500. When the Szechwan gibbon gives one cry,
     it brings boats to a halt along the moon-brightened gorges;
     when the barbarian horse suddenly neighs,
     you lose your way among the deserts of yellow sand.

KUNG-CH'ENG I

PROSEPOEM ON SADNESS

501. Blocking the sun, the evening mountains
     stand in clusters, green;

touching the sky, the autumn waters
stretch in vastness, white.

PO CHÜ-I

> In the title, "Hsing-chien" is Po's younger brother, Po Hsing-chien,
> himself an important writer best known for his story "The Tale of Li
> Wa," one of the masterpieces of T'ang dynasty fiction.

502. Reflected fires from fishing boats
  in coldness burn the ripples;
sounds of bells along the station road
  at night pass through the mountain.

TU HSÜN-HO

> *Tu Hsün-ho wen-chi* (the poet's collected works, in a recently pub-
> lished facsimile edition) reads "return to the cold shore" for the sec-
> ond part of line 1 (so that the entire line would read "Reflected fires
> from fishing boats return to the cold shore"), offering a far less inter-
> esting image than the conceit of "burning the ripples" found here.

503. The mountains seem a painted screen,
  the river seems a mat,
striking the gunwales, we come and go
  within the bright moonlight.

LIU YÜ[-HSI]

504. The plants and trees now flourish:
spring winds comb these hairs of the mountain god!
The fish and turtles frolic as they swim:
the autumn waters nurture these subjects of the River Earl!

[ŌE NO SUMIAKIRA]

> Numbers 504, 505, and 506 all are from the same work by this poet.
> They are wrongly attributed to Ōe no Asatsuna, who is in fact the
> *father* of Sumiakira. Number 457 is from the same work.

505. The place where Han K'ang went to perch alone

still has flourishing herbs as of old.
The spot where Fan Li moored his little boat
displays misty waves that seem quite fresh.

[ŌE NO SUMIAKIRA]

> Both men are famous hermits of the past who withdrew after selling
> herbs in the city (Han) or serving in government (Fan).

506. Mountains after mountains:
what craftsman carved the forms of these green cliffs?
Rivers after rivers:
what master dyed the colors of these emerald streams?

[ŌE NO SUMIAKIRA] WRONGLY ATTRIBUTED TO
ŌE NO ASATSUNA (SEE NOTE TO NUMBER 504)

507. Place where clouds open among distant trees
     around a mountain station;
time when the sun breaks clear
     above a solitary village on the seaside.

TACHIBANA NO NAOMOTO

508. The mountains become illuminated
     front and back in setting sun;
the river appears to flow upstream
     among the whirling rapids.

ŌE NO ASATSUNA

509. *The banks of Mimuro Mountain,*
Where the sacred trees grow,
Must be crumbling,
For the waters of the Tatsuta River
Are soiled and muddy.

ATTRIBUTED TO TAKAMUKO KUSAWARU

> Mount Mimuro is in present-day Nara Prefecture.

Bodies of Water (with Fishermen appended)

510. Grazing horses at the frontier town neigh and neigh again;
      the level sands stretch far.
      Traveling sails on their river journey all have vanished;
      the distant shore is hazy.

HSIEH KUAN

PROSEPOEM ON THE DAWN

511. The islets are perfumed by fragrant lilies
          extending their stems so delicate;
      the sand is warm where mandarin ducks
          spread out their wings and sleep.

PO CHÜ-I

> "Spring at K'un-ming" is one of Po's *New Yüeh-fu* poems, describing
> how the artificial K'un-ming Lake (an imperial preserve) was revital-
> ized by being filled with water after having dried up. In keeping with
> the general program of the fifty *New Yüeh-fu* poems, Po wishes to
> make a point: he hopes that just as the residents of the K'un-ming
> Lake area are allowed to fish and otherwise enjoy the benefits of the
> lake tax free, the imperial largess will extend to the entire empire, and
> all citizens will be disburdened of taxes on such goods as tea or silver.
> The lake thus becomes a symbol of the good society as envisioned by
> Confucianism, that is, one in which the government places as little
> burden as possible on the citizenry while at the same time ruling
> benevolently in accordance with the will of Heaven.

512. Your sail will unfurl on Green Grass Lake, as you travel along;
      your clothes will be dampened by "Yellow Plum" rains,
          as you journey on your way.

PO CHÜ-I

> "Yellow Plum" is a poetic term for the rainy season (generally, the
> fourth lunar month, although there are varying interpretations and
> the actual rainy season differs, of course, from region to region). In
> "seeing off" poems such as this—one of the most common topics in

Chinese poetry—the poet often imagines what the journey will be like for the person to whom he is saying good-bye. The next example is similar.

513.   At the water station, your route will pass
          the moon at Child-Speak Inn;
       the flowered boat will be piloted
          through Woman's-Tomb Lake in spring.

PO CHÜ-I

> Both place-names allude to legendary events of the past, variously interpreted by commentators. According to one version, "Child-Speak Inn" marks the spot where the son of King Kou-chien of the ancient state of Yüeh first spoke at the age of one. Although the place was on the territory of the rival state of Wu, after Kou-chien succeeded in conquering Wu, he changed the previous name of this location to "Child-Speak Pavilion [or Inn]." One version of the second allusion has it that another ancient king, Ho-lü, was once picnicking with a concubine. He gave her a half-eaten steamed fish to eat, at which she became so offended that she committed suicide. Ho-lü had her buried and flooded her tomb to form the artificial "Woman's-Tomb Lake." Both locations are in the Suchou region, hence their appropriateness in a poem in which the poet is seeing off an official (probably Liu Yü-hsi, himself a major poet also represented in the *Wakan rōei shū*) who has just been appointed to a position in Suchou.

514.   With a ladle of gourd, you pour out wine
          that thickens in the spring;
       with a tiny skiff, you ride the tides
          that rise and swell at night.

TU HSÜN-HO

[PLAYFULLY SENT TO] A FISHERMAN

> In this poem Tu Hsün-ho playfully refutes the idea that the fisherman's life is a difficult one. He ends by riding his horse back to the capital city of Ch'ang-an, where presumably life is actually much more difficult because of political pressures and factionalism.

515. This place of retirement—to whom does it belong?
To the lord of the Purple Imperial Hall!
Autumn waters—in what spot do they appear?
At the new residence of Vermilion Bird Courtyard.

SUGAWARA NO MICHIZANE

LIVING IN RETIREMENT AND ENJOYING THE
AUTUMN WATERS

> This and the following passage, from the same work, describe the
> retirement villa of Emperor Uda (r. 887–897).

516. The one who casts the fishing line now gets no fish:
quietly, he contemplates the pleasure of their swimming.
The one who moves the oar hears only wild geese above:
from far he's moved by the timeliness of their distant journey.

SUGAWARA NO MICHIZANE

517. Along the sand are etched the marks of gulls
    where they have stepped;
Reflected in water, copies of words
    written by passing geese.

ŌE NO ASATSUNA

> Wild geese flying in formation are often said to form the word *person*
> (formed like an inverted "V" with the left-hand stroke extended above
> the apex); hence the geese often remind the poet of some yearned-for
> friend, wife, or lover.

518. Sunbeams lie gentle on the ripples: sunset on the lonely isle;
wind blows from afar along the shore: the traveler's sailboat is cold.

TAIRA NO SUKEMOTO (DATES UNKNOWN; THE GRANDSON
OF A PRINCE)

519. *As each year comes in succession*
The water [of the pond],

Reflecting the flowers as a mirror,
Clouds over as the petals fall.

LADY ISE

520. *The headwaters steadfast,*
Your august reign
Continues again in the clear waters
Of the Horikawa River.

SONE NO YOSHITADA

> Written on the second occasion on which the Emperor En-yu (r.
> 969–984) moved to his palace near the Horikawa River in Kyoto.

The Forbidden City

521. Behind the Phoenix Pond appears the new autumn moon;
before the Dragon Tower-Terrace, mountains in setting sun.

"PO CHÜ-I"

522. The autumn moon hangs high beyond the azure void;
this immortal youth serenely enjoys the world
    behind the forbidden gates.

PO CHÜ-I

523. Of those thirty immortals, which one could have heard
the sounds of pipes and strings that played
    in a corner of Han-yüan Hall?

CHANG HSIAO-PIAO

> While thirty men were concentrating on taking the grueling *chin-shih*
> (presented scholar) examinations, they could not hear musicians who
> were playing in the Han-yüan (Containing the origin) Hall of the
> Forbidden City, perhaps to celebrate the victory of government forces
> against rebels who had been holding the town of Tung-p'ing. Either
> the candidates were too engrossed in their work to hear, or they were

too far away. An alternative reading is "three thousand immortals,"
which is a more realistic figure for the number of *chin-shih* candidates
on a given occasion.

524. The "rooster man" cries out at dawn:
the sound awakens the enlightened monarch from his sleep.
Master Fu's bell rings out at night:
its echo penetrates all hearing beneath a darkened sky.

MIYAKO NO YOSHIKA

The "rooster man" was a kind of night watchman. "Master Fu" is said
in the Confucian classic *Chou li* (The rites of Chou) to have invented
a type of bell. Both allusions are to old Chinese books and do not nec-
essarily describe realities of the Heian court.

525. Rushing to court muster—the sun's so high,
their caps fall from their heads!
patrolling at night—the sand's so thick
their clogs make hurried sounds.

LINKED VERSE

The authors of this couplet are unknown. In a linked verse, two or
more poets collaborate to write a single poem, alternating in accor-
dance with elaborate formal and aesthetic rules. In the case of this sin-
gle couplet, presumably one poet wrote each of the lines. For more on
this subject, see Earl Miner, *Linked Verse* (Princeton, NJ: Princeton
University Press, 1979), and Hiroaki Sato, *One Hundred Frogs* (New
York: Weatherhill, 1983).

526. *My fire is not like the one*
The imperial guards tend at the palace;
Yet in my heart, my own thoughts
Are always burning.

ANONYMOUS

Variants of this poem have been attributed to Ōnakatomi no
Yoshinobu.

527. *Even here the light*
Of the autumn moon shines down,
Yet how much brighter must it be
Where our sovereign stays!

FUJIWARA NO NOBUOMU

THE NIGHT OF AN AUTUMN MOON BANQUET

The Old Capital

528. Green grasses now become a park for deer to wander;
red flowers certainly once the site
of men playing pipes and strings.

SUGAWARA NO FUNTOKI

529. *When I come to look on*
The ruins of that ancient capital at Isonokami,
I find those flowers used the decorate the hair
[of that nobility long gone]
Continue on, blooming afresh.

ANONYMOUS

Isonokami was as ancient capital site of the fifth century, located in
present-day Nara Prefecture. In regard to the flowers in the hair, see
poem 25.

Old Palaces (with Deserted Mansions appended)

530. Forming dark ranks, ancient willows and sparse locust trees,
in spring showing no spring colors.
Crumbling away, tottering windows and collapsing roofs,
in autumn making autumn sounds.

KUNG-CH'ENG I

PROSEPOEM ON THE LIEN-CH'ANG PALACE

531.   The terrace is collapsing, only a few steps of polished stone remain;
    the curtains are tattered, not even enough pearls are left to take a
        single hook.

PO CHÜ-I

532.   Mighty Wu faded, ah! only brambles left;
    the dew is thick and moist on Ku-su Terrace.
    Cruel Ch'in withered, ah! no more tigers or wolves;
    the mist hangs in tatters over Hsien-yang Palace.

MINAMOTO NO SHITAGŌ

533.   The old crane has always been the vehicle
        of this cave of the immortals;
    cold clouds in the past were robes
        for this tower of dancing girls.

SUGAWARA NO MICHIZANE

534.   A solitary flower drips with dew, weeping
        over faded rouge;
    an evening bird perches in the wind,
        guarding the deserted hedge.

KORENAGA NO HARUMICHI

535.   On the deserted hedge appears the dew—
        autumn orchids weeping;
    deep within this "cave," wind is heard—
        old junipers grieving.

MINAMOTO NO FUSAAKIRA

536.   Toward dawn on tops of curtains forms the white dew;
    all night beneath the beds can be seen the dark sky.

"ZENSŌ" (? POSSIBLY MIYOSHI NO YOSHIMUNE)

537. *You have left this life,*
And through the boards of the roof
Of your house, now in ruin,
The moonlight pours in,
And my sleeves have become wet with tears.

ANONYMOUS

538. *You have left this life,*
And at the bay of Shiogama,
Where the salt fires have died away,
The world now seems desolate.

ANONYMOUS

Shiogama is located in Matsushima Bay in present-day Miyazaki Prefecture.

539. *In days gone by,*
It was you who mourned
The passing of the flowers;
Now, the blossoms themselves
Grieve for times past.

FUJIWARA NO KORETADA

Written on the death of Fujiwara no Atsukata (906–943), minister of the left and a noted *waka* poet himself.

The Immortals (with Taoists and Hermits appended)

540. There is a world inside a jar, beyond mere heaven and earth; my life and name pass in a dream, between the days and nights.

YÜAN CHEN

The idea that there is a magical world "inside a jar" (the Chinese word, *hu,* is an ancient one describing a type of vessel represented among the standard bronze ceremonial vessel types of the Shang dynasty) is widely disseminated in Taoist and other literature.

541. His herb brazier glows with fire;
          the elixir must be hidden within!
      his cloud pestle is held by no man;
          water works it by itself!

PO CHÜ-I

> Strange though it may seem, "Failing to Find a Hermit at Home" is a
> standard motif in Chinese poetry. The surprising phrase "cloud pes-
> tle" is explained by Po Chü-i himself in a poet's note to the line in his
> collected works: "In the Lu Mountains, there is much 'mother-of-
> cloud' [that is, mica]; therefore when a water-operated pestle is used
> to pound silk, it is commonly referred to as the 'cloud-pestle.'" This
> sounds very much like an attempt to explain a local phrase that is
> closer to guesswork than a true etymology.

542. Beneath the mountains, they gathered ferns—
          the clouds did not reject them;
      in the caves were planted trees—
          the cranes the first to know.

"WEN T'ING-YÜN"

543. The Three Jar-Worlds float like clouds:
      the distance of seventy thousand miles
          divided by the waves.
      The Five Walled Cities surge up like mists,
      their structures with twelve towers
          penetrating the sky.

MIYAKO NO YOSHIKA

> The magical places referred to here are the three Isles of the Immortals
> located far out at sea, and the cities of the immortals in the K'un-lun
> Mountains in the distant west.

544. Strange dogs bark among the flowers;
      the sound flows to the banks of red peach blossoms.

A sudden breeze shakes the leaves;
the fragrance spreads through forests of purple cassia.

MIYAKO NO YOSHIKA

> From the same work as number 543. The imagery here is derived pri-
> marily from T'ao Ch'ien's famous *Peach Blossom Spring*. In this par-
> adise on earth, a Taoist utopia such as the one described in the *Tao te
> ching* can be found. The dogs and chickens of one village can be
> heard in the next, and yet the people are so content that they never
> want to visit the neighboring villages.

545. Mistakenly they entered the realm of the immortals,
and though they stayed as guests for only half a day,
how fearful the return to their old village:
they met descendants only in the seventh generation!

ŌE NO ASATSUNA

> The imagery here derives from several famous accounts of encounters
> with the immortals but most notably from the story of Liu Ch'en and
> Juan Chao, who are said to have climbed Mount T'ien-t'ai, where they
> encountered two immortal women. After returning to their homes,
> they found that seven generations had passed. There are variations on
> this story, including several collected by folklorists in the twentieth cen-
> tury (see Wolfram Eberhard, *Folktales of China* [Chicago: University
> of Chicago Press, 1965], story 44).

546. In the elixir-brazier has formed the *Tao*;
in the mountains, brilliant colors beneath the lunar aura!

SUGAWARA NO FUNTOKI

> The imagery is derived from Taoist alchemy, here probably a mere lit-
> erary convention, as this branch of Chinese religion does not appear
> to have come to Japan, at least in organized form. The *"Tao"* here
> would be the cinnabar-based elixir of immortality. This couplet plus
> the following three (numbers 547, 548, and 549) together constitute a
> complete eight-line regulated-verse poem entitled "In the Mountains
> There Is a Stone Cave-House," or "In the Mountains There Is a
> House for Immortals."

547. A stone bench remains in the cave,
          emptily brushed by vapors;
      a jade desk has been discarded in the woods,
          where a bird now sings alone.

SUGAWARA NO FUNTOKI

> See the note to number 546.

548. The peach and plum trees say no word—
          how many nights in spring?
      the mists and vapors show no trace—
          who perched here in the past?

SUGAWARA NO FUNTOKI

> See the note to number 546.

549. Once this Prince Ch'iao departed hence,
          the clouds cut off the spot:
      sooner, later the sounds of his sheng
          will return to his old stream.

THE ABOVE [FOUR PASSAGES] CONSTITUTE FOUR RHYMES

> This poem has four rhymes (see the note to number 546). As even-
> numbered lines rhyme, an eight-line poem has four rhymes in all,
> although sometimes the first line also participates in the rhyme
> scheme, yielding a total of five. Prince Ch'iao was a famous player of
> the *sheng* (Jpse. *shō*), or mouth organ, who attained immortality and
> ascended into heaven.

550. At Shang Mountain as the moon descends
          their autumn whiskers whiten;
      along Ying River where waves ripple
          his left ear is purified!

ŌE NO ASATSUNA

> These lines allude to famous recluses of the past, the Four White-
> heads of Shang Mountain, and Hsü Yu, who used river water to clean
> out his ears after he had been offered a government position.

551. The deserted stream produces sound,
       its cold gurgle bubbling;
    the former mountain residence has no master now—
       the evening clouds are orphaned.

KI NO HASEO

THE MOUNTAIN HAS NO RECLUSE

552. Seen in dream—deep in the night,
       moonlight in vine-covered cave;
    seeking the traces one spring evening—
       dust on the willow gates.

SUGAWARA NO FUNTOKI

   It was Fu Yüeh, a sage of antiquity, who was discovered living in a cave
   as a consequence of a prophetic dream, and T'ao Ch'ien, the poet,
   who called himself "Mr. Five Willows" and had a willow gate in front
   of his retirement residence.

553. *In the instant*
    It took my robe to dry,
    Brushed by the dew from the chrysanthemums
    On this mountain path,
    Could it be that, for me,
    A thousand years have gone by?!

SOSEI

Mountain Residences

554. The bell of the Temple of Bequeathed Love—
       I hear it striking against my pillow;
    the snow on top of Incense Burner Peak—
       I see it through the rolled-up blind.

PO CHÜ-I

555. You in the "Orchid Bureau" at this time of flowers
       beneath the embroidered curtains;

me, here in Mount Lu on a rainy night,
    inside my thatched hut...

PO CHÜ-I

"Orchid Bureau" was a popular name for the Shang-shu sheng,
the Department of State Affairs, also sometimes referred to as the
Secretariat.

556. The fisherman in his evening boat
        fishes shore by shore;
    the herd boy plays on his cold flute
        as he lies back on the ox.

TU HSÜN-HO

Tu Hsün-ho ends his original poem with the boast that his poem
captures the beautiful scene more successfully than could be done
in painting:

Should a painter wish to paint this,
    then let him paint away:
even six pictures would have to yield
    to the eight lines of this poem!

557. Secretary Wang's "Orchid Bureau" was lovely
        as far as loveliness goes,
    but alas! he had only red-cheeked guests;
    Hsi Chung-san's Bamboo Grove was secluded
        as far as seclusion goes,
    but we must regret that his guests were not scholars
        of truly noble discourse.

SUGAWARA NO FUNTOKI

THE GATHERING OF ESTEEMED ELDERS

"The Gathering of Esteemed Elders" was superior to those held by
two famous scholars, Wang Chien and Hsi K'ang, of the Six Dynasties
period in China. The event took place in a mountain villa, hence its
appropriateness to this category, "Mountain Residences."

558. Gazing south, there stretches the length
        of the road toward mountain passes:
    travelers and journeying horses are seen flowing past
        from under blue-green blinds.
    Looking east, there too the marvel of tree-lined embankments:
    purple ducks and white gulls frolicking
        before the vermilion balustrades.

    MINAMOTO NO SHITAGŌ

    SHIRAKAWA PALACE

559. The mountain road as the sun sets:
    filling the ears, sounds of woodcutters' songs
        and herd boys' flutes.
    The valley mouth as birds return:
    obscuring the vision, colors of bamboo mist and pine-tree fog.

    KI NO TADANA

560. Among the flowers I seek for friends—
        bush warblers exchange words with me;
    into a cave I move my home—
        cranes become my neighbors.

    KI NO HASEO

561. After clearing, blue mountains draw near, coming to my window;
    as rain starts, white waters flow toward me, entering the gate.

    MIYAKO NO YOSHIKA

562. Touching stone, spring clouds arise, just above my pillow;
    swallowed by the ridge, the moon at dawn
        emerges at my window.

    TACHIBANA NO NAOMOTO

563. *True enough, it is sad to live*
    In this mountain village,

Yet how much better here
Than in the world of woe.

ANONYMOUS

564. *In this mountain village,*
The winter's loneliness grows greatest;
The grasses are withered, it seems,
And no eyes are here to see them.

MINAMOTO NO MUNEYUKI

Farmers

565. Along the fringes of emerald carpet—
early rice sprouts emerge;
along the sash of a green gauze robe
unfold the new cattails.

PO CHÜ-I

566. Guarding the house, a single dog,
barking to greet someone;
let out to graze in the fields, a herd of cows,
resting with their calves.

MIYAKO NO YOSHIKA

567. In the fields they pour the "mulberry-leaf dew,"
wine at 6:oo A.M.!
On mountain paddies, wind through rice-sprout flowers
on this early autumn day.

KI NO TADANA

Wine at 6:oo A.M. was thought to rouse the spirits.

568. How desolate, this place where the playing of a flute
is carried by the village breeze;

so mournful, journey-stage where the fulling of the clothes
    is neighbor to the moon.

TAKAOKA NO SUKEYUKI

569. *I will leave*
The planting of spring fields
To others; today, amidst the flowers,
I cultivate my heart!

ANONYMOUS

570. *Time passes;*
Before the rice seedlings grow too quickly,
Farmers, never mind the rain!
[For they must be transplanted.]

KI NO TSURAYUKI

571. *It seems only yesterday*
The rice seedlings were transplanted;
Now, suddenly,
Their leaves rustle
And the autumn wind blows.

ANONYMOUS

Neighbors

572. On nights of bright moonlight, we will enjoy
        walking the three paths together;
    our green willows should share
        a springtime of two households.

PO CHÜ-I

573. Nor will it be only us two,
        visiting the rest of our lives:

our sons and grandsons forever will be
    men who live next door.

PO CHÜ-I

> This and the preceding couplet are from the same poem and allude
> to two famous retired scholars of earlier periods: Chiang Hsü, who
> had three paths running through his place of hermitage, and Lu Hui-
> hsiao, whose residence shared two willows with that of his friend and
> neighbor, Chang Jung.

574. This estate, beside the pond—who is it that lives here?
     I've heard it said that Lu and Chang once were neighbors in
        this place.

SUGAWARA NO FUNTOKI

575. Falling to my pillow, sounds of waves
        divide between dreams on two shores;
     before the blinds, the willow colors
        share spring between two households.

SUGAWARA NO FUNTOKI

> This and the previous passage come from the same poem. Lu and
> Chang are the same pair of neighboring recluses already alluded to in
> number 572.

576. The spring mists share back and forth
        their colors before our blinds;
     the dawn wavelets secretly divide
        their sounds to both our pillows.

TACHIBANA NO NAOMOTO

577. *Will there be none who come to see*
     Before they fade
     Those iris which, like a fence,
     Divide your house from mine?

KI NO TSURAYUKI

Mountain Temples

578. Beneath a thousand pine trees, the temple of double peaks;
inside this single little boat, this body of ten thousand miles!

"PO CHÜ-I" (ACTUALLY BY CHAO KU [CA. 810–CA. 856])

579. Not a single vulgar thing to face a person's eyes;
there is only the sound of a waterfall to cleanse my heart!

PO CHÜ-I

580. No change in the gate from which I once paid court,
but now it is a place to seek the Vehicle;
just as before, the bridge for viewing the stream,
except it has become a path to the Other Shore!

ONO NO TAKAMURA

THE TEMPLE OF COMPASSIONATE KINDNESS

   The proprietor of a private estate has donated the property for a
   Buddhist temple, a fairly common occurrence in Heian Japan.

581. When I urged on my horse and came here,
I was thinking only of how enjoyable would be
      the windswept mist;
then I met the monks, and we had a talk:
gradually, I cam to realize that the world and its ways
      all are empty.

MINAMOTO NO FUSAAKIRA

582. The people emerge, like birds on pathways through the clouds;
the land is a "dragon gate" following the stream we ascend.

SUGAWARA NO MICHIZANE

   This couplet is a good example of a perfect grammatical parallelism
   in the original Chinese that must be compromised in the translation.
   Underlying this image of a "dragon gate" is the comparison of candi-

dates in China's civil service examinations with fish that ascend the stream and finally are transformed into dragons as they pass the examinations. The name of the temple where the poem is set is in fact Ryūmonji (Chin. Lung-men ssu), or Dragon-Gate Temple.

583. The Three thousand–fold Chiliocosm is exhausted before our eyes; the twelvefold karmic chain turns empty in our hearts.

MIYAKO NO YOSHIKA

This couplet employs two technical concepts of Buddhist thought, appropriate here because the poet and his associates are visiting a Buddhist temple. The "Three thousand–fold Chiliocosm [thousand-fold world]" is a term referring to the entirety of the universe (or "Buddha world") we inhabit. There are other Buddha worlds as well. The "karmic chain" is fundamental to Buddhist psychology and describes a circular sequence of cause and effect by which sensation leads to craving, which in turn leads through various stages to attachment and eventually death and rebirth, upon which the whole cycle begins again. The goal of Buddhism is liberation from the cycle, achieved through meditation leading to the realization of the "empty," or illusory, nature of the whole process. For more information about both of these concepts, consult W. E. Soothill and Lewis Hodous, A Dictionary of Chinese Buddhist Terms (originally published in 1937 and continually reprinted by Ch'eng-wen Publishing Company, Taipei), pp. 42–43, 61.

584. The waterfall flies down, its rainfall purifying
the dreams of the Śrāvakas;
the leaves fall, wind blowing through the autumn
of this material world.

TAKAOKA NO SUKEYUKI

Again, two technical terms from the Buddhist lexicon are employed here. "Śrāvakas" are disciples of Buddha who have "heard his voice" (the literal meaning of the Sanskrit term), here referring to the monks. The "material world" (Chin. se-hsiang, "form-and-attribute") is the world around us, which is ultimately illusory. See Soothill and Hodous, Dictionary, pp. 220, 461–462.

585. *Each time I hear the ringing*
      Of the mountain temple bell
      I hear the melancholy finish
      Of still another autumn day.

      ANONYMOUS

586. *[Traveling,] I dwell beneath the trees,*
      And so it is [when spring comes]
      I become like all the others,
      Happy to view the flowers.

      EMPEROR KAZAN

      A Buddhist pilgrim's poem.

                                                    Buddhist Matters

587. The moon is hidden by layered mountains, ah!
      we lift a fan to show it;
      the wind blows through the great void, ah!
      by swaying trees we teach it.

      [*MO-HO*] *CHIH-KUAN*

      The *Mo-ho chih-kuan* ([Treatise on] the great cessation and contem-
      plation) is one of the key texts of T'ien-t'ai (Jpse. *Tendai*) Buddhism.
      It consists of the teachings of the great Chinese Buddhist monk
      Chih-i (538–597) of the Sui dynasty. *Chih-kuan* refers to the Sanskrit
      Śamatha-vipaśyanā, or "cessation and contemplation," a term inter-
      preted by Buddhist teachers as the serenity achieved by practicing a
      combination of physical and spiritual techniques, including various
      forms of meditation. In this passage, the moon and wind represent
      the truth, which is hidden or obscured—or is simply invisible in this
      world. But teachers can demonstrate the presence of the wind by not-
      ing its effect on the trees, and they can use a Chinese fan—round or
      oval in shape—to symbolize the moon. Similarly, Buddhists can use
      "expedient means" (*upāya*) to convey the truths of Buddhism that are
      otherwise inexpressible. See Soothill and Hodous, *Dictionary*, pp.
      154, 158.

588. I vow to take the error of the wild words and decadent diction of my
worldly literary enterprise in this life and transform it into the karma of
praising the Turning of the Wheel of Dharma of Buddha's Vehicle for
ages and ages to come.

PO CHÜ-I

This passage is in prose.

589. For thousands and millions of *kalpas* to come,
    you have planted the tree of *bodhi*;
for eighty-three years now, a forest of merit is yours.

PO CHÜ-I

In this poem, as well as in others in the series of five from which it
derives, Po Chü-i demonstrates his impressive knowledge of Bud-
dhism by using Sanskrit technical terminology (transliterated, of
course, into Chinese). *Kalpas* are enormously long eras of time.
Bodhi is the wisdom achieved by Buddha as he meditated beneath a
"*bodhi* tree" and striven for by all Buddhist practitioners. Ju-man, the
man to whom the poem was written, was eighty-three years old (by
Chinese reckoning; actually eighty-two or eighty-one) at the time of
this writing, as Po informs us in a note to the poem's title. He also tells
us that this venerable Buddhist had been a monk for sixty years.

590. Among the Buddha lands of the ten directions,
    the west is cynosure;
of the lotus thrones of all nine levels,
    even the lowest suffices.

YOSHISHIGE NO YASUTANE

The west is the direction of Amitabha (Jpse. *Amida*), Buddha's
Western Paradise, where in Pure Land Buddhism the pious achieve
rebirth on a lotus throne. Each of the three divisions has three subdi-
visions, for a total of nine, arranged hierarchically in accordance with
the spiritual levels of different devotees. These nine sections of par-
adise were depicted in paintings, for example, at the magnificent
Byōdōin temple in Uji, dating from 1053. The "ten directions" are the
four cardinal directions, the intermediary directions (northeast, south-
east, southwest, northwest) plus the zenith and the nadir.

591. Though you may have committed all ten deadly sins,
   ah! still will he take you in,
   more readily than a brisk wind will sweep off clouds or fog.
   Though you make even a single recitation,
   ah! he will incvitably respond;
   compare it to the vast ocean absorbing a drop of dew.

PRINCE TOMOHIRA

> These lines praise Amida Buddha's Vow of Compassion to accept all
> into the Western Paradise. The "ten sins" are (1) killing, (2) stealing,
> (3) lust (or adultery), (4) lying, (5) lascivious language (including dou-
> ble entendre), (6) foul language (such as cursing), (7) "double
> tongue" (hypocrisy, disingenuousness), (8) covetousness, (9) anger,
> and (10) false views. Only a single recitation of the *nembutsu* (formula
> of praise addressed to Amida Buddha) spoken with true devotion will
> result in Amida's acceptance of the sinner into paradise.
>   The word *inevitably* (Chin. *pi*) was dropped from the *Wakan rōei
> shū* text, but the editors added it, on the basis of other texts of this work
> by Prince Tomohira.

592. Formerly, when Buddha went on a ninety-day retreat
      in the Trayastrimśā Heaven,
   there was carved a statue modeling his honored visage
      in red sandalwood.
   Today, two thousand years since he entered Nirvana
      by the banks of the Hiraṇyavatī,
   with scintillating red gold image, we perform a ceremony
      to the Double-Honored One.

ŌE NO MASAHIRA

> The anniversary of Buddha's death is celebrated by dedicating a gold
> image of him. The legend of the creation of the first Buddha image
> is alluded to in the first two lines of this passage: When Buddha went
> to the "Heaven of the Thirty-three Devas" (Skt. *Trayastrimśā*) to
> observe the traditional ninety-day rainy season retreat and to preach
> the dharma to his mother, his presence on earth was missed, and so
> the sandalwood image was carved to represent him. There are various

interpretations of the phrase "Double-Honored." It might mean "by both gods and men" or "by all two-legged creatures."

593. Waves may wash them completely away,
   and yet [the children] whip up their bamboo horses
      and pay no heed;
   rain may bludgeon them into pieces,
   and yet [the children]
      set mustard-seed cocks to fight each other
      and forget forever.

YOSHISHIGE NO YASUTANE

THEY GATHER SAND AND MAKE IT INTO BUDDHA STŪPAS

Yasutane developed into a poem a line from the Lotus Sutra, one of the most popular and influential of all Buddhist sacred books. The occasion for this exercise was a sermon on the Lotus Sutra that must have centered on this passage. In Chapter 2 of the Lotus Sutra, entitled "Expedient Devices" (as translated by Leon Hurvitz), Buddha is exhorting his followers to gain merit by such pious activities as making images of him or erecting *stūpas* (reliquary monuments) in his honor. He is making the point that such activities are easy; children perform them as a game. But even these children gain merit through this unwittingly pious activity:

> There are even children who in play
>   Gather sand and make it into Buddha stūpas.
> Persons like these
>   Have all achieved the Buddha Path.

(From Leon Hurvitz, trans., *Scripture of the Lotus Blossom of the Fine Dharma* [New York: Columbia University Press, 1976], pp. 38–39.)

Mustard seeds are said to have been spread on the feathers of fighting cocks, presumably to increase their belligerence.

Yasutane appears to be orchestrating the point, implicit in the Lotus Sutra, that even though the children's pagodas (the Chinese or Japanese form of the stūpa) are impermanent and the children them-

selves forget about them and turn to other games, they still earn merit
by building them, because of Buddha's great compassion.

594. Recalling the Lord of the Paradise of Supreme Joy, one night
the mountain moon was perfectly full;
setting the precedent, the Gathering at Kou-ch'ü
   lasted three days—
now magic-cave flowers again are soon to fall.

KI NO TADANA

THE GATHERING TO ENCOURAGE STUDY

> The original work is based on the meeting of a Lotus Sutra study
> group. The moon reminds them of Amida Buddha, and the flowers at
> the temple where they have gathered are reminiscent of a famous
> episode in the life of a certain Mao Ying of the Han dynasty. Mao was
> actually a practitioner of "alchemical Taoism" rather than of
> Buddhism; on the day he was about to ascend to heaven after having
> successfully concocted the elixir of immortality, he set a date to return
> to earth for a reunion with two of his disciples at Mount Kou-ch'ü.
> "Magic caves" play a significant role in Taoist lore. The mixing of
> Buddhist and alchemical–Taoist allusions is most unusual. Perhaps it
> seemed acceptable in Japan for the very reason that Taoism never
> really developed as a practiced religion there but has remained essen-
> tially a source of literary allusion.

595. The jade chime stones remind us of the playing of pipes
   and strings;
monks dressed in cassocks take the place
   of courtiers in elegant silks.

MIYAKO NO YOSHIKA

> At a gathering to hear the recitation of the Lotus Sutra, the courtiers
> wear monk's robes in place of their usual court dress and hear the tem-
> ple chimes instead of courtly "pipe and string" music. The passage is
> also wrongly attributed to Ono no Takamura.

596. His lotus eyes—were they nurtured
        by waters pure and clear?
    His full-moon face retains always
        the night of the fifteenth.

KI NO TADANA

ĀNANDA

> Ānanda was Buddha's greatest disciple, eulogized here through the
> use of nature imagery. His eyes are like lotuses, and his face is like a
> moon perpetually full, not only on the fifteenth night of the lunar
> month, when the ordinary moon becomes perfectly full.

597. Even with the aid of Buddha's divinity,
        how could you drain it dry?
    Even after billions of ages,
        would this river all flow into the ocean?

ŌE NO MOCHITOKI

> This couplet praises the limitlessness of the bodhisattva Avaloki-
> teśvara's (Kannon's) vow to postpone enlightenment until all sentient
> beings can reach it. The doctrine is reminiscent of the view expressed
> by Origen (185?–254?) that eventually all people will be saved, which
> the Church declared to be heretical.

598. Breaking through ice, he carried firewood—
        moonlit nights in cold valleys;
    brushing off frost, he gathered every last piece of fruit,
        among the clouds of evening mountains.

YOSHISHIGE NO YASUTANE

> This couplet praises the earnestness of Śakyamuni Buddha when, as a
> king in a past life, he renounced his realm in order to engage in the
> search for the teachings of the true dharma. Buddha himself describes
> his ordeal in chapter 12 ("Devadatta") of the Lotus Sutra: "For
> Dharma's sake I abandoned realm and title . . . and to the beat of a
> drum I announced to the four quarters. . . . 'Whoever can preach the
> Great Vehicle to me, for him I will render service and run errands for
> the rest of my life!' "

[When a sage appears and offers to teach him, the king] "then straightaway followed the seer, tending to whatever he required: picking his fruit, drawing his water, gathering his firewood." Hurvitz, trans., *Scripture of the Lotus Blossom of the Fine Dharma*, p. 195.

599. Having completed a thousand years of unprecedented labors,
he finally chanced to obtain the writings of the One Vehicle,
so difficult to encounter!

YOSHISHIGE NO YASUTANE

The Lotus Sutra states that underlying all of Buddha's apparently disparate teachings there is a single truth, called the One Vehicle. These "writings" would be the Lotus Sutra itself.

600. *Once I thought to pluck the young herbs*
For your pleasure;
Today I must pick them
To honor the laws of Buddha.

EMPEROR MURAKAMI

Written by the daughter of the wife of Emperor Murakami at her mother's death in 955.

601. *I have heard*
That the paradise of Buddha
Is far away indeed,
Yet in prayer,
It comes as quickly
As the morning itself.

KŪYA

602. *May all the omniscient Buddhas*
Bless what I set out to build
On these tree-filled mountains.

DENGYŌ DAISHI

Written on the occasion of the construction of a temple on Mount Hiei, north of Kyoto.

603. *If you plant the seeds*
Of enlightenment in this world,
You must surely be drawn up [to the Western Paradise]
By Amida Buddha himself.

SASHŌFU

The reference is to the Pure Land sect of Buddhism.

Monks

604. When clearing starts of patches of foggy rain—
a cold spit of land where an egret stands.
Where breaks appear in layers of mountain mists—
an evening temple and monks returning home.

ATTRIBUTED TO CHANG TU

PROSEPOEM ON LEISURE

605. At temples in the countryside I visit monks,
way back lit by moonlight;
to fragrant forests I conduct my guests;
drunk, we sleep in flowers.

PAO JUNG

606. At home there is your honored mother:
do not, therefore, linger beneath the moon of Central Sky!
In your temple are signs of your master's presence:
do not, therefore, rest overlong among the clouds of Five Terraces!

YOSHISHIGE NO YASUTANE

AT A FAREWELL BANQUET FOR A MONK ABOUT TO
JOURNEY TO CHINA

"Central Sky" is a term from Buddhist cosmology referring to north-central India, that is, the land where Buddha actually lived. The monk in question may have been intending to extend his journey that far or to visit a temple of the same name on Fei-lai (Flew Here) Peak at Hangchou. The Five Terraces Mountains, in Shansi Province, were associated with visionary appearances by the boddhisattva Mañjuśrī (Jpse. *Monju*) and were a major pilgrimage site.

607. A bright mirror, suddenly revealed, that illuminates
         everywhere;
      without taint of the slightest cloud,
         you come down from the mountain.

ONO NO TAKAMURA

> This couplet praises the brilliant wisdom and purity of a Buddhist monk.

608. Contemplating emptiness, these pure monastic brothers
         have minds like moons suspended;
      seeing out old age, the monks of high rank
         shave frost from off their heads.

MINAMOTO NO SHITAGŌ

609. The crane is serene; his wings he arranges,
         thousand-year-old snow!
      the monk is old; his eyebrows hang,
         frost shaped like an inverted "V"!

MINAMOTO NO TAMENORI

> In the original, the inverted V is "the character *pa*." *Pa* is the word for "eight" in Chinese and does resemble an inverted V, but with a slight gap between the two sides instead of a pointed joining.

610. *My mother,*
      Thinking it might be so,
      Must never have stroked my black hair
      When I was a child
      [hoping I would become a monk].

RYŌSŌJŌ

611. *In this world,*
      If no oxcart existed,
      How might we ever escape
      This earthly house of carnal passions?

ANONYMOUS

> This poem is a reference to the celebrated Parable of the Burning
> House found in the Lotus Sutra.

612. *Purifying myself*
      In the clear stream of Mount Miwa,
      Let my reputation in this world
      Lose every stain.

ATTRIBUTED TO GENBIN

> Mount Miwa, south of Nara, contains one of the most famous Shintō
> shrines in Japan. There is a legend that this poem was written by the
> monk Genbin on the occasion of his retiring as a teacher of the Law.

Living in Retirement

613. Here I do not merely record the doings of a retired old man, living in
      leisurely peace in Walk-the-Way Neighborhood in the eastern capital,
      but I also show how, during the years of the Great Harmony period of
      the imperial T'ang dynasty [827–835], there were heard sounds of the
      serene music of harmonious society.

PO CHÜ-I

> This passage is in prose.

614. The Palace Carriage once departed,
      towers and terraces, all twelve, perpetually deserted!
      The "colt past a crack" is hard to pursue;
      the silks and satins, three thousand in all, secretly turn old.

ATTRIBUTED TO CHANG TU

PROSEPOEM ON LEISURE

> The first line refers obliquely to the death of an emperor. Chuang Tzu,

a great Taoist philosopher, compared time to a "colt seen galloping past through a crack in a wall." Number 615 comes from the same source.

615. My deep thoughts unending,
far down the alleys, where no one comes at all;
my sad heart about to break,
at my tranquil window, as the moon appears.

ATTRIBUTED TO CHANG TU

PROSEPOEM ON LEISURE

616. When I open the crane's cage, I see the sovereign;
as I unfold my book scrolls, I encounter old friends.

PO CHÜ-I

Po here is describing the consolations of a life in retirement. Although cut off from the outside world, he "sees" the emperor in his pet crane and "meets" friends by reading.

617. The glory of this human realm—its karma is quite shallow;
the hidden leisure beneath the trees—its flavor is quite deep.

PO CHÜ-I

618. The path of officialdom—from this time forth,
my heart says good-bye to it!
Worldly affairs? From now on, my mouth will not discuss them at all.

PO CHÜ-I

619. With orchid sash and robe of vines
I'll pluck out my official hat pin north of North Mountain!
With epidendrum sweep and scull of cassia
I'll beat the gunwales east of the Eastern Sea!

ŌE NO ASATSUNA

The poet uses imagery derived from the great Chinese poetic anthology the *Ch'u tz'u* (Songs of the south), based on the shamanistic religious poetry of the ancient state of Ch'u (see the complete translation

by David Hawkes [Harmondsworth: Penguin, 1985], and Arthur
Waley's study, *The Nine Songs* [London: George Allen & Unwin,
1955]). In those poems, dating from the fourth century B.C. and later,
a shaman-poet decks himself in the floral costuming characteristic of
such garb and travels in a magic boat of sacred plants, in preparation
for an encounter with a deity. In the later poems, this imagery is
exploited for the purpose of political allegory. Here it creates a general
atmosphere of withdrawal and seclusion from the world.

620. Of the gate tower of the prefect's residence
    I see only the colors of the roof tiles;
of the Temple of Kannon Bōsatsu,
    I hear only the sound of the bell.

SUGAWARA NO MICHIZANE

I DON'T GO OUT THE GATE

621. I've hid my traces but not rejected
    the moonlight on the path of moss;
I've fled the racket, yet still lie near
    the wind through the bamboos at the window.

TAIRA NO SUKEMOTO

622. At T'ao's gate, all traces cut off
    on spring mornings of rain;
in the boudoir, colors fade,
    on autumn evenings of frost.

ŌE NO MOCHITOKI

    In the first line, the poet compares himself with T'ao Ch'ien. In the
    second line, he compares himself with an aging imperial concubine.

623. *So overgrown now,*
There is no longer a path to my home
While I have waited
For my heartless lover.

BISHOP HENJŌ

Views and Vistas

624. Wind ripples the white wavelets—flowers, a thousand petals!
geese mottle the blue sky—words, a line of writing!

PO CHÜ-I

625. Emerging from the purple portal, eastward I gaze:
mountain peaks are half-submerged in the obscurity of cloud roots.
Climbing the blue-green ridge, westward I look:
my hometown is completely hidden in the depths of misty trees.

TACHIBANA NO ARITSURA

> "Cloud roots" usually mean mountaintops or cliffs, from which
> clouds were thought to be generated. In this context, it seems to refer
> to the lower portions of the clouds themselves.

626. I see Mount T'ien-t'ai's high cliffs:
forty-five feet of waves, all white!
I gaze at Ch'ang-an City's distant trees:
hundreds, thousands of stems of shepherd's purse, all green!

MINAMOTO NO SHITAGŌ

> The editors speculate that the poet is using famous Chinese place-
> names to refer to the capital city of Heian and to Mount Hiei. The
> "waves" refer to a waterfall, and the comparison of trees seen in the dis-
> tance to shepherd's purse derives from a passage in the Chinese philo-
> sophical book *Yen-shih chia-hsün* (Family instructions of the Yen clan).

627. River mists on the other shore,
      smoke from homes is far;
the lake's water reaches sky
      where wild geese dot the distance.

TACHIBANA NO NAOMOTO

628. A single line of slanting geese
      fades at the edge of clouds;

in the second month, remaining blossoms
  fly beyond the wilds.

MINAMOTO NO SHITAGŌ

629. My old eyes are easily confused in fragmentary rain;
  Spring feelings are hard to hold just before the dusk.

FUJIWARA NO ATSUMOCHI

630. *As I gaze out,*
  Cherries and willows are mixed together;
  The capital itself
  Becomes a spring brocade.

SOSEI

Farewell Gatherings

631. When will our next meeting be,
    where will it take place?
  Please, this morning, take this wine
    and drink a cup for me.

PO CHÜ-I

632. The road ahead stretches far for you;
  your thoughts race to the evening clouds of Wild Goose Mountain.
  A later meeting? The date far off,
  we moisten hat strings in tears this morning
    at the court of diplomacy.

ŌE NO ASATSUNA

> The poet is at a farewell banquet for a Chinese emissary who is about
> to return home. The "court of diplomacy" was responsible for enter-
> taining foreign visitors of state.

633. Once we gathered "red birds"
  to grasp each moment for fifteen whole years!

Now you are escorted by the "painted bear";
we part hands after three hundred cups of wine.

MINAMOTO NO SHITAGŌ

> This passage is a tissue of literary allusions. A diligent but impover-
> ished scholar once gathered fireflies ("red birds") in a lantern so that
> he could continue studying by their illumination at night, because
> he could not afford lamp wicks and oil. "Fifteen years" is the amount
> of time another scholar was said to have studied before being
> appointed to a position. According to the regulations of the Han
> dynasty, the crosspiece of a feudal lord's carriage was supposed to be
> ornamented with the painted image of a crouching bear. Here the
> image refers to the official carriage in which the poet's friend is con-
> veyed to his post as *kokushu* (governor's executive officer). The "three
> hundred cups" conjures up the memory of the Han scholar Cheng
> Hsüan, at whose farewell banquet there were three hundred guests,
> each of whom wished to drink an individual parting toast with
> Cheng. Cheng managed to consume three hundred cups of wine,
> we are told, "without collapsing."

634. At Yang's crossroads the way flows easily:
I've been seeing people off for many years.
At Li's Dragon Gate, the waves are high:
when will people ever see me off?

ŌE NO MOCHITOKI

PREFACE: AT A FAREWELL BANQUET FOR SEVERAL FRIENDS

> There are two key allusions here: the ancient philosopher Yang Chu
> is said to have wept tears at the sight of a crossroads, and the Han
> scholar Li Ying had a gateway to his residence called "Gate of the
> Ascending Dragon." On passing the examinations, successful candi-
> dates for the *chin-shih* degree are compared to carp that have passed
> upstream through the "Dragon Gate" (Lung-men) of the Yellow River
> to be transformed into dragons. The passage may therefore be para-
> phrased as "Yang Chu may have wept at the metaphysical problem of
> fate and choice implied by a crossroads, but for me, the farewells that
> take place at a crossroads have flowed all too easily as friends have
> passed the examinations and been appointed to positions. But I still
> have not succeeded and wonder when I ever will."

635. Ten thousand miles you came to the east—
        will you ever come again?
      The rest of my life I'll be gazing west—
        such will be my constant feelings.

ONO NO TAKAMURA

636. The nine-stemmed lamp has burned out now—
        we only expect the dawn;
      your boat will fly, a single leaf
        that did not wait for autumn.

SUGAWARA NO MOROCHIKA

637. We may wish to plan another meeting
        in this floating life,
      but I lament this flickering flame
        that's struck from stone in wind!

SUGAWARA NO MICHIZANE

638. *There seems nothing whatsoever*
      That can keep my thoughts from you,
      However those white clouds on the peaks
      May try to distance us.

TACHIBANA NO NAOMOTO

639. *Every year*
      I feel the sadness of spring partings
      As I send off my friends,
      For it is I who remain behind.

KIYOHARA NO MOTOZANE

640. *If life itself*
      Could indeed be made
      To suit our human hearts

Then my grief at parting
Might be less intense.

SHIROME

Travel

641. While I stay the night in this lonely inn,
        the wind sprays earth with rain;
    in the spot where a distant sail heads home,
        water joins with sky.

HSÜ HUN

642. Journeying, journeying, and again journeying—
    the dawn colors of Bright Moon Gorge go on forever!
    Vastly sounding, vastly sounding—
    the evening tones of Long Wind Bank still deep.

MINAMOTO NO SHITAGŌ

643. At dawn we enter a cave among tall pines;
    the cliffside waterfall splashes with the songs of gibbons.
    At night we sleep by the waves of the distant shore;
    green mountain breezes blow coldness from the frosty moon.

ATTRIBUTED TO YOSHISHIGE NO TAMEMASA OR FUJIWARA
NO TAMEMIYA

644. At the crossing, the ferry boat
        sets out as the wind settles;
    across the waves, beneath clearing skies,
        I see my place of exile.

ONO NO TAKAMURA

645. Nighttime rain in the islet reeds—
        tears of homesickness!

Autumn wind through the riverside willows—
feelings of the distant frontier!

TACHIBANA NO NAOMOTO

646. Over the green waves, the way is long—
clouds for a thousand miles!
in white fog, the mountains are deep—
a single birdsong is heard.

TACHIBANA NO NAOMOTO

647. *Dimly*
In the morning mists
Over Akashi Bay,
I think of a boat moving
Hidden behind the islands.

ANONYMOUS

648. *I have rowed*
Into the vast seas,
Toward a myriad of isles—
Can you take back that message,
You on the fishing boats?

ONO NO TAKAMURA

The poet was being exiled.

649. *If some means presents itself,*
Tell them in the capital
That today,
I have crossed the Shirakawa Barrier.

TAIRA NO KANEMORI

The Shirakawa Barrier, the gate to the northern regions, marked for
many the edge of civilization. Even after its functions were aban-
doned, the gate remained a famous site, visited by Bashō in his

famous *Narrow Road to the Deep North*, written in the late seventeenth century.

Kōshin

Kō and *shin* (Chin. *keng* and *shen*) are two of the cyclical characters used to name the years, days, and hours of the day, among other things. Here the reference is to a practice derived from Chinese Taoism but also followed in popular Buddhism, of going without sleep on *kōshin* nights because on such nights, the three "corpse bugs" believed to inhabit the person are supposed to report to the Lord on High that person's evil deeds. The purpose of the wake is to help sweeten the report. Pictures of the Three Monkeys ("See no evil, Hear no evil, Speak no evil") are hung, as is a popular Buddhist figure known as the "Blue Warrior."

650. Advanced in years, it's always confusing
     to reckon the chia and tzu;
     the night so cold, for the first time together
     we keep the keng-shen wake.

HSÜ HUN

Years in East Asia were always named in accordance with two sets of cyclically repeating characters, one of twelve (beginning with *tzu*), and one of ten (beginning with *chia*). A given pair repeated every sixty years. The same system was used to designate the day; *keng-shen* (Jpse. *kōshin*) is one such pair. One added a year to one's age not on one's birthday but, instead, on New Year's Day. Because of the calendrical system, it was difficult to determine the date of an event or even one's own age.

651. The year *kiyū* draws to a close, few winter days are left;
     on this *kōshin* night, as midnight comes—
     dawn light still far away!

SUGAWARA NO MICHIZANE

Kiyū is another of the cyclical combinations used to name the years. In this case, the year 889 is meant (the previous *kiyū* year would have been 829, and the subsequent one, 949). Michizane lived from 845 to

903, so 889 would have been the only *kiyū* year to occur in his life-
time. Of course, in winter, *kōshin* nights would have been even more
difficult than usual to endure, as the nights were longer.

652. *In the offing*
The fishing boats
Never fail to land a catch;
do the fishermen come first,
Or do the fish?

ANONYMOUS

In the original Japanese, this poem has untranslatable puns on *kōshin*.

Emperors and Princes

653. With his three-foot sword, Emperor Kao-tsu of Han
just sitting there regulated the feudal lords.
With his book of only a single scroll, Chang Liang
immediately became tutor to the heir apparent.

"HOU HAN SHU" (HISTORY OF THE LATER HAN DYNASTY)

Wrongly attributed; actually by Fujiwara no Masaki.

654. Hsiang Chuang at the feast of Hung-men
showed his feelings to all the assembled guests;
when Kao-tsu of Han returned to P'ei County,
he expressed his sadness through the winds of all four directions.

"HOU HAN SHU"

Wrongly attributed, as in the previous entry. In this passage (from the
same source as 653), Masaki alludes to two famous passages from the
"Basic Annals of Hsiang Yü" and the "Basic Annals of Emperor Han
Kao-tsu," in China's greatest work of historiography, the *Shih chi* by Ssu-
ma Ch'ien. Both passages describe important moments in the war for
control of China between Hsiang Yü, the king of Ch'u, and Liu Pang,
the king of Han, who ultimately prevailed and become the founder and
first emperor of the Han dynasty. At the "feast of Hung-men," Hsiang
Yü has his clansman Hsiang Chuang get up to perform a sword dance,

in the course of which he is supposed to assassinate Liu Pang, who is
present as a guest (at this point in the story, the two men are supposedly
allies against the failing Ch'in dynasty). Emperor Kao-tsu is also known
for a short poem that he recited while visiting his hometown of P'ei:

A great wind blows, ah! clouds fly and rise;
my power imposed on all within the seas,
    Ah! I return to my hometown.
How can I obtain brave warriors,
    Ah! To guard all four directions!

655. The peace or danger within the four seas
        he holds in the palm of his hand;
      the order or chaos of a hundred princes
        hangs inside his heart.

PO CHÜ-I

THE MIRROR OF A HUNDRED REFININGS

The poem by Po Chü-i is another from his great series of fifty *New
Yüeh-fu* and is subtitled "Distinguishing the Mirror of the Monarch."
Po's purpose is to distinguish a figurative from an actual mirror. After
elaborately describing a magnificent mirror recently presented to the
emperor—an example of the exquisitely crafted and ornamented pol-
ished bronze or silver mirrors of the T'ang dynasty—he urges the
emperor to consider that more important than this mirror for reflect-
ing one's face is the mirror of history. If the monarch fully understands
the historical records, he will be able to learn from them how to
achieve order in the realm. It is this mirror that he should "hold in his
hand" and "hang inside his heart."

656. Happily I live in an age of Yao and Shun—
        effortlessly transformed!
      I've gotten to be a subject
        of Fu Hsi or even before!

PO CHÜ-I

Living in retirement, the poet feels as if he has been transported to the
golden age of the ancient sage emperors, whose moral charisma was

such that they were able to rule "effortlessly" (*wu-wei*, "doing noth-
ing," "nonaction") and yet the people would be "transformed" (*hua*)
into a perfectly moral citizenry. It is instructive that here Po combines
concepts from Confucianism (*hua*) and Taoism (*wu-wei*—a term from
the Taoist classic, the *Tao te ching*), as the two schools of thought—
though otherwise quite different—shared the ideal of a "passive"
ruler, one whose positive influence would be achieved nonactively.
By contrast, the so-called Legalists (Fa-chia) called for an activist ruler
who would use statutes and measures of various kinds, in a manner
reminiscent of Machiavelli.

657. May His Sagely Majesty continue serenely
        in the Palace of Long Life;
    no need to visit the Isles of Paradise
        or the home of the Queen Mother of the West.

YANG HENG

658. His benevolence expands beyond the Autumn-Ford Continent;
    His wisdom flourishes more greatly than the shades
        of Mount Tsukuba.
    The voices of stagnant pools transformed into noisy rapids
    have turned silent, closed their mouths;
    the praises of grains of sand that grow to become cliffs
    profusely fill our ears.

KI NO YOSHIMOCHI

[CHINESE] PREFACE TO THE *KOKINSHŪ*

This elaborate encomium to the emperor is based on a series of allu-
sions to phrases from the great imperial anthology of poetry to which
Yoshimochi wrote the Chinese-language preface. The better-known
Japanese-language preface to the same book is by Ki no Tsurayuki.
"Autumn-Ford Continent" is a poetic name for Japan.

659. The ancient revels of Emperor Yüan of Liang!
    —Again, the moon of Spring Prince Terrace slowly sinks.
    A modern gathering of King Mu of Chou!

—The clouds of the Queen Mother of the West
  are now about to leave.

SUGAWARA NO FUNTOKI

A contemporary gathering is compared with two famous ones of
antiquity.

660. Courts in which decrees are promulgated
in elegance may not match mountains and gardens of paradise,
but both of these are combined in this spot!
Eras of love for literature
in moral transformation may not be as glorious
    as the reigns of the Yellow Emperor
    and the Divine Husbandman,
but both of them are combined in our sovereign!

SUGAWARA NO FUNTOKI

PREFACE TO THE COLD SPRING PAVILION

The pavilion where a gathering is taking place is compared with leg-
endary places referred to in the Chinese classics, and the emperor is
compared with two of China's ancient sage emperors.

661. Jung Ch'i-ch'i in singing of three joys
still did not reach the gate of Eternal Joy;
Huang-fu Mi in narrating a hundred kings
remained ignorant of the way of the king of the dharma!

ŌE NO ASATSUNA

The poet is praising Emperor En'yū (r. 969–984) for leaving the throne
and becoming a Buddhist monk. His action demonstrated his greater
wisdom by comparison with the legendary Taoist figure Jung Ch'i-ch'i
and the Confucian historian Huang-fu Mi (215–282). According to the
Taoist classic *Lieh Tzu* (contains material ranging in date from fourth
century B.C. to fourth century A.D.), when "Confucius" expressed
amazement at Jung's apparent happiness despite his poverty and his
extreme old age, Jung responded that he had three reasons for joy: hav-
ing been born a human being, having been born a man, and having

lived to the age of ninety. (Jung is also alluded to in number 484.) Huang-fu Mi was noted for his various works of history and biography, including "Generational Annals of Emperors and Kings."

662. On the jade screen the sun is shining, and
         patterned phoenixes appear;
      when vermilion banners flap in the breeze
         painted dragons rise.

FUJIWARA NO KORECHIKA

PAYING MORNING COURT

663. The punishment whips of reed have rotted:
         fireflies fly off to the sky.
      On the drum of petition, the moss grows deep:
         the birds are never startled.

[FUJIWARA NO] KOKUFŪ

> This couplet uses allusions to praise the emperor for his humane regime. The kind official Liu K'uan of the Han dynasty is said to have used reeds to make whips for punishing criminals, as they cause no pain. But the current emperor's moral charisma is so great that there are not any criminals to be punished, so the reed whips have rotted away and turned into fireflies, in accordance with an old belief. The sage emperor Yao is said to have set up a drum for petitioners to beat, but now conditions are so good that no one has anything to complain about, so the drum is overgrown with moss, and the birds are never startled by its sound.

664. *At the Bay of Naniwa*
      The plums are in blossom!
      Before in winter hibernation,
      Now they bloom
      To say that spring is here.

ATTRIBUTED TO WANI

> This poem has a political message as well. According to the Japanese

preface to the *Kokinshū*, where the poem appears, the poet wrote the poem as a means to urge Nintoku (r. 313–399), then living at Naniwa, to take the throne.

665. *The blossoms may fall,*
Yet when spring returns
They flower again,
Even for a thousand years;
And when they have finished,
We will still look to you, our sovereign.

> A poem presented at the ascension of Emperor Komitsu (r. 884–887).

Princes (with Royal Grandchildren appended)

666. In low-slung carriages and sedan chairs,
        noble princes!
With perfumed shirts and delicate horses,
        young men of great families!

PO CHÜ-I

THE PEONIES SO FRAGRANT

> "The Peonies So Fragrant" is another of Po's *New Yüeh-fu* series and follows a rhetorical pattern that he uses in several of his protest poems. First he describes at length and quite brilliantly the seductive attractions of some worldly pleasure, and then he unexpectedly cautions that it is a sign of decadence, helping erode the Confucian virtues that are the basis of society. In this case, Po uses the virtual craze for peonies that was characteristic of T'ang dynasty society. This couplet describes the princes and wealthy young men coming to view the displays of flowers.

667. Ts'ang of Tung-p'ing's "cultivated tolerance":
was he not the incomparable younger brother
    of the Han emperor and highly rewarded by him?

Shuo of Kuei-yang's "literary diction:" indeed he was the eighth son
of the emperor of Ch'i, so beloved of him.

SUGAWARA NO FUNTOKI

THE EIGHTH PRINCE'S COMMENCEMENT OF STUDY

> "Commencement of Study" was a ceremony held when a prince was
> six or seven years old, to celebrate the formal beginning of his educa-
> tion. The *Classic of Filial Piety* was most often the text used. In this
> couplet, the poet praises the prince by comparing him with famous
> Chinese princes who were also eighth in the generations to which
> they belonged.

668. The prince of Chiang-tu's love of nimble skill
was such he leaped a seven-foot screen—how vain the height!
The prince of Huai-nan's quest for the immortals led to the day
he ascended on a cloud—but what good was that?

MINAMOTO NO SHITAGŌ

> This passage praises a prince for eschewing such superficial skills as
> those pursued by the princes of Chiang-tu and Huai-nan. There was
> a long-standing tradition of criticizing or questioning the quest for
> immortality as futile or escapist.

669. Opening the book, already you comprehended
the Way of being a son;
in autumn wind, sadly you gaze
toward the clouds of Tripod Lake.

YOSHISHIGE NO YASUTANE

> The prince is praised for his filial piety; the book he opened is an edi-
> tion of the *Classic of Filial Piety* annotated by the emperor. Tripod
> Lake, in Honan Province, was the location of the ascension into the
> sky on the dragon back of the Yellow Emperor. Before departing, the
> Yellow Emperor forged the bronze tripods that came to symbolize
> imperial legitimacy. The second line therefore alludes to the prince's
> mourning for the late emperor, his father.

670. Our prince's filial conduct:
     to where does it first extend?
     —To Ts'ang-wu peaks, in autumn wind,
     a little strip of mist.

SUGAWARA GAKI

> Like the previous passage, this one praises the filiality of a prince whose father, the emperor, has died. It was Shun, one of the legendary sage emperors of China, who was buried in the "wilds of Ts'ang-wu," so again the deceased emperor is being compared with one of the founders of Chinese civilization.

671. "This flower was not planted in the world of men":
     it is the second blossom on the branch of a jeweled tree!

ŌE NO ASATSUNA

A FAMOUS FLOWER IN THE QUIET COURTYARD

> A prince is praised by being compared to a flower growing on a magical tree in the realm of the immortals. The first line was apparently presented for elaboration to several courtier poets, including Sugawara no Funtoki (see the next entry).

672. "This flower was not planted in the world of men":
     again they've raised a strip of mist at Level Terrace!

SUGAWARA NO FUNTOKI

SAME THEME AS ABOVE

> Level Terrace was a famous summer palace built by Prince Hsiao of Liang.

673. *Should even the flowing waters*
     Of the Tominogawa at Ikaruga run dry,
     We will never forget the name
     Of our great prince.

ATTRIBUTION UNCERTAIN

> Written on the death of Prince Shōtoku Taishi (573–621).

Prime Ministers (with Executive Officials appended)

674. Chi Wen-tzu's concubines never wore cotton or silk,
and the people of Lu thought this worthy of praise.
Kung-sun Hung's person was clothed in plain cloth,
but Chi An criticized him for being full of pretense.

HOU HAN SHU

> The passage, from the *tsan*, or eulogy, for a certain Wang Liang in the
> *Hou Han shu* (Official history of the later Han dynasty), names two
> prime ministers famous for their abstemiousness and frugality. It is
> unclear from this passage whether Chi An's criticism of Kung-sun
> Hung was justified.

675. Pai-li-hsi was begging for food on the road
when Duke Mu conferred the government on him;
Ning-ch'i-tzu was feeding his oxen beneath the cart
when Duke Heng entrusted the nation to him.

HAN SHU

> Two examples of destitute men recognized by enlightened rulers
> as potentially great ministers. From the biography of a certain
> Tsou Yang.

676. Kung-sun Hung's side door was boisterous,
never lacking in guests;
Fu Yüeh's boat was constantly busy—
he never lent it to people!

PO CHÜ-I

> Two prime ministers: one (cited for a different reason in 674) was
> famous for being able to combine business with pleasure, and the
> other, for being too busy to do so.

677. Where mats hang as doors in the western capital:
that was the ancient residence of Prime Minister Ch'en.
Along the magic-fungus gullies of the southern mountains:

was that not the hidden hermitage of the minister of education of
the gardens?

ŌE NO ASATSUNA

The "minister of education of the gardens" was one of the Four
Whiteheads who left the world during the Ch'in dynasty. One of
them called himself the "duke of the Eastern Garden."

677a. The following passage is number 678 (pp. 224–225) in the *Nihon koten
bungaku taikei* edition, but it does not appear in the *Shinchō Nihon koten
shūsei* edition, the one that we are using for our translation. For this reason,
from this point to the end, the entries in our book are one number lower
than those in the *Nihon koten bungaku taikei*, and the total number of our
entries is 803 rather than 804.

The duke of Chou, Tan, was the son of King Wen
    and the younger brother of King Wu;
he knew his own nobility.
The duke of Loyal Humaneness was the ancestor of an emperor,
    the father of an empress;
generations have praised his benevolence.

ŌE NO ASATSUNA

From a memorial on the resignation of Fujiwara no Tadahira (880–949)
as regent.

678. Although the vapors of Master Fu's cliff
    turned windswept cloud after the dream of Yin,
    the waters of the rapids at Yen's embankment
    maintained the distinction between muddy and clear
        when Han issued the invitation.

SUGAWARA NO FUNTOKI

Fu Yüeh did accept the invitation to become prime minister to King
Wu Ting of the Yin (Shang) dynasty, after the king recognized him
from a dream. But Yen-kuang turned down a similar offer from
Emperor Kuang-wu of the Han dynasty and continued to fish at the
embankment named after him.

679. As spring passes and summer fades,
    at the home of Minister of Education Yüan,
      the snow-bound roads will certainly become passable.
    "In the morning, southerly, in the evening, northerly":
    the winds at Captain Cheng's stream have become known to all.

SUGAWARA NO FUNTOKI

> Yüan An was appointed minister of education after he was discovered
> sleeping in his home without having cleared the snow from the
> street. When young, Cheng Hung was gathering firewood when he
> discovered the arrow of an immortal. Upon returning it to the
> immortal, he was granted a wish, and he wished for southerly winds
> in the morning and northerly winds in the evening to blow along the
> stream. Both anecdotes demonstrate the selflessness of these two
> great officials.

680. *How I have enjoyed the colors*
    Of the mountain cherries
    To the fullest!
    And in these [peaceful] times
    There is no reason
    For the wind to scatter the blossoms.

TAIRA NO KANEMORI

> In praise of a minister of state.

Generals

681. A three-foot flash of sword light:
      ice is in his hand!
    a single arc of bow force:
      the moon is at his chest!

LU HUI (NOTHING IS KNOWN ABOUT THIS MAN)

682. In the snow, he let the horse loose—
      at dawn it found the way;

beyond the clouds he heard the goose—
at night he shot it by sound.

LO CH'IU

> Both these images are allusions to the Chinese classics; these are the
> kinds of deeds one expects from great generals.

683. Coming and going over a thousand *li*—
the war horse is haggard;
living apart for ten years now—
friends few and far between.

HSÜ HUN

684. At Mount Lung the clouds hang heavy:
such was General Li at home!
At Ying River the waves are calm:
such the life of Ts'ai, campaigner for prisoners,
before he was employed!

SUGAWARA NO FUNTOKI

> Nature imagery is used to evoke the feeling of great generals before
> their recognition.

685. In profession he ranks with the Tiger Teeth,
although his martial valor actually surpasses
the twenty-eight great generals of Han!
His scholarship puts forth the unicorn horn,
and so he savors the literary beauties
of the twenty chapters of Lu!

MINAMOTO NO SHITAGŌ

> A general is praised for combining martial and civil arts. The "Tiger
> Teeth" were the Imperial Guards, of whom this general was one. The
> "twenty chapters of [Confucius's home state of] Lu" refers to the *Lun
> yü*, the Confucian *Analects*.

686. Male sword at his waist,
     when he draws it: three feet of autumn frost!
     "Female ocher" from his mouth,
     when he chants, indeed a sound of cold jade!

MINAMOTO NO SHITAGŌ

> As in the previous entry, Shitagō praises a general for combining mar-
> tial with civilian cultural values. *Tz'u-huang*, "yellow ocher" (literally,
> "female yellow"), is cleverly used here in parallel with "male sword."
> According to legend, a famous pair of male and female swords was
> once forged by a great swordsmith when his wife sacrificed herself by
> leaping into the furnace. As mentioned in the note to number 140, yel-
> low ocher was used to correct errors in literary texts. A man from
> whose mouth such corrections issue is thus a man of great literary dis-
> cernment. The general also chants poetry as beautiful as the sound of
> an ancient ceremonial jade chime: cold, clear, and pure.

687. Snakes, startled by his sword's mere shadow,
        slither away, evading death!
     His horse, hating the fragrance of his robe,
        wants to bite the man!

MIYAKO NO YOSHIKA

> Again, a general is praised for combining military and, by implica-
> tion, civilian qualities. The second line of the passage alludes to
> Ts'ao P'i, Emperor Wen of the Wei dynasty (r. 220–227), famous for
> his elegance and literary accomplishments, including the writing of
> the *Lun wen* (Discussing literature), considered the first work of true
> literary criticism in China. On one occasion, the famous physiogno-
> mist of horses, Chu Chien-p'ing, upon examining the emperor's
> horse, declared that he discerned signs of imminent death. As the
> emperor was about to mount his chariot, the horse, disliking the fra-
> grance that emanated from the emperor's elegantly perfumed robe,
> made as if to bite his knees, at which the emperor, incensed, had the
> horse killed.

688. *I have not seen you*
     For these two years;

Yet I never thought
I would see you still
Dressed in crimson robes.

FUJIWARA NO KINTADA

> This was written to a friend who, despite his bravery, was passed over for promotion. The incident is described in detail in episode 4 of the *Tales of Yamato*. See the translation by Mildred Tahara (Honolulu: University of Hawaii Press, 1980), pp. 5–6.

Provincial Governors

689. The songs and mouth organs of youths and lasses,
        just right for the moonlight!
The gold and purple of the governor,
        perfect complement to the flowers!

PO CHÜ-I

> Liu Yü-hsi (Meng-te)—Po's great friend and himself a major T'ang poet, mentioned in the title—was governor of Suchou at this time. As such, he would have worn a *gold* seal of appointment attached to his belt by means of a *purple* cord.

690. Brilliant, enlightened: comparable to the pearls of Ho-p'u!
Incisive, decisive: even the sword of K'un-wu not as sharp!

MONK KENG (OR HSÜAN)-HSÜAN [A T'ANG DYNASTY MONK-POET ABOUT WHOM NOTHING IS KNOWN; ALSO RECORDED AS CHIH-HSÜAN OR CHEN-HSÜAN]

> An interesting case of a Buddhist monk's praising a Confucian official for his enlightened, just administration.

691. Even three hundred cups, do not decline!
—The frontier is not a land of intoxication!
These lines—two or three—you'd best keep repeating:
that northern land is hardly a country of poetry.

YOSHISHIGE NO YASUTANE

692. *Climbing to the roof*
      And gazing out,
      Indeed the smoke does rise
      From the hearths of the people
      In their prosperity.

FUJIWARA NO TOKIHIRA

> The poem refers to a famous passage in the *Nihongi* (Chronicles of Japan), book 11, which records the virtues of Emperor Nintoku (r. 313–399), who sacrificed himself for the prosperity of his people.

Singing of History

693. The lamp darkens—several rows of tears
          down Miss Yü's face;
      the night deepens—on all four sides
          the sounds of songs of Ch'u.

TACHIBANA NO HIROMI

> This couplet describes the scene in the tent of Hsiang Yü, the king of Ch'u, shortly before his final defeat at the hands of Liu Pang in 206 B.C. With the collapse of the previous Ch'in dynasty, several contenders attempted to conquer China and become the founder of a new dynasty. Liu Pang and Hsiang Yü emerged as the two final rivals. As the great Chinese historian Ssu-ma Ch'ien describes the scene in his biography of Hsiang Yü, Hsiang and his concubine, Miss Yü, were spending their last night together in his tent when they heard the songs of Ch'u being sung by the ranks of Han troops that had them surrounded. Hsiang Yü thereby realized that his own men had been captured or had gone over to the other side. Liu Pang eventually became the first emperor of the Han dynasty.

694. The journeying goose had a letter attached—
          Autumn leaves were falling;
      waiting for male sheep to produce some milk—
          the years passed into void.

KI NO ARIMASA

This couplet is based on the biography of Su Wu as recounted in the *Han shu* (the official history of the Han dynasty). Sent as an emissary to the Hsiung-nu nomads in the north, Su Wu was taken prisoner and made to herd sheep. He was told he would be released when a male sheep produced milk. On one occasion, when the Han emperor was hunting in the Shang-lin Imperial Hunting Park, he shot down a goose and found attached to its leg a letter from Su Wu.

695. In younger days he did escape the tiger's jaws of Ch'in;
in later years he first bowed to the dragon's face of Han.

KI NO HASEO

Shu-sun T'ung was a reluctant official at the court of Ch'in. Eventually he managed to escape and came to serve the first emperor of the Han dynasty.

696. *How moved our Great Parents*
Must have been;
For indeed they remained below
For three years.

ŌE NO ASATSUNA

A reference to a legend in book 1 of the *Nihongi* concerning the birth of the Leech Child to the gods Izanagi and Izanami. After three years, the child could still not stand upright.

Wang Chao-chün

The story of Wang Chao-chün, versions of which are related in various sources, is one of the most famous in all of Chinese history, inspiring countless poems, plays, paintings, and musical compositions. Wang was a palace concubine during the reign of Emperor Yüan (r. 48–31 B.C.) who, for diplomatic reasons, was married off to the khan of the Hsiung-nu nomads after she refused to bribe a court painter. The painter had been instructed to paint portraits of the palace ladies so that a relatively unattractive one might be chosen for the dreaded fate of marriage to the khan. The other women bribed him to depict them as attractively as possible, but Wang refused, so the painter rendered her as ugly. When the emperor actually saw Wang Chao-chün, he realized how beautiful she really was and fell hopelessly in love, but it was too late; she had already been promised to the Hsiung-nu. Wang died among the barbarians, although one version of the story has her committing suicide during her journey north. As recently as the 1950s, China's leading modern playwright, Ts'ao Yü (Cao Yu), wrote a play based on Wang Chao-chün's life, transforming her into a symbol of willing personal sacrifice for the purpose of national service and international relations.

697. With grief and pain, with bitterness
      she's withered quite away:
      now, alas, she really looks
      as she did in that painting!

PO CHÜ-I

> When Po wrote his two *chüeh-chü* (quatrains) on Wang Chao-chün, he was sixteen years old; hence they were written in 788. This fact prompted a Sung dynasty admirer of the poems to declare, "The ancients have written many poems on Wang Chao-chün. But my own favorite is a *chüeh-chü* by Lo-t'ien [Po Chü-i]. In feeling it is free and easy, unconstrained. And yet when Lo-t'ien wrote this poem, his years were very few." This passage is quoted by Wang Li-ming, the Ch'ing dynasty commentator on Po's poetry (his preface to the complete collection is dated 1702), from the Sung dynasty encyclopedia of poetics, *Shih-jen yü-hsieh* (Jade dust of the poets), compiled in the thirteenth century by Wei Ch'ing-chih. The comment is telling because it is indeed unusual for juvenilia to be included in the collected works of any Chinese poet, excluding perhaps short-lived poets such as Li Ho (791–817) or Wang Ling (1032–1059). It was generally believed that years of practice were necessary to master the difficult technical aspects of the art, as well as to develop a style with aesthetic integrity. This passage from the *Shih-jen yü-hsieh* expresses astonishment that such a young poet could have written with such freedom and technical mastery. That Po himself, or perhaps one of his early editors, was proud of the achievement is indicated by the note inserted immediately below the title of the pair of poems in Po's collected works: "At the time, seventeen [sixteen by Western count] years of age."

698. Her body perished—soon became rotted bones
      in barbarian land;

her house remained, but to no avail—
a deserted homestead of Han.

KI NO HASEO

699. Blue-green eyebrows, rouge-tinted cheeks,
        robes of embroidery:
    weeping, she follows the sand and dust
        away from home and country!

ŌE NO ASATSUNA

> This and the following three couplets together constitute a complete
> *lü-shih* (regulated-verse poem) by Asatsuna.

700. Frontier winds blow to tatters
        the strings of her autumn heart;
    Dike River's waters, flowing, add
        to streaks of tears at night.

ŌE NO ASATSUNA

701. A single blare of barbarian horn—
        awake from frost-chilled dreams;
    the palace of Han, ten thousand miles—
        heartbroken beneath the moon!

ŌE NO ASATSUNA

702. If only Chao-chün had paid that man
        the bribe of yellow gold,
    certainly she'd have lived out her life
        serving the emperor!

ŌE NO ASATSUNA

703. Several streaks of secret tears
        beyond the lonely clouds;

a single speck of grief-stricken eyebrow
   beside the descending moon.

ATTRIBUTED TO MINAMOTO NO FUSAAKIRA OR SUGANO
NO MEIMEI

704. *The nightingale,*
Hiding himself in the deep mountains,
Pours out his sounds of weeping
With no one to hear.

FUJIWARA NO SANEKATA

This poem refers to poet's emotions while in exile.

Singing Girls (or Concubines)

705. Her face recalls her uncle,
this niece of P'an An-jen!
In temperament like her elder brother,
this younger sister of Ts'ui Chi-kuei!

CHANG WEN-CH'ENG (CHANG CHO)

P'an An-jen (or P'an Yüeh) and Ts'ui Chi-kuei (or Ts'ui Yen) were
men famous for their attractive looks and demeanor. The writer is
praising a beautiful woman by comparing her with them. Chang Cho
was the author of a pioneering love story, *Yu hsien k'u* (A journey to
the dwellings of the immortals), from which this poetic passage is
taken. The work was known from an early period in Japan and is
reflected in both the *Man'yōshū* and the *Tale of Genji*. In his *Chinese
Literature—A Historical Introduction* (New York: Ronald Press, 1961),
Ch'en Shou-yi describes the work as follows: "It was an account of
how he [the author] in his young manhood traveled to Hoyüan on
official duty and how on his way he had sought lodging in a huge
mansion one night where he met two young women with whom he
had a pleasant banquet and wrote poetry through the night...[an]
unprecedented experiment in the telling of a love story." A complete
English translation of *Yu hsien k'u* was published in 1965 by Howard
S. Levy under the title *The Dwelling of Playful Goddesses: China's*

First Novelette (Tokyo: Howard S. Levy). In this edition the author's name is rendered Chang Wen-ch'eng, using his *tzu*, or courtesy name, as is also done in the *Wakan rōei shū*.

706. Others do not realize she's receiving royal favor—
 except that from her robe of gauze
  wafts the imperial fragrance.

"YÜAN CHEN"

707. Delightfully charming—hair on my two temples,
  wings of an autumn cicada!
 Elegantly lovely—moth-antenna eyebrows,
  the curve of distant hills!

PO CHÜ-I

> The poem from which this couplet comes, "From the Well Bottom We Draw the Silver Vase," is another of Po's fifty poems of moral exhortation, the *New Yüeh-fu*. The poet's subtitle for this poem reads, "An Exhortation Against Loosely Running Off [Elopement]." The poem is recited by a young woman who complains that after she and a young man fell in love at first sight and she eloped with him, his parents refused to acknowledge her as his official wife, because of their elopement. The couplet in the *Wakan rōei shū* comes from the passage early in the poem in which she is describing herself. The title of the poem compares the young woman to a silver vase in a well: as the vase is being drawn up, the rope breaks and the vase falls back down again.

708. Don't be amazed at laughter from the face
  behind the veil of red:
 it is a peony indeed, blown into blossom by the spring wind!

"PO CHÜ-I"

> At first, readers thought she was a peony flower, but then she laughed, and they were surprised to discover that she was in fact a person. But the poet insisted that she was a flower and that the laugh was the moment of blossoming.

709. Li Yen-nien's eulogizing of his clan member
was so he could start to fly himself, bolstered by her beauty!
Lady Wei Tzu-fu, when she waited on the emperor,
was forever distinguished from the mass of ugly ladies.

ONO NO TAKAMURA

> This passage is based on two allusions to famous court women of the
> Han dynasty. Li Yen-nien was a musician at the court of Emperor
> Wu of the Han dynasty. He eulogized in song his younger sister, thus
> drawing the emperor's attention to her, whereupon he made her
> Lady Li, his favorite concubine. Li Yen-nien himself, of course, ben-
> efited from her position. Lady Wei Fu-tzu was Empress Wei to
> Emperor Wu.

710. On an autumn evening, awaiting the moon—
then we see its pure radiance emerging from the mountain!
On a summer day, thinking of the lotus—
then first seeing its red loveliness breaking the water's surface!

SUGAWARA NO MICHIZANE

PREFACE TO THE POEM "HURRYING TO PUT ON MAKEUP"

> The two images of moon and lotus represent metaphorically the
> beautiful concubine or singing girl first appearing at a gathering or
> performance at court with newly applied makeup.

711. His Majesty wishing to select a woman
combining looks and talent,
while she's not yet emerged from the "makeup tower,"
keeps sending urgent summons.

SUGAWARA NO MICHIZANE

> This and the following three entries together constitute a complete
> eight-line *lü-shih* (regulated-verse poem).

712. Doubled topknot—she's still arranging
the softness of spring clouds;

delicate eyebrows—just now emerges
the sliver of dawn moon.

SUGAWARA NO MICHIZANE

713. Silken sleeves—there's no time left!
Send back the heated iron!
Phoenix hairpiece—she's mortified!
Still locked in its fragrant case!

SUGAWARA NO MICHIZANE

714. A gentle breeze first wafts to us
hints of her fine perfume
as we catch glimpses through blue-green blinds
of a lovely room in red.

SUGAWARA NO MICHIZANE

715. She hesitates to lift the broidered curtain,
wishing to keep in the scent of musk;
she hates to roll up the pearl-studded blind,
wanting to linger at arranging her hairpin.

"PO CHÜ-I"

716. To provide a meal for the newly empty stomach of today,
weeping, she sells the zither
presented to her by a former monarch.

KI NO HASEO

A poignant variation on the theme of the aging concubine who has
lost her imperial favor. The most famous literary treatment of this
theme was Po Chü-i's *Song of the P'i-p'a*, one of the most frequently
painted scenes in Chinese literature.

717. *Winds of heaven,*
Blow closed

The path they follow through the clouds;
Keep the apparition of these maidens here
Just a bit longer!

BISHOP HENJŌ

> The poem refers to the Gosenchi dancers, mentioned in the *Tale of Genji*.

Pleasure Girls

718. The autumn waters have not set tinkling
          pendants worn by pleasure girls;
       cold clouds alone now fill
          the "Husband-Viewing Mountain."

HO·LAN SUI

> Neither the divine "pleasure girls" who appeared to two friends one day in the mountains nor the devoted wife who turned to stone atop a mountain as she watched for the return of her long-absent husband is now to be found.

719. Although completely different from the ten thousand ceremonies
       for betrothing blue-green eyebrows in the red boudoir,
       here in a boat on the waves,
       a lifetime of happiness is still the same!

ŌE NO MOCHITOKI

> The poet sings the joy of a carefree life with his "pleasure girl," considering it the equal of formal marriage.

720. Her Japanese zither she slowly tunes,
          overlooking a pond of moonlight,
       or her Chinese oars she loudly rows,
          pushing off into misty waters.

MINAMOTO NO SHITAGŌ

721. *I pass my life*
     Where the white waves
     Approach the strand;
     A fisherman's child,
     I have no fixed abode.

ANONYMOUS

Old Men

722. Once I was a resident of Ch'ang-an and Lo-yang,
         enjoying fame and glory;
     now I am an old man among rivers and lakes,
         fallen on bad times.

PO CHÜ-I

723. My aging eyes now open early—
         there's still nighttime to spare;
     the force of illness withers me
         before my years advance.

PO CHÜ-I

724. If I keep thinking about you, it's for no other reason
     than that the men from T'ien-pao now
         are becoming fewer and fewer.

PO CHÜ-I

725. Red blossoms flourish, yellow leaves fall:
     one tree's spring colors and autumn sounds!
     Tying on the cord, removing the hat pin:
     one man's heart in youth, thoughts in old age!

SUGAWARA NO FUNTOKI

> The third line refers to entering official service by tying on the cord
> from which one's official insignia are suspended, and then to remov-
> ing the official hat pin upon retirement.

726. Younger than Lo-t'ien by three years,
     still I've reached the age of decrepitude;
     that I've been able to visit this wonderful spot
          for even a single day:
     is this not a blessing of old age?

SUGAWARA NO FUNTOKI

> Funtoki and his associates formed the Society to Honor Old Age on
> the model of a similar "society" described by Po Chü-i (Lo-t'ien) in his
> poem "The Society of the Seven Old Men" (*pu-i/ hsia*, 1a). In his
> poem, Po tells us he was seventy-four years old at the time. Funtoki
> was seventy-one when he wrote his poem. (These ages, of course, are
> based on the practice of considering the newborn child to be one year
> old and then adding a year on each subsequent New Year's Day.)

727. When T'ai-kung-wang encountered King Wen of Chou,
     the ripples of the banks of the River Wei
          patterned his face;
     When Ch'i-li Chi advised Emperor Hui of Han,
     the moon of Mount Shang hung at his brows.

ŌE NO MASAHIRA

PRESENTATION TEXT [ON OLD AGE]

> Both men are famous examples from Chinese exemplary history of
> old recluses who were discovered and invited to emerge from reclu-
> sion and serve the ruler. The poet has cleverly worked into his
> metaphors for the marks of old age (facial wrinkles like wavelets,
> white eyebrows like crescent moons) the names of the actual places
> where these men had been residing.

728. The rivers have no evening of return—
          tears for flowing years!
     How could the flowers return to last year's spring?—
          makeup in old age!

SUGAWARA NO FUNTOKI

SOCIETY FOR HONORING OLD AGE

729. Through forest fog, compare the sound—
      the warbler's still unaged;
    in riverbank wind, consider strength—
      the willow still stands firm.

SUGAWARA NO FUNTOKI

> That is, nature continues apparently ageless while the poet withers
> away.

730. Drunk, I face the falling flowers,
    my heart grown quite serene;
  lying in bed, I think of my remaining years,
    as tears start to redden my eyes.

SUGAWARA NO GAKI

731. *When I look into the depths*
Of the polished mirror,
In that instant I feel I meet
An old man I have not known.

ŌSHIKŌCHI NO MITSUNE

732. *Where can I take myself*
In this world,
Old as I am?
For there are none
Who do not despise the aged.

FUJIWARA NO TAMEYORI

Friends

733. Lute, poetry, wine—my friends
    all have deserted me;
  snow, moon, flowers—these seasons,
    I most often think of you.

PO CHÜ-I

734. These songs of *Yang*-force in the spring:
     so noble, hard to echo!
     Feelings of friendship like limpid waters
     only in old age I've come to know.

PO CHÜ-I

> In this poem, "echo" refers to writing poems in harmony with the
> theme of a poem by someone else, a standard literary practice.

735. In former years you looked at me
     directly—pupils dark;
     now, I meet you, and I find
     your hair has turned to white!

HSÜ HUN

> The first line alludes to the third-century poet Juan Chi, who looked
> at men of character directly, showing them the "blacks" of his eyes—
> while showing the whites to vulgarians.

736. K'uai-chi Magistrate Hsiao, on passing the ancient shrine,
     forged a friendship across the eras;
     Vice Director Chang, in valuing fresh talent,
     promoted it and formed a friendship transcending age.

ŌE NO ASATSUNA

> Both these are allusions to the *lieh-chuan*, or biographies of two men
> from the *Book of Ch'en*, the official history of the short-lived Ch'en
> dynasty (557–589). Hsiao Yün, magistrate of K'uai-chi, when passing
> the shrine of Chi Cha (a famous sage-statesman of the Spring and
> Autumn period), offered a sacrifice and thus formed a friendship with
> a man of a different era. Chang Tsuan was noted for presenting at court
> the younger man, Chiang Tsung, and becoming friends with him.

737. Descendant of P'ei of the Bureau of Documents—
     I have heard of you for years!
     Orphan of the attendant gentleman of the Ministry of Rites—
     you see me today for the first time.

SUGAWARA NO ATSUSHIGE

The poet is the son of Sugawara no Michizane, now deceased. He is greeting P'ei Ch'iu, an envoy to Japan from the kingdom of Po-hai (between China and Korea), who arrived in Japan in 908 (Michizane had died in 903). The poet recalls that P'ei T'ing, the father of P'ei Ch'iu, also had arrived in Japan as a Po-hai envoy (in 883) and had been greeted at that time by the poet's own father, Michizane. Hence the two families were linked for two generations. The first line refers to P'ei Ch'iu; the second line, to the poet himself.

738. *You and I—*
What promises must we have made
In a former life—
How I would like to know!

ANONYMOUS

739. *Who may I call my comrade now?*
For even the aged pines at Takasago
Cannot replace the friends of yore.

FUJIWARA NO OKIKAZE

Nostalgia for Men of the Past

740. Beneath the yellow earth, how could you know of me?
With head of white hair, alone I think of you.
All I can do is let my aged tears
sprinkle these writings of yours, my friend.

PO CHÜ-I

741. Into the long night, you gentlemen have gone first;
remaining years—how many left to me?
Autumn wind, tears covering my shirt:
beneath the Springs, so many of my friends!

PO CHÜ-I

"The Springs": the "Yellow Springs," or underworld (also in next poem). The phrase "yellow earth" in number 740 has the same meaning.

742. Past experiences—vague, unclear—
      all are like a dream;
      old friends—lost and scattered—
      half gone to the Springs.

PO CHÜ-I

743. The boat we moored at Suchou then
      is old, its dragon prow darkened;
      The Wang I Bridge has fallen down,
      aslant like teeth or geese.

PO CHÜ-I

744. At Gold Valley—place of intoxication with flowers—
      the flowers every spring turn fragrant,
          but the host never returns;
      at the southern tower—where a man once whistled at the moon—
      the moon meets autumn's time, but where has the man disappeared?

SUGAWARA NO FUNTOKI

> The poem contains two allusions to men of the Chin dynasty, Shih
> Ch'ung, who was famous for his wealth and his magnificent estate at
> Gold Valley, and Yü Liang, who used to climb the southern tower to
> enjoy the moon. The character *ch'ao* in the text, meaning "to ridicule"
> or "to satirize," is here assumed to be an error for *hsiao*, "to whistle," as
> in the name of Ishikawa Jōzan's "Tower for Whistling at the Moon" at
> the Shisendō (built in 1641).

745. Upon Prince Chin's ascension as an immortal,
      later men built a shrine
          in the moonlight of Mount Kou;
      upon the early passing of Grand Mentor Yang,
      passersby wept tears in the clouds of Mount Hsien.

MINAMOTO NO SUKENORI

PREFACE AT THE ANRAKU-JI TEMPLE

> Again, this passage is built on two allusions to men of the Chin
> dynasty: Prince Chin, who ascended in broad daylight as an immor-

tal and then returned to appear at Mount Kou, where a shrine was
erected to him; and Yang Hu, whose epitaph at the top of Mount
Hsien, where he had loved the scenery, always drew tears from the
eyes of travelers.

746. The good tree cut short in years—
     lament its collapse!
but the sweet pear tree of lingering love—
     they sing, "Don't cut it down!"

ONO NO YOSHIKI

The first line is based on Chuang Tzu's famous parable of the useless
tree, which gets to live a long life, whereas the tree whose wood is use-
ful to the carpenter is likely to be cut down young. The second line
derives from poem 16 in the *Shih ching* (Book of songs), which relates
that the pear tree under which Prince Shao rested should never be cut
down but should remain as a memento of that great man.

747. *This water,*
     Once clear running in the fields
     Is tepid now;
     But those who remember
     Still come to scoop it.

ANONYMOUS

748. *I have determined not to worry over*
     Things of the past;
     Yet even so, how strangely,
     My eyes fill with tears!

EMPEROR MURAKAMI

A poem presented to Fujiwara no Saneyori on the death of his daugh-
ter, who had been in service at the court of Emperor Murakami (r.
946–967).

749. *There are those*
     Who would think even now
     To go on living in this world;

Yet how many who have had these thoughts
Have already passed away.

FUJIWARA NO TAMEYORI

Describing Sentiments

It is clear from the following passages that the "sentiments" in question have mostly to do with the vicissitudes of history and personal fate, especially with regard to the perennial Confucian problem of how the good man should respond to bad times.

750. The passionate intensity of Chuan-chu and Ching K'o,
the self-sacrifice of Master Hou and Master Yü:
their hearts were motivated by benevolence received,
their lives they held lightly because of righteousness.

HOU HAN SHU

> Chuan-chu, Ching K'o, and Yü all were failed assassins. The first two men died in the attempt, and Yü committed suicide by falling on his sword. But Hou committed suicide out of remorse that he was too old to follow his lord's troops into battle. His death was intended as a farewell gift to his departing lord.

751. Fan Li took the blame before Kou-chien,
riding off in a tiny boat to the Five Lakes;
Chiu-fan apologized for his faults to Duke Wen,
then he, too, withdrew to the riverside.

HOU HAN SHU

> Both men were loyal officials who served their lords truly and well and then withdrew to a life of seclusion after they had achieved success, blaming themselves for their faults.

752. One who revels in a rocky stream
and never has peered into a jade abyss
—how can he know where the black dragon coils?

One who is accustomed to an obscure town
  and has never seen a leading capital
is one who has no idea where heroes reside.

WEN HSÜAN (LITERARY ANTHOLOGY)

> The text from which this is drawn is the *Prose Poem on the Capital of Wu* by Tso Ssu (ca. 250–ca. 305). For a complete translation of this work, see David R. Knechtges, *Rhapsodies on Metropolises and Capitals*, vol. 1 of *Wen xuan or Selections of Fine Literature* (Princeton, NJ: Princeton University Press, 1982), pp. 373–428.

753. Disaster and fortune in this human realm
  I'm too foolish to foresee;
wind and waves in this world of ours
  with old age still continue.

PO CHÜ-I

754. Before the carriage, the thoroughbreds are ill—
  jaded nags are at liberty;
on the perch, the falcon is at rest—
  sparrows fly freely about.

HSÜ HUN

> The symbolism here refers to a situation in which the bad circumstances of good men lead to the activities of petty men.

755. In every affair, nothing achieved,
  my body ages now;
if not to the land of intoxication,
  where then should I go?

PO CHÜ-I

756. "Fan Li took the blame—"
then, rowing off in a little boat,
  escaped the world of fame.
Hsieh An declined pursuit of accomplishment—

then urged his horse to the solitary clouds
　　where he'd cultivate his mind.

ŌE NO ASATSUNA

> Fan Li was introduced in number 751 in the same passage from the
> *Hou Han shu*. Hsieh An is yet another example of a man who withdrew
> from the world after having helped his lord defeat invading forces.

757. Ascending to the palace is appointment
　　　beyond phenomena:
vulgar bones may never tread the clouds of Paradise!
"Imperial secretary" is the aspiration of the world:
men of ordinary talent may never climb
　　　to the moon of those terraces and pavilions.

TACHIBANA NO NAOMOTO

> The writer is petitioning for appointment. In effect, he is saying,
> "Although I do not really deserve it, nevertheless I humbly make
> my petition."

758. My age is second only to that of Yen Ssu:
I've lived through three regimes and still remain obscure.
My disappointment resembles that of Po-luan:
I sing the "Five Laments" and prepare to depart.

TACHIBANA NO MASAMICHI

> Yen Ssu, a man of the Han dynasty, failed to rise above a relatively low
> position, although he served under three emperors (Wen, Ching, and
> Wu). When Emperor Wu (the "Martial Emperor") asked him why, he
> replied, "Emperor Wen [the "Civil Emperor"] loved civil affairs, and
> I love martial affairs; Emperor Ching loved beauty, and my face is
> ugly; Your Majesty loves youth, and I am an old man." Moved by these
> words, Emperor Wu promoted Yen to a high position. Liang Hung
> ("Po-luan"), disappointed with the current state of affairs, withdrew
> with his wife to a life of quiet husbandry in the mountains, compos-
> ing the "Five Laments" upon his departure.

759. Hidden in people's words, secretly there burns
　　　a fire to melt one's bones;

cloaked in smiles, surreptitiously are sharpened
   knives to cut one's flesh.

KORENAGA NO HARUMICHI

760. Riding in a carriage full of ghosts—
      what's so scary about that?
   rowing a boat down the three gorges of the witch—
      that's not dangerous at all!

PRINCE KANEAKIRA

   Neither of these things can compare with the frightening dangers
   posed by the treachery or backbiting of one's enemies at court.

761. San-lü of Ch'u may have been sober,
      but ultimately, what good did it do him?
   Po-i of Chou may have starved himself to death,
      but he was still not necessarily seen to be a sage.

TACHIBANA NO YORIHIRA

   Ch'ü Yüan declared himself to be the only sober man in the realm,
   but he ended up drowning when he leaped into a river after an old
   fisherman berated him for his unyielding, rigid sense of purity. Po-i
   (and his brother Shu-ch'i) starved when they ate ferns rather than the
   grains of the new Chou dynasty—such was their loyalty to the defunct
   Shang dynasty. And yet Ssu-ma Ch'ien, in his famous biography of
   them, raises the question of whether they were really sages (that is,
   whether they were acting out of real serenity or mere resentment).
   Thus, no matter how far one goes to establish one's transcendent
   purity, it is possible to be questioned about the value of one's actions
   or motives.

762. *What could I have been doing—*
   I've grown old, to no purpose.
   What do you make of this,
   You years through which I have passed?
   How ashamed you must have been for me.

ANONYMOUS

763. *In this life,*
     Whether this or that,
     All becomes the same:
     We can live out our lives
     In a palace or a straw hut.

ATTRIBUTED TO SEMIMARU

764. *So painful*
     Does this world seem to live in;
     How we may truly envy
     The clear moon shining above.

FUJIWARA NO TAKAMITSU

> This poem is said to have been composed when the poet became a Buddhist monk. The moon is often a symbol for religious enlightenment.

Congratulations

765. With sword and pendant, *you* rush each dawn
     to the double phoenix towers
     while among the misty waves, *I* sleep at night
     in a little fishing boat.

PO CHÜ-I

> "Yüan the Eighth," named in the title of this poem, is not Po's great friend Yüan Chen but, rather, a lesser-known figure by the name of Yüan Tsung-chien, as noted by the editor and commentator Wang Li-ming, whose edition of Po's poetry—one of the best in existence— was prepared in 1702.

766. Ch'ien-t'ang is three thousand *li*
     away from this capital:
     I'll view the scenery each step of the way
     with real satisfaction!

CHANG HSIAO-PIAO

> There is some doubt about the attribution of this and the following couplet to Chang, but if the attribution is correct, we may imagine

that the poet, who had just passed the *chin-shih* examinations in the
capital city of Ch'ang-an, was looking forward to his homeward jour-
ney. Chang's hometown of T'ung-lu was indeed in the region of
Ch'ien-t'ang (Hangchou, the mouth of the Che River, and environs),
approximately one thousand miles (a *li* being one-third mile) from the
capital. The first thing the successful examination candidate was
expected to do was return home to share his glory with his parents.

767. I can well imagine that the elders
        down south of the Yangtze
   will use you, sir, as an exemplar
        when they urge their children to study.

CHANG HSIAO-PIAO

> Having congratulated himself in the previous couplet for passing the
> examinations, Chang here (if the attribution is accurate) congratu-
> lates a friend who also has passed.

768. Attendant gentleman in the Ministry of Personnel—
        a position in the imperial office!
   Wearing the madder, for the first time
        you emerge from the Palace of Subtle Purple.

TACHIBANA NO MASAMICHI

> This and the following three entries together constitute an eight-line
> regulated-verse poem congratulating a man on his promotion to a
> fifth-level position, thereby allowing him to wear the madder (or deep
> purple) robe, silver fish–embroidered pouch, and robes with crane
> patterns.

769. The silver fish hanging from your waist
        parts from the springtime waves;
   the silken cranes on your coat
        trail through the morning mist.

TACHIBANA NO MASAMICHI

770. Moon and flowers we shared together once
        at a single window;

now, ten thousand miles part clouds from mud—
    my eyes cannot see that far!

TACHIBANA NO MASAMICHI

771. When I consider my own position, I feel ashamed
        to have known you so long:
    you, a childhood friend—in the beginning
        we rode bamboo horses together!

TACHIBANA NO MASAMICHI

THE ABOVE [FOUR PASSAGES] CONSTITUTE FOUR RHYMES

772. *In ancient times*
Happiness was enfolded
In the sleeves;
Tonight, it cannot be contained,
It overflows from within me.

ANONYMOUS

> This poem is based in turn on an anonymous poem, number 805 in the
> *Kokinshū*, in which happiness is said to be wrapped in sleeves of Chi-
> nese brocade. The "happiness" may refer to an advancement at court.

Felicitations

773. This wondrous time, these supreme months—
        joy without an end!
    ten thousand years, a thousand autumns—
        happiness that never stops.

HSIEH YEN

774. In the Palace of Long Life,
        rich in springs and autumns;
    before the Gate of Never Aging,
        the days and months pass slowly.

YOSHISHIGE NO YASUTANE

775. *May my lord's life endure*
      A thousand generations,
      Eight thousand generations,
      Until a pebble
      Becomes a boulder
      Covered with moss.

ANONYMOUS

> This poem is used as the text of the present Japanese national anthem.

776. *The cries for a long reign*
      Can be heard from Mikasa Mountain itself,
      For under the heavens,
      All is peaceful, refulgent.

PRIEST CHŪSAN

> This poem was written for Emperor Murakami (r. 946–967).

Love

777. For you I scented my clothing—
      but you smelled no fragrance in orchid or musk!
      For you I carefully made up my face—
      but you saw no beauty in jade or kingfisher!

PO CHÜ-I

> These lines come from "The T'ai-hang Road," another of Po's great
> series of protest poems, the *Hsin yüeh-fu* (New music bureau poems).
> Like the others, this one's subtitle reveals its symbolic meaning:
> "Using the Relationship Between Husband and Wife to Protest the
> Inconstancy of the Relationship Between Sovereign and Subject."
> The poem is recited by a wife who has been rejected or abandoned by
> her husband, even though she continues to love him. Toward the end,
> Po himself draws this analogy:

In recent times, the relationship between sovereign and subject has
   also been like this.
Do you not see, sir, that the adviser of the left and the censor of the right

in the morning receive the imperial favor, and that evening are
    sentenced to death?
The difficulty of traveling the roads
lies not in bodies of water,
nor in mountains,
but in the inconsistency of human emotions!

778. The watch draws on, the night is calm:
      the Long Gate is silent and never opens.
      The moon is cold, the wind autumnal:
      the round fan deserted and cast aside.

"CHANG WEN-CH'ENG"

Although number 705 is an authentic passage from Chang's "Journey
to the Dwellings of the Immortals," the immediately preceding lines
do not appear in that work and so are of uncertain attribution. In the
Han dynasty, "Long Gate Palace" was the setting for a famous *fu* or
prosepoem written by Ssu-ma Hsiang-ju on behalf of a deserted impe-
rial concubine. The "round fan" in line 4 derives from an equally
famous poem by concubine Pan (Pan *chieh-yü*, fl. ca. 48–46 B.C.), in
which she compares herself to a round, white silk fan used in sum-
mer, only to be cast aside in colder weather.

779. As his palace was transported, he'd see the moon,
      its heartrending colors!
      As it rained at night, he'd hear the gibbons,
      their gut-wrenching cries!

PO CHÜ-I

This and the following two couplets come from Po's most famous
work and probably the best-known poem of love in all of Chinese lit-
erature. "The Song of Everlasting Sorrow" is based on the poignant
tale of frustrated love between Emperor Hsüan-tsung, or Ming-
huang, of the T'ang dynasty (r. 713–756) and his beloved concubine
Yang Kuei-fei. Although they both are historical figures, the details
of the story are at least partially legendary. The emperor's infatua-
tion with Yang enabled the rebel general, An Lu-shan, to invade the

capital, Ch'ang-an, driving the emperor, Yang Kuei-fei, and their forces to flee west toward Szechwan. This is the "transported palace" that Po refers to. Furious at Yang Kuei-fei because of her influence on their emperor, his troops refused to move until she and her uncle, Yang Kuo-chung—who had been appointed prime minister through her influence—were executed. The emperor reluctantly agreed to this, and these couplets describe his undying love for Yang Kuei-fei. Note that Po's collected works reads "bells" for "gibbons," so that the second line would read "he'd hear the bells, their gut-wrenching sounds."

780. In spring wind, on days
        when peach and plum opened their blossoms;
      in autumn dew, at times
        when paulownia trees dropped their leaves...

PO CHÜ-I

At such times as these, the bereaved emperor would remember his beloved Yang Kuei-fei.

781. In the nighttime palace hall, as fireflies flew,
        he would yearn for her grievously;
      when autumn lamps had wicks picked to the end,
        still he could not sleep...

PO CHÜ-I

782. They soar to the south, then head back north:
      hard to send news of cold and warmth with the autumn geese!
      It emerges in the east, then flows toward the west:
      I'll just entrust my yearning gaze to the moon of dawn.

ŌE NO ASATSUNA

LETTER TO THE KING OF WU-YÜEH

783. I have heard that in your garden,
        a flower grows, so fair:

please, sir, would you pluck for me
a branch of this springtime?

ANONYMOUS

> This is the only Chinese passage in the *Wakan rōei shū* attributed to
> "Anonymous." Borrowing a phrase from the English composer
> William Walton, we may say that this is a case of "anon. in love."
> Perhaps the poet is writing to the father of a beautiful woman, asking
> her hand in marriage.

784. I lie alone in this cold boudoir—
　　　there's not one sound of husband;
　　nothing prevents the young master Hsiao
　　　from turning his horses this way.

> This passage has no attribution, but one annotator identifies it as the
> response of a certain *uneme* (a kind of court waitress) to a love letter
> from a young man she refers to poetically as "young master Hsiao,"
> using a Chinese convention for referring to a young male lover.

785. Chaste Woman Gorge is empty—
　　　only moonlight there;
　　Lovely Lady Embankment, old—
　　　just the sounds of waves.

MINAMOTO NO TAMENORI

> The poet's wife has died, and he expresses his grief through parallel
> references to places in China.

786. *I do not know*
　　Where my love is going,
　　Or how it may end,
　　I only know
　　To meet will be its culmination.

ŌSHIKŌCHI NO MITSUNE

787. *I ask you to come,*
　　But the nights go by

Without a visit;
I have decided to wait no longer,
A choice more painful still than waiting!

KAKINOMOTO NO HITOMARO

788. *"I'll come soon!" you said,*
Yet how I have waited,
Only to see the moon at dawn
In the longest month of the year.

SOSEI

> The ninth month in the lunar calendar was considered the longest of the year.

Impermanence

789. Examine one's life: at river's edge,
    a reed snapped from the root;
discuss one's fate: along the stream,
    a boat tied to no mooring.

"LO WEI" (WRONG FOR YEN WEI, A POET OF THE
MID-EIGHTH CENTURY)

790. Year after year, season after season,
    the flowers look the same;
season after season, year after year,
    people completely different!

SUNG CHIH-WEN

791. What do we struggle for,
    here on the horns of a snail?
—this life of ours, lived in the spark
    of light struck off a stone!

PO CHÜ-I

> These are the first two lines of the poem; the final two read

Whether rich or whether poor—
simply take pleasure in it:
a man who doesn't open his mouth and laugh
is a foolish man.

> The reference to the horns of a snail comes from the *Chuang Tzu*,
> chapter 25. Here a sage named Tai Chin-jen develops this parable in
> a discussion with King Ying of Wei. See Burton Watson, *The
> Complete Works of Chuang Tzu*, pp. 283–285.

792. That which lives must fade:
even Śakyamuni—the Honored One—could not avoid
      smoke from the *candana* wood!
When joy is done, sadness comes:
even the heavenly *devas* encounter
      a day of Five Decays.

ŌE NO ASATSUNA

> Śakyamuni—the Buddha—was cremated on a pile of *candana* wood,
> a type of sandalwood. The *devas*, Buddhist angels, do eventually die,
> an event signaled by five types of decay: the flowers in their hair fade;
> dirt appears on their heavenly garments; perspiration flows from their
> underarms; their vision blurs; and they become dissatisfied with their
> place of residence. The modern novelist Mishima Yukio derived the
> name of the fourth novel in his tetralogy from this concept: *Tennin
> gosui* (The decay [literally, "five decays"] of the angel).

793. Morning, you have ruddy cheeks,
      the pride of worldly roads!
Evening, you've become white bones
      rotting in plains beyond city walls.

GENERAL FUJIWARA NO YOSHITAKA

> Number 229 is a *tanka* by the same poet.

794. Although we see the reflection
      of the autumn moon in waves,

so hard to escape the springtime flowers,
   fame within a dream!

ŌE NO ASATSUNA

   The moon reflected in the water is a Buddhist image for the ephemer-
   ality of human life, and the flowers symbolize worldly pleasures.

795. *To what should I compare this world?*
      It is like the wake left behind
      Of a ship being rowed
      Through the mists at dawn.

PRIEST MANSEI

796. *The reflection of the moon*
      Caught in the water
      Scooped into my hand,
      Fleeting and evanescent,
      As my very life itself.

KI NO TSURAYUKI

797. *Like dew on the tips of branches,*
      Or a trickle from the roots themselves,
      Such is the way of this world,
      That sooner or later
      We all must [fade away.]

BISHOP HENJŌ

Whiteness

798. The emperor of Ch'in sighed in amazement:
      the day of Prince Tan of Yen's departure—the crow heads!
      The emperor of Han grieved in lamentation:
      the time of Su Wu's return—crane hairs!

HSIEH KUAN

PROSEPOEM ON WHITENESS

> The emperor of Ch'in held Prince Tan of Yen as a hostage, saying that only when crow heads turned white and horses grew horns would he release him. Prince Tan then raised a cry to heaven, upon which both of these miracles occurred, forcing the emperor to release him. Su Wu was held prisoner by the Hsiung-nu barbarians for nineteen years. Upon his return, all his hair had turned as white as crane feathers.

799. The Silvery River sparkles in brightness
       whitening the autumn sky;
   and we also see the fullness of the white dew
       throughout the wooded garden.

MINAMOTO NO SHITAGŌ

> This and the following three couplets constitute a complete regu-lated-verse poem, "Whiteness." The "Silvery River" is the Milky Way.

800. Mao Pao's turtle returned
       beneath the chilly waves;
   Wang Hung's messenger stood
       before the late-year flowers.

MINAMOTO NO SHITAGŌ

> According to the official history of the Chin dynasty, Mao Pao bought a white turtle in the marketplace, raised it, and then, when it had grown to adulthood, released it into the river. Years later, after being defeated in battle, when Wang jumped, armor and all, into the river to escape the enemy troops, he landed on the back of the turtle, who had returned to help him and who carried him safely to the other shore. Wang Hung sent a white-robed messenger to bring wine to T'ao Ch'ien, so that the destitute poet would have something to drink among the chrysanthemums.

801. Among the reedy islets, moon colors
       flood with the tide;
   in the Pamirs, cloud-skin
       links with snowy peaks.

MINAMOTO NO SHITAGŌ

802. Frosty cranes, gulls on sand—
        all of these are lovely!
    I hate only the temple hairs
        that grow hoary with the years.

MINAMOTO NO SHITAGŌ

THE ABOVE [FOUR PASSAGES] CONSTITUTE FOUR RHYMES

803. *With white hair*
    In the white of the moonlight
    Pushing through the white snow
    To break off a white plum.

ANONYMOUS

3

The *Wakan rōei shū* and Its Impact on Japanese Literature

Jin'ichi Konishi (translated by J. Thomas Rimer)

Around the tenth century, an abundance of Chinese literary texts were imported into Japan. In the case of poetry, however, the complete works of any given poet were not easily available, one reason being that during this period, paper was still a precious commodity. Except for those in the upper nobility, it was extremely difficult to obtain enough paper to make copies. A more important reason is that the Japanese themselves preferred the shorter poetic forms. Although *chōka* (long poem) continued to be written until around the eighth century, in the ninth century this form lost favor, and from the tenth century onward, the thirty-one-syllable *waka* became the representative form of Japanese poetry. Those Japanese who enjoyed Chinese poetry did not choose, therefore, entire texts but, rather, one or possibly two verses as the focus of their appreciation.

From the inception of Chinese poetry to the first decade of this century, the poets used strategies to express their ideas and thoughts. Thus even poetry that is primarily emotional in content also contains (sometimes hidden) some social criticism, while such complexity is difficult to achieve in a waka poem of thirty-one syllables—usually no more than about fifteen words. The shortest form in traditional Chinese poetry uses four lines (about twenty words), and the most common shorter form uses eight lines (about forty to sixty words). And much longer poems were even more common.

The way that the Japanese liked to read Chinese poetry was to extract just one or two lines, a method that radically diverged from the way in which these poems were originally conceived. The Japanese attitude thus contradicted the Chinese poetic urge to advance an ideology or to support a statement of public opinion concerning history or social values. Rather, Japanese readers attempted to take from Chinese poetry its personal and private feelings about or responses to the experience of natural beauty. In Chinese poetry as well, of course, the poet offered his personal feelings about and responses to nature as a means of expressing more general themes, and it was these sections that the Japanese poets extracted. What was therefore only a means for Chinese poets became a larger purpose of poetry for the Japanese.

This does not mean, however, that Japanese had no sense of public opinion during this period. Rather, they tended to address such issues in prose rather than in poetry.

The practice of selecting for appreciation one line from a longer Chinese poem is referred to as *kudai waka*, "waka on verse topics." The poet composed waka appropriate to the emotions expressed in a single line of Chinese poetry that he had chosen. The earliest examples of this technique can be found in the *Ōe no Chisato shū* (Collected waka of Ōe no Chisato), compiled in 894. All the waka in this collection are based on single lines of Chinese poetry. Other examples of this technique can be found through the thirteenth century and beyond.

With these works as a foundation, the Japanese extended their use of single lines of Chinese verse as subjects for kudai waka. But they found it difficult to form another vocabulary in Japanese as a technique to embellish the Chinese original. The reason was that Chinese poets were extremely fond of parallelism, going to considerable lengths to express their sentiments in parallel expressions. The Japanese recognized that to appreciate fully these two-line Chinese sequences, one line no longer was emotionally sufficient. Therefore, in a collection like the *Wakan rōei shū*, many of the Chinese lines were selected to illustrate this two-line parallelism. (Longer segments are included in the *Wakan rōei shū* as well, as exceptions to this general principle.)

In the *Wakan rōei shū*, certain lines of Chinese poetry were chosen in order to harmonize with the Japanese sense of beauty. Therefore, the way in which the poems are grouped reveal a very Japanese (or, to be more precise, a waka-like) sensibility, one that Chinese poets might have considered unsatisfactory.

The *Wakan rōei shū*'s divisions and categories of subject matter, such as the four seasons and human affairs, are similar to those in a number of the imperial waka anthologies. But the *Wakan rōei shū* does not display the finely graded sense of progression or delicate association of images found in an anthology like the *Kokinshū*. The main reason is that during this period, Japanese poets were not able to consult enough Chinese poetic sources and collections to find a sufficiently rich selection of such lines in Chinese. Then, too, those who read Chinese poetry tended to use these texts as sources for their own poems, in either Chinese or Japanese, instead of appreciating the collection as a whole.

The poems in the *Kokin waka rokujō* (Six volumes of waka, old and new), compiled toward the end of the tenth century, are meticulously classified. By that time, the anthology assembled by Ou-yang Hsün (557–641), entitled *I-wen lei-chü* (Literary references) may have become available in Japan and, with it, the Chinese influences on its system of classification.

Later Japanese poets in the medieval period found such methods of classification to be very helpful. Indeed, they used Chinese works in much the same way that writers in the vernacular such as Chaucer, Thomas Hoccleve, Robert Henryson, or John Lydgate used classical Latin works as sources for allusions. The later Japanese poets, however, did not refer to the Chinese works directly but, rather, consulted such works as the *Wakan rōei shū* that were based on them. Likewise, the quotations used in the medieval *nō* drama were taken from the *Wakan rōei shū*, not from the original sources.

This cultural practice of altering Chinese methods of expression to suit the Japanese sensibility provides crucial material for studying the history of Japanese style. The first important issue, as I have already explained, is that apparently no one noticed that only those portions of Chinese verse were chosen that accorded with Japanese sensibility. The second and perhaps more fundamental issue is how modern Japanese understand and evaluate the *Wakan rōei shū* as part of their own tradition. Their attitude is undoubtedly quite different from that of the Western reader.

My views regarding the first issue are not my own; until now, all Japanese have consistently taken the same position. Despite the many books of commentary on the *Wakan rōei shū* from the seventeenth century until today, none of them—to my knowledge—explicate the Japanese waka selected. The reason commonly cited is that all the waka chosen were extremely well known, verses for which no explanations were deemed necessary. Indeed, the compiler of the collection turned his attention instead to the Chinese verses to be included. His purpose was to show that Japanese waka were capable of expressing sentiments similar to those in the examples of Chinese poetry selected. But if the compiler merely intended to show that certain types of waka did exist, then he surely would have selected a greater number of Japanese poems to demonstrate this. Because he had many collections of waka available to him, he probably assumed that his readers could consult these other collections for additional examples.

In regard to the second issue—how modern Japanese understand and evaluate the *Wakan rōei shū*—I have no particular position that I wish to stress. But I will point out that when the Japanese have used only their own resources, they have not produced their best works of literature. Rather, it has been in times of outside influences (which, before the Meiji period, beginning in 1868, were largely confined to the Chinese) that the melding of the Japanese with a continental sensibility has given birth to the greatest Japanese works of literature. Thus the kind of Chinese verse cited in the *Wakan rōei shū* was able—indeed, until the Meiji period—to inspire the most admirable expression in the literature of our civilization.

4

Singing the *Wakan rōei shū*

Stephen Addiss

POETRY AND SONG

In the West we are accustomed to reading poems instead of hearing them spoken or declaimed. For the Japanese, however, poetry has traditionally been meant to be sung, to the extent that one of the reasons for compiling verses was to make them available for musical performance, as the title of the *Wakan rōei shū* makes clear. Indeed, music was so important to poetry that the classical five-line Japanese verse known as the *tanka* or *waka* is also often called *uta* (song), and other poetic forms were also given melodies in order to complete their emotional expression.

Japan's earliest known poems were songs. The first books compiled in Japan, the *Kojiki* (Records of ancient matters, 712) and the *Nihonshoki* (Chronicles of Japan, 720), contain 113 and 131 songs, respectively, intermingled with prose in the texts in order to give them a narrative context. These songs came from an earlier oral tradition, maintained through religious ceremonies and also preserved into the eighth century by both entertainers and professional reciters. In preliterate Japan, these reciters held an important role in society, but when a writing system was introduced from China, they gradually disappeared.

Even though they were written as poems in the earliest books, the songs of prehistoric Japan betray their musical origin by their rhythmic repetition of words and sometimes also by their extra vocalizing syllables. The songs often tell of the mythic days of the gods, like the five-line lyric that celebrates the building by the god Susano-o no Mikoto of an auspicious palace for his princess bride:[1]

Where eight clouds arise	*Yakumo tatsu*
in Izumo, eight-sided balustrades	*Izumo yaegaki*
to receive my wife,	*tsumagomi ni*
eight-sided balustrades I've built,	*taegaki tsukuru*
these eight-sided balustrades, O!	*sono yaegaki o*

This lyric follows the 5–7–5–7–7 syllable pattern of classical Japanese court verse, leading some scholars to suspect that it is not one of the older songs in the *Kojiki*, but it also is possible that the compilers adapted the original words to the more refined form. The other poems in the two early collections have a variety of meters, but in general, songs tended to be built of either groups of even lines, having roughly equal syllable counts, or groups of uneven lines, most often alternating between five and seven syllables. It was this latter group that led to the development of the classical Japanese waka.

When discussing the early songs recorded in the *Kojiki* and *Nihonshoki*, Edwin Cranston notes that they "can be traced back to a social matrix in which they were not individual creations, but served the purpose of ritual, entertainment, or the perpetuation of myth."[2] In total, almost five hundred of these early lyrics have been gathered from early sources, and they comprise songs of love, work, travel, victory, praise, and children at play. As such, they often are personal, even if they were sung at social and ritual occasions, and they anticipate the subjects of much later Japanese poetry.

In the Heian period, when the *Wakan rōei shū* was compiled, the arts continued to be closely intertwined. Both music and calligraphy added new dimensions to the appreciation of poems, giving them new expressions. When written in a beautiful hand, a verse can be appreciated instantly as a visual image. In addition, anyone trained in calligraphy can also recreate the actual writing of the poem, beginning with the first word on the upper right and following the movement of the brush down the columns to the lower left. The viewer can detect the varied timing, showing when the rhythms are quick and when they pause or move more slowly, and can also see where the lines are thicker because of more pressure and where they are thinner because of a lighter touch. In this way, both writing and viewing calligraphy can be a creative as well as a recreative art, just like singing and listening to song.

This ability to present and enjoy the poems in calligraphy and music, both of which extend the verse through time, may explain why the Japanese have favored short poetic forms such as the five-line waka and, later, the three-line *haiku*. It also may be one reason that Japanese connoisseurs have often preferred short Chinese poems, or even shorter excerpts from Chinese poems, as seen in the *Wakan rōei shū*.

A later chapter will discuss calligraphy; this chapter will focus on how the poems from this great anthology were sung. The verses offer at least three different kinds of vocal presentations, ranging from spoken to chanted to sung. A lover would whisper a poem to his or her beloved, at which point the affair might be ruined if the recipient did not respond in kind. Poems could also be chanted, on a single tone or two or three different notes. The most complex presentation, however, was putting the verse into full melody, and this was often done both spontaneously and in more formal ways.

Little is known about the melodies for the earliest songs, but some of the songs are listed in the *Kojiki* as "floating songs" or "rustic songs," perhaps suggesting categories of melody. To learn what the old songs might have sounded like, we can turn to the folk and ritual songs that are still performed at traditional occasions in Japan, as they may retain some of the ancient flavor. It was not until some of the old folk songs had been incorporated into court music that any specific melodies were known, and these may be quite different from their original tunes. There are two types of such court settings of Japanese poems, one called *saibara* (horse tender's music), which combines old folk songs and Chinese musical styles, and one called *ōuta* (great song), which preserves some of the characteristics of Japanese ritual music. A third form, having the generic name of *rōei*, indicates the singing of poems written in Chinese by either Chinese or Japanese poets.

To know what Heian period waka might have sounded like, we could look to the current performance of saibara, although the melodies are now sung so slowly that they have lost much of their vigor. Furthermore, the music has been extensively reconstructed and therefore does not offer a very reliable indication of what the original melodies may have been. But what we can see clearly in saibara is how even earlier forms of Japanese verse were amalgamated into the thirty-one–syllable form, with extra nonsense syllables (similar to our "fa-la-la") added to fit the music's framework.

Saibara is now sung by a soloist, who keeps time with wooden sticks called *shakubyōshi*, along with a chorus that enters with the instrumental accompaniment after a few measures. Once the others have entered, the timing is strict. The formal and rather solemn performance might partially reflect how Japanese poems were sung in concerts held at the Heian court, but today's reenactment probably is quite different from that of a tenth-century courtier privately singing a love poem that he has composed for his paramour, or that of a few carefree young men at court entertaining themselves with a song contest in which they must continuously write new lyrics. Nevertheless, saibara offers at least a small window into the world of early Japanese song. We should note, too, that one of the most famous early singers of this form was Princess Hirō (777–856), indicating that this music was performed by women as well as men.[3]

Unlike the earliest Japanese lyrics, the poems of the Heian period did not exist solely as songs. Indeed, the development of a court culture led to many changes in Japanese aesthetics, including those of poetry and music. Certainly the development of a writing system, based on the Chinese one, that could conveniently record the Japanese language was crucial to the development of waka, and to some extent it was responsible for the gradual separation of verse and song. In any case, the most famous Japanese statement on poetry—written by Ki no Tsurayuki around 905 as a preface to the *Kokinshū*—confirms the close ties between poetry and singing:

> The poetry of Japan has its roots in the human heart and flourishes in the countless leaves of words. Because human beings possess interests of so many kinds, it is in poetry that they give expression to the meditations of their hearts in terms of the sights appearing before their eyes and the sounds coming to their ears. Hearing the warbler sing among the blossoms and the frog in his fresh waters—is there any living being not given to song?[4]

It is not surprising that Japanese loved to sing their native poetry or, conversely, that the lyrics that they loved to sing were themselves poems, but it may be surprising that they also sang Chinese verses. After all, Chinese was not their native tongue, and even though it is one thing to read poems using the same characters that are used in Japanese, it is quite another to sing them when they were originally composed in a totally different language. Nevertheless, singing rōei was very popular in the Heian period, and despite the vicissitudes of history, the practice still exists. In her excellent study entitled *Rōei: The Medieval Court Songs of Japan*,[5] Eta Harich-Schneider offers transcriptions into Western notation of the fourteen remaining rōei, at least one of which has been issued in Japan in recorded form.[6] However, we must again ask whether current performance practice reflects how the poems were sung a millennium ago. From comments in novels and diaries of the Heian period, it seems that rōei were, at times, sung very freely and only later put into more formal and stylized forms. But the fact that we still have some music (as well as the poems) of a thousand years ago is a remarkable testament to Japan's ability to preserve the past while embracing the future.

RŌEI IN LITERATURE

How, why, and where were rōei originally sung? The evidence from literary sources—including the world's first novel, Lady Murasaki's *Tale of Genji*—is that some performances were private and informal. In the chapter of *Genji* entitled "Yūgao," Prince Genji is recalling a lover who has died:

> Even the clamor of the cloth beater's mallets that they had heard together now became a dear memory, and as Genji leaned on his pillow, he sang to himself the verse of Po Chu-i:
>
>> In the eighth month, in the ninth month,
>>   just when the nights are long,
>> a thousand poundings, ten thousand poundings,
>>   it never has an end![7]

Here Genji is reminiscing about the brief affair he had with Yūgao before her tragic early death, and significantly it is a Chinese poem that comes to mind as he hears the typically autumn sound of cloth being beaten. We can imagine him singing softly and sadly to the accompaniment of the fullers' mallets in nearby houses.

In the later chapter "Suma," Genji is now in exile. One night he recalls the public performances of rōei and other music that took place back in the capital, and again it inspires him to sing the poetry of Po Chu-i:

> A splendid moon had risen, and Genji realized that on this night of the full moon there would be concerts at the Imperial Palace. Perhaps his previous companions, gathered for a midnight party with beautiful court ladies, might be thinking of him.
>
>> Two thousand miles away,
>>   the heart of my friend.[8]
>
> So he sang and could not hold back the tears.

Again the mood is sad nostalgia, and Genji sings a rōei alone in memory of the more formal music, including rōei, that he could no longer share with his friends in the capital.

Other early texts also indicate that rōei were sung at both private and public occasions. The *Pillow Book* diary of the court lady Sei Shōnagon, written at the end of the tenth century, has several interesting references to rōei, including an anecdote about the emperor and his courtiers singing Chinese poems informally in the gardens of the palace, intended in part as a flirtation with the ladies-in-waiting. Another description of rōei is quite different, taking place after a memorial ceremony attended by the entire court:

> After the ceremony was over, we were served wine, and Chinese poems were recited and sung. Fujiwara no Tadanobu beautifully sang this rōei:
>
> The moon meets autumn's time, but where has the man disappeared?[9]

The fact that when they were moved by the deep emotions evoked by a memorial service, the courtiers sang Chinese poetry shows how deeply rōei had penetrated the Japanese spirit.

EARLY PERFORMANCE PRACTICE

At many formal concerts at the Imperial Palace, rōei would be sung toward the end of the performance. It seems to have been the court nobles who sang on such occasions, with professional musicians providing the accompaniment. Although these instrumentalists were attached to the court, they represented a much lower social class than the nobles. Whereas a nobleman might show his skill by picking up and playing an instrument, the professional musicians do not seem to have been allowed to sing at court.

Two entries in the diary of Fujiwara no Michinaga (966–1024) indicate two ways in which rōei were performed, one with accompaniment by professionals and one with accompaniment by courtiers. In the entry for the fifteenth day of the first month of 1011, Michinaga notes that "when the merry circle of high guests had finished their meal and enjoyed their sake, the servants entrusted with the music were summoned. They accompanied the songs of the higher and lower courtiers who all sang together, and after some musical numbers the servants all received rewards." On the thirteenth day of the fourth month of 1010, he wrote that "in the presence of the Empress Dowager in the Biwa-tei, wine was served and the courtiers made music. Four or five courtiers who were experts in instrumental music kneeled near the seats of the higher nobles and sang *rōei* with string accompaniment."[10]

Almost three centuries later, rōei continued to be sung in a very similar fashion at court, although it now was not unusual for court ladies to accompany the singing on string instruments. Lady Nijō, who was born in 1258, writes in her autobiographical narratives about an elaborate party in 1281 when two retired emperors both sang and joined five other noblemen and court ladies in performing music on wind and string instruments, including rōei from the *Wakan rōei shū*. The ability to choose exactly the right poem for the moment was highly prized:

> As the night deepened, the mountain wind moaned through the nearby pines and sounded in the halls of the palace. The nearby bell of the Jokongō Temple tolled and GoFukakusa began to sing:

> > On the gate tower of the prefect's residence
> >   I see only the colors of the roof tiles;
> > of the temple of Kannon Bosatsu,
> >   I hear only the sound of the bell.

> This was so appropriate and moving that for a while all amusements stopped.[11]

Later in the same narrative, Lady Nijō discusses a concert at the temple Saionji in 1285. Again, retired emperors join other court nobles, including the crown prince, in singing rōei from the *Wakan rōei shū*.[12]

In addition to such formal occasions, rōei were sung freely as the spirit moved a courtier, or a group of courtiers, and rōei often seem to have been performed just for the sheer enjoyment of singing.

Another thirteenth-century source, the *Kokonchomonshū* of Tachibana Narisue, contains an unusual and amusing use of rōei:

> One evening the minister Myōon-in secretly brought a lady to his mansion. He told his vassal Owari no Kami Takasada: "When dawn breaks, please give us a discreet warning."

> Not too early, not too late, but just at the exact moment Takasada went into the garden and sang:

> > As guests drink in the hall,
> > the garden dew is still moist;
> > servants are waiting at the gate—
> > the peak of Mount Chi-lung blushes at first light.

> How tactful! Takasada was surely a loyal and useful vassal.[13]

Another entertaining anecdote from the same source tells how a rōei was sung at a Buddhist meeting by a high-ranking monk who made a mistake in the words of the poem.[14] Instead of singing "five hundred grains of dust" (representing the virtues of the Buddha), he sang "eighty grains." Even as he was intoning the word *eighty*, a witty court lady named Owari who was listening from behind a curtain commented: "You have just dropped four hundred and twenty grains."

Although this story is included in the *Kokonchomonshū* as an example of mental alacrity, it also tells us several things about the social and cultural atmosphere in Japan at the beginning of the Kamakura period. First, the original words of the poem must have been familiar to this court lady, indicating that men were not the only ones to study Chinese poetry, even though for most of Japanese history, expertise in Chinese cultural pursuits was considered a male domain. Women, on the other hand, took the lead in writing prose in Japanese, joining monks and courtiers in composing fine waka. But what is officially supposed to be happening is often different from actual events, and although there are no recorded examples of women singing rōei, they certainly must have known how to do so. Thus the comment by Lady Owari has an extra element of humor: Not only is the monk satirized by being corrected by a female, but she also seems to think that she could have done better, had it been considered appropriate for her to sing rōei in public.

Second, no matter how quick the lady's wit, the monk could not have been singing very fast. Two ways to compose suitable musical settings for short texts of two or four lines of Chinese poetry are, first, to hold some notes for a long time and, second, to sing several notes for one syllable; this is called a *melisma*. This kind of slow melismatic vocal practice is related to how rōei are now sung, and this anecdote indicates that more than seven hundred years ago, rōei were probably sung in a similarly slow manner.

Third, the setting of this story during a Buddhist service indicates that in the thirteenth century, rōei were sung outside court circles. This was an era in which the warfare that had erupted between two major clans caused a great deal of personal tragedy, and to many Japanese, religion became even more important than before. Buddhist vocal practice offered the first form of notation used for rōei, and Buddhist chant may have influenced the music of rōei as well.

Finally, this story poking fun at a monk with aspirations to high culture surely represents some of the tensions accompanying the loss of court dominance in Japan during the Kamakura period. Humor is often an effective way of dealing with trouble, and it must have reassured the courtiers that they remained the cultural elite, even if they no longer held political power. Furthermore, this anecdote would certainly have fed their sense of aristocratic superiority, all the more precious for being threatened.

These final two points are supported by a third anecdote from the same collection, in which the nobleman Takamichi Ason happens to hear an unknown monk singing a rōei with a Buddhist text.[15] When he courteously compliments the monk on his skill, the monk tells him that he is good because he studied with Takamichi Ason himself! As before, a rōei is being sung in a Buddhist context, and again the nobility is honored over commoners through the medium of humor.

THE MUSIC OF RŌEI

The *Wakan rōei shū* is the oldest compilation of rōei in Japan, and it is still the most celebrated. But this collection offers no clues to how the rōei were sung, although most of its poems were probably selected at some time for musical performances. Later rōei collections often include a form of musical notation that derives from Buddhist chant (*shōmyō*) notation. Lines called *neumes* are drawn next to the words, indicating upward, downward, or more complex up-and-down movements of the voice (see figure 4.1). Sometimes red dots are also used, indicating the phrasing. Although this kind of notation is not very precise—for example, it says little about the speed at which notes were sung—it nevertheless outlines the rōei's melodic contour. Tradition, in the form of standard performance practice, would fill in the gaps, so that an experienced singer would know how a particular poem was to be sung.

Notation is, of course, a great help to performers, but it also has potential drawbacks. The kind of improvisation that seems to have been typical of Heian period rōei singing was codified in the Kamakura period, with the singing of rōei consequently losing some of its freedom at that time. Once a piece has been published with notation, it is less likely to undergo many changes. This certainly helps preserve it, but it discourages creative transformation. Similarly, the spread of rōei singing beyond court nobles in the Kamakura period encouraged its broader diffusion though Japanese culture, but at the same time, rōei began to lose its prime group of both performers and listeners. Perhaps this was inevitable; the Japanese court has never regained the cultural dominance that it enjoyed during the Heian period.

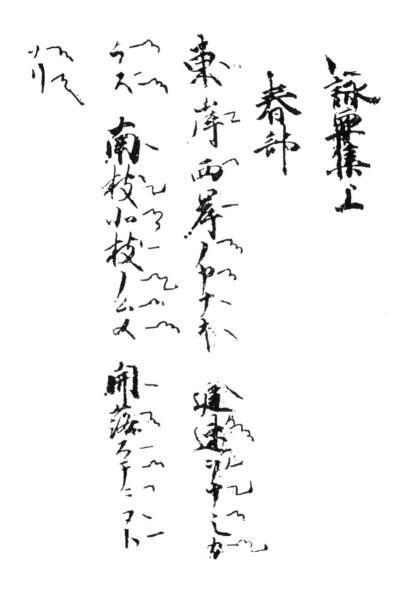

Figure 4.1   "Tōgan" from the *Rōei yōshū* of 1292.

A fifteenth-century document, the *Rōei kyūjishushō* of 1448, has a more complete notation system than the earlier sources do, with the neumes in black ink and the phrasing, ornaments, and intervals in red. A few of the rōei melodies were considered secret, however, and so no neumes were given for them. This volume also contains an interesting passage on the development of rōei, commenting that during the reigns of Emperors Daigo (898–930) and Suzaku (930–955), rōei were very popular. As the form developed, it separated into two different traditions, the Minamoto style, with more than one hundred rōei, and the Fujiwara style, with more than two hundred.

> But the vicissitudes of time have left of all the luxuriant leaves of the Fujiwara tree only the last heir, Munenobu. During his childhood his father died. Lonely in the world, he was unable to foster the arts, and the rōei tradition became extinct. What an inexpressibly bitter loss! The true rōei style is therefore preserved uniquely in the house Minamoto.

This sad comment on the loss of an aristocratic tradition mirrors the loss of power and prestige in the court during an age of warrior control of Japan.

Finally, a postscript to this collection has the following comment: "This scroll was provided with neumes because I am slow of mind and forgetful and therefore have to disregard the scorn of more perfectioned musicians."[16] This excuse for adding notation is surely too modest, but it indicates that there was some opposition to the broader dissemination of rōei through written sources. Like many traditions in Japan, the singing of rōei became more and more fixed into a lineage that would preserve the past through hereditary right and closely supervised training. Prince Go-Sukō-in (1372–1456) wrote in his diary that an elaborate ceremony was held when the time came for him to learn "secret" rōei, and only then was he allowed to copy a scroll containing these special rōei and to receive other secret instructions.[17] By this time, some rōei were traditionally sung solo, and others had instrumental and choral parts. In contrast, during earlier eras, a rōei could be sung freely with or without accompaniment.

Rōei did not fare well in the Tokugawa period (1600–1868), but since then, there has been some attempt to revive the form. At present, fourteen rōei have been preserved and occasionally are sung at court occasions, using the lyrics of four Chinese and eight Japanese poets, none later than the early eleventh century. The music is based on a pentatonic (five-note) scale, with occasional passing tones adding to the variety of pitches. Originally, a poem could have been sung at any pitch, as long as the melodic intervals remained the same, but now the pitches are more fixed, in part to facilitate the instrumental accompaniments.

In current practice, rōei are divided into three parts, although the original poems have two parts, usually couplets or quatrains. This form very likely reflects the Japanese penchant for asymmetry, as opposed to the regularity and balance of most Chinese aesthetics. In a four-line poem, for example, the first two lines become the first part of the rōei, with the third and fourth lines of the poem constituting the second and third parts of the music. As now performed, the beginning of each rōei section is sung solo, and the chorus and accompaniment join in after the first phrases.

In the Heian period, there was a great freedom in the choice of instruments used to accompany rōei. Transverse flutes (*ryūteki*) and reed mouth organs (*shō*) were most common, but oboes (*hichiriki*) and stringed instruments were also frequently used. Currently, the three wind instruments accompany the male soloist, along with a chorus of other male voices. The instruments and the chorus perform the same basic melody as the solo singer, but with slightly fewer subtleties of melodic movement. In the tenth and eleventh centuries, it was surely more difficult to accompany rōei because of the greater use of vocal improvisation, and one early text cautions the instrumentalist not to attempt exact precision with the singer.[18]

When singing rōei, each line of the Chinese poem becomes a separate musical phrase, with a pause as each phrase concludes. Surprisingly enough, each of the fourteen surviving rōei has a similar basic melody. For example, in the first line of each poem, the melody rises, lingers, and then falls in a similar manner. Having such similar melodies does not make the fourteen rōei the same, however, because of subtle changes in how the melodies move and how they are vocally ornamented. Furthermore, certain traditions of vocal ornamentation generally prevail. For example, the lowest and "resting tone" of the scale is usually ornamented with a slight break of the voice to a higher note and immediately back to the original tone, sung halfway through the holding of the note. This "grace note" is so subtle that it can almost pass unnoticed, but it adds a special effect to the note that helps establish it as the "resting tone" on which rōei always end.

In contrast, the fifth higher note—which is actually the fourth note in the pentatonic scale over the "resting tone"—is typically ornamented by a slow trill with the note below it. A series of other ornaments are possible, most for specific notes in the scale. However, a few effects, such as a sudden vocal aspiration, can occur on any note. These various ornaments are crucial to the rōei's emotional expressiveness; without them, the music would merely be slow melodic chanting without much relation to the specific meanings of the texts. And like most fine vocal music, the texts are the emotive springboards for the music to enhance and amplify.

As an example of current performance practice, the rōei now generally entitled "Tōgan" (Eastern shore), the eleventh poem in the *Wakan rōei shū*, is presented here in Western notation (see figure 4.2):

Figure 4.2   Score of "Tōgan."

Willows of the eastern shore,	*Tōgan seigan no yanagi*
the western shore—	
slowly, quickly, not the same;	*chisoku onajikarazu*
plum blossoms on the southern	*nanshi hokushi no ume*
branches, northern branches—	
opening, falling, there's a difference.	*kairaku sude ni kotonari.*[19]

Although the text was originally composed in Chinese by Yoshishige no Yasutane (934/35–977), it is sung with both Sino-Japanese pronunciations and Japanese verb endings. The transcription here shows how the melody can be varied and ornamented, although no notation can show all the vocal subtleties of an actual performance. For example, the rhythm is much more complex and sung more freely than this notation can capture. In addition, some tones are variable in pitch, such as the second note of the scale, which is sung as E*b*, E, and F, as well as pitches between them. This suggests that the usual pentatonic scale, which is used in China and many other countries, has been partially displaced by the pentatonic scale particularly favored by the Japanese, which contains two half-steps, here notated as D to E*b* and A to B*b*. This scale is typical of much Japanese traditional music, and its characteristic sound seems to have a melancholy feeling (see figure 4.3).

This music is very freely organized, and the vocal phrases have many different lengths. It is held together by both the repetition of ornaments and certain melodic motifs and miniphrases that return throughout the piece but are never exactly the same (see figure 4.4). This is another example of the traditional Japanese love of asymmetry and allows both the musicians and the listeners to have some sense of pattern without being confined to a rigid structure.

These patterns and the melodic outline would be generally similar in any contemporary rendition of "Tōgan," but even now, when the form has become somewhat rigid, each performance would be slightly different. For example, Eta Harich-Schneider's notation for "Tōgan"[20] is quite different from mine, indicating the varieties of possible performance practice.

We may well regret that we do not know more about how either waka or rōei were sung a thousand years ago and that so much of the music for the magnificent poems of the *Wakan rōei shū* has now been lost. However, we are fortunate that fourteen complete musical rōei settings still remain in Japan, with neumes and other indications for still more poems. Compared with our knowledge of how Western poets sang their verses, this is remarkable. Not only do we lack the music of Homer as he chanted his great epics, but even for as recent a poet as William Blake (1757–1827), who sang his "Songs of Innocence" and "Songs of Experience," we know nothing of the tunes. So we may be grateful that some melodies for the great classical Chinese and Japanese poems still exist, and when we read the verses to ourselves, we can imagine not only that they once were, but that they still are, music.

Usual pentatonic   **Japanese pentatonic**

Figure 4.3   Scales for "Tōgan."

Figure 4.4   Melodic motifs.

5

The Art of Calligraphy and the *Wakan rōei shū*

Ann Yonemura

By the middle of the Heian period (794–1185) when the poems of the *Wakan rōei shu* were gathered and arranged, writing with brush and ink had attained the status of a fine art that embodied and transmitted to later times the central cultural values of Japanese aristocrats. Three arts—poetry, calligraphy, and music—were studied and practiced nearly universally by the men and women of the Japanese imperial court.[1] Accomplishment in these arts was expected of anyone who aspired to high social standing; the common pattern of education for the elite and confined society of the Heian court ensured that the standards for performance in the arts were widely understood and respected and that the practice and mastery of artistic skills were fostered and rewarded.

Chinese characters and the tools of Chinese calligraphy—brush and ink—were the basis of the first written language to be adopted in Japan, beginning around the fourth century.[2] Japanese mastery of the Chinese written language was undoubtedly hastened by the sixth-century introduction of the Buddhist religion with its extensive corpus of Chinese manuscripts of sacred scriptures (sutras) and treatises, which were copied in prodigious numbers during the seventh and eighth centuries. Writing the Japanese language, however, compelled significant alterations in the use of Chinese characters, such as the reading of a Chinese character to represent one or more sounds of the Japanese language without reference to the meaning associated inseparably with the character in Chinese.[3]

The birth of Japanese literature, especially poetry—in which sequences of sounds and meanings coexisted in complex and subtle associations—stimulated the transmutation of Chinese characters to represent phonetically the sounds of the Japanese language. Writing itself was appreciated for its aesthetic qualities as Japanese writers struggled to master for practical purposes the techniques and forms of Chinese scripts and began to write with conscious artistic intention. Calligraphy came to be respected in Japan, as it had been for centuries in China, as a skill to be cultivated in both execution and connoisseurship, as a manifestation of cultural erudition and individual character, and, at its highest level, as the most elevated of the visual arts.

Between the eighth and tenth centuries, Japanese calligraphers created a practical, elegant, and graceful phonetic script that was derived from the cursive forms of Chinese characters. This script—called *kana*, *sōgana* (cursive kana), or *hiragana*—simplified and abbreviated the Chinese cursive forms of characters beyond the conventions of the Chinese models, enabling Japanese writers for the first time to write the sounds of their own language swiftly and intelligibly. In the hands of the men and especially of the women of the Heian court, for whom kana was often the sole means of written communication, kana script came to possess aesthetic qualities that clearly distinguished it from the cursive Chinese script from which it had been derived.

In the early eleventh-century "Kōyagire" manuscript of the *Kokinwakashū* (figure 5.1), which is regarded as a classic expression of mature kana calligraphy, slender lines accentuated by graceful loops and angular turns flow from the tip of a long, narrow brush that seems barely to touch the paper. The columns of calligraphy are spaciously arranged and are often composed in sequences of irregular length that are not aligned along a horizontal "margin" at the top of the page, as was customary in Chinese calligraphy. There is no counterpart in Chinese calligraphy to the forms and styles of Heian period kana.

The compilation of the *Wakan rōei shū* in the early eleventh century fortunately happened to coincide with the maturation of kana calligraphy as a fully developed Japanese art with its own aesthetic principles. Two distinct modes of artistic writing, one Chinese and one Japanese, were thus available to the first calligraphers, who turned to the *Wakan rōei shū* as a source for artistic expression.

Among the surviving early manuscripts of the *Wakan rōei shū* from the eleventh century are some of the most beautiful and esteemed works in the history of Japanese calligraphy.[4] No extant manuscript is now regarded by scholars as having been written during the lifetime of Fujiwara no Kintō (966–1041), and not even a fragment survives from his original draft of the anthology. However, the accomplished elegance of the calligraphy and the colorful and luxuriously decorated papers incorporated in manuscripts dating from around the middle of the eleventh century brilliantly communicate—almost one thousand years after their creation—the prestige and stature attained by the *Wakan rōei shū* in the first decades following its compilation.

The name of Fujiwara no Yukinari (or Kōzei, 972–1027), the preeminent calligrapher of the mid-Heian period, has traditionally been associated with many of the earliest surviving manuscripts of the *Wakan rōei shū*, even with some now regarded by modern scholars as having been written a century or more after Yukinari's death. Although none of the extant manuscripts or fragmentary manuscripts can be identified authoritatively as being in Yukinari's hand, he is mentioned in a Heian period record as the calligrapher who produced the first clean copy of the anthology, in the format of a pair of handscrolls placed in a *tebako*, a finely made box usually of lacquered wood, for presentation to Fujiwara no Kintō's son-in-law as a gift to celebrate his marriage to Kintō's eldest daughter.[5]

Yukinari's cultivated calligraphic style in both Chinese and Japanese scripts profoundly influenced contemporary calligraphers and became a standard model for later calligraphic practice. The consummate elegance associated with Yukinari's kana calligraphy may be expressed in the Kōyagire manuscript of the *Kokinwakashū*, for which Yukinari is likely to have been one of its three calligraphers.[6] Japanese calligraphy in the style associated with Yukinari was so widely emulated by court calligraphers during and immediately following his lifetime that it permeates the surviving calligraphic works of the period, including the earliest manuscripts of the *Wakan rōei shū*.

Most of the surviving Heian period manuscripts of the *Wakan rōei shū* were written on sheets of paper joined to form continuous handscrolls, following the two-part organization of Fujiwara no Yukinari's lost archetype. One noteworthy exception is the "Detchōbon" manuscript in the collection of the Imperial Household Agency (figure 5.2) The two-volume Detchōbon manuscript is considered by scholars to be one of the earliest extant texts of the *Wakan rōei shū*, and it is named for its format, a book in which individual sheets are folded vertically at the center and joined by pasting the back edges of the center folds to adjacent sheets. A third likely format in which the calligraphy of selected poems of the *Wakan rōei shū* might have been executed, but for which no examples survive from the Heian period, is the *shikishi*, a nearly square sheet of paper suitable for writing a single verse. Heian period literary sources describe shikishi bearing poems in fine calligraphy that were mounted on folding screens (*byōbu*) for display.[7] The brevity of the Japanese poems and most of the quotations from Chinese poems in the *Wakan rōei shū* was particularly suitable for calligraphy in the shikishi format, so the lack of Heian period examples in this format probably reflects the poor preservation of folding screens, which are subject to greater exposure and environmental stresses than are the smaller books and scrolls, which were enclosed in protective boxes.

Each calligraphic work constitutes a unique performance or interpretation of a text. The brush of the calligrapher expresses the text in time and space, controlling the visible tempo and dynamics just as a musician controls sound. Aesthetic preferences governed by the taste of an individual or community are expressed in the choice of script style and in the variations in the scale, composition, rhythm, tempo, and tonality made visible by the ink traces that record each nuance of movement of the supple brush. The calligrapher's brush reveals discrimination, aesthetic sensitivity, and originality against the foundation of a disciplined mastery of character forms, script styles, and composition.

For the calligrapher, the text of the *Wakan rōei shū*, which alternates frequently between sequences of Chinese characters (*kanji*) and Japanese kana, is particularly challenging, like a musical score that demands a high level of technical skill and virtuosity for performance. The close juxtaposition of poems written in substantial and structurally stable Chinese characters to *waka* verses written in slender, insubstantial lines of kana demands of the calligrapher a parallel and articulate mastery of both calligraphic modes. To write the *Wakan rōei shū* with grace and style, the calligrapher must shift imperceptibly between two calligraphic systems, each of which requires a different physical and intellectual focus for the formation of characters according to discrete principles of technique and execution. Writing kana requires focusing physically on the control of fine movements at the tip of the brush; in the composition of individual characters and sequences, line and space possess equal value. Calligraphy of kanji utilizes more fully the body of the brush, which contacts the paper in firm, relatively broader brushstrokes that incorporate considerable internal movement. In regard to composition, calligraphy in kanji is dominated by the positive forms of the characters themselves, the balance and proportion of their structures. Writing the *Wakan rōei shū* text also compels attention to scale, style, and composition, all essential to a harmonious and unified result.

Calligraphers working during and immediately after Fujiwara no Yukinari's lifetime around the mid-eleventh century established harmony between the Chinese and Japanese elements of the text by choosing a similar scale for individual Chinese characters and phonetic symbols of the Japanese kana syllabary, and a relatively even, wide spacing between columns of characters in either script. Thus, the slender, simple forms of kana appear relatively large in scale and thereby create a visual parity with the more complex and substantial forms of the Chinese characters. A common device to maintain proportion and balance was to write each Chinese couplet of fourteen characters in a single vertical column and to write in two columns a thirty-one-syllable waka poem, requiring thirty-one kana symbols. Names of poets are often noted or abbreviated in smaller characters following each verse. Greater compositional variation is apparent in the waka passages, in which the length of the second column of a poem may be somewhat shorter than the first. Heian period calligraphers of the *Wakan rōei shū* usually maintained, with disciplined regularity, the proportions of characters and the spacing between columns, placing the columns evenly across the joints between the sheets of paper, which often were colored or decorated with contrasting patterns. The characteristically balanced proportion of Chinese and Japanese characters and spacing observed by most Heian calligraphers may be related to the common practice—as an act of personal religious devotion—of copying Buddhist sutras, which are conventionally written in columns of seventeen Chinese characters each.

One fragment of an eleventh-century manuscript of the *Wakan rōei shū*, written on tinted paper and decorated with particles of mica, gold, and silver, features characters of larger proportions, which led to its nickname, the "Daiji" (Large character) manuscript (figure 5.3). The calligraphy of the Daiji manuscript segment, a registered Important Art Object in the Tokyo National Museum, shows well-formed, regular, and semicursive Chinese characters spaced thirteen to each column, so that a typical fourteen-character couplet must have its last character carried to the top of the next column. The kana passages of this manuscript are similarly proportioned in relatively widely spaced columns.

Most calligraphers in the Heian period also elected to diminish rather than enhance the potential stylistic contrasts between Chinese and Japanese calligraphic forms, by favoring for the Chinese poems the flowing, continuous brushstrokes of the semicursive (Jpse. *gyōsho*, Chin. *hsing-shu*) or cursive styles (Jpse. *sōsho*, Chin. *ts'ao-shu*) of the Chinese scripts, rather than the standard script (Jpse. *kaisho*, Chin. *k'ai-shu*), with its architectonic emphasis on individually executed horizontal, vertical, and diagonal brushstrokes. Even when standard script is occasionally used for the Chinese verses, the Heian calligrapher emphasizes curves rather than angles and graceful internal movements of the brush producing elegant flourishes that complement the loops and fluent lateral gestures of the Japanese kana passages.

A prominent feature of Heian period manuscripts of the *Wakan rōei shū* is their extensive employment of colored and decorated papers of the most luxurious types then available. Heian period aristocrats, who were both the producers and the audience for these luxurious calligraphic works, were discriminating connoisseurs of poetry, calligraphy, paper, music, flowers, and incense. In their world of refined connoisseurship and heightened sensory awareness, even personal correspondence demanded the selection of an appropriate paper, the composition of a poem suitable for the season or the occasion, a calligraphy that would properly reflect the sensitivity, accomplishment, and character of the writer, and the selection of a fresh flower or plant sprig to attach to the message.[8]

The high demand among aristocrats in Kyoto for fine paper for correspondence—the principal means of personal communication—and for the artistic production of fine calligraphy scrolls, books, and shikishi for mounting on folding screens inspired and supported the production of an exceptional range of specialized papers in an unprecedented variety of hues and patterns. As is frequently the case in the Japanese visual arts, the luxurious Heian period manuscripts of the *Wakan rōei shū* illustrate the achievements of unnamed masters of the craft of paper production and decoration.

Surviving manuscripts of the *Wakan rōei shū* that are especially noteworthy for their opulent array of decorated papers include the Detchōbon volumes, the two scrolls constituting part 2 of the *Wakan rōei shū*, which is known as the "Konoe" manuscript, a registered National Treasure in the Yōmei bunko Foundation; the "Sekido" manuscript, now a single scroll made up of segments from the original pair of scrolls, a registered Important Cultural Property; the "Kansubon" manuscript, a complete transcription of the anthology in two scrolls in the collection of the Imperial Household Agency (figure 5.4); and the "Masuda" manuscript (figure 5.5), a single scroll representing part 2 of the anthology, a registered Important Cultural Property in the Tokyo National Museum. The first three of these manuscripts appear from their calligraphic attributes to have been produced around the middle of the eleventh century, very soon after the compilation of the *Wakan rōei shū*; the Kansubon and the Masuda manuscripts were probably produced in the early twelfth century. Not only the calligraphy of these manuscripts, which closely follows the classic style associated with Fujiwara Yukinari, but also the taste for color and pattern expressed in the selection and arrangement of paper communicates tangibly and directly many characteristics of the complex and now somewhat enigmatic aesthetic ideals of the Heian period during a period of intense creativity in literature, calligraphy, and the visual arts, and, although less directly documented, in the performance of music and dance.

All these manuscripts are made up of sheets of colored and decorated paper joined in sequences in which each sheet contrasts with the next. Whereas continuity and harmony are emphasized in the calligraphy, the underlying designs and colors of the paper shift conspicuously sheet by sheet from neutral tones to deep or light tones of red, yellow, blue, purple, and green; color was applied to paper by dyeing or applying pigments. The decoration ranges from simple sprinklings of gold, silver, or mica particles to patterns such as geometric tortoiseshell designs, stylized plant and floral scrolls, and delicate landscapes. Patterns printed on the paper using a stencil process to apply luminous mica powder were especially favored. Paper of this kind, which was imported from China, was termed *karakami* (Chinese paper). Karakami was highly valued in Heian society, and its extensive use in early *Wakan rōei shū* manuscripts underscores the prestige of the anthology in the period following its compilation.

Japanese papermakers also produced distinctive papers with areas dyed in hues of blue and purple to form irregular, cloudlike patterns termed *kumogami*, "cloud paper." Kumogami sheets are interspersed in scrolls such as the Sekido and Masuda manuscripts with sheets of paper, including karakami, of contrasting colors or patterns. One early manuscript in the collection of the Imperial Household Agency is written entirely on paper of this type and is known today as the "Kumogami" manuscript (figure 5.6).

Hand-painted underdrawings also appear on some Heian period manuscripts of the *Wakan rōei shū*, such as the eleventh-century "Atakagire" manuscript, part of which survives, with the largest section in the collection of the Imperial Household Agency (figure 5.7); the two scrolls of the eleventh-century "Ōtagire" manuscript in the Seikadō Foundation; and the "Ashide shita-e" or "Eiryakubon" manuscript, a complete text in two scrolls registered as a National Treasure in the Kyoto National Museum (figure 5.8). Gold and silver—which assume great importance in the evolution of Japanese painting from the Heian period onward—are extensively employed for the paintings of the Atakagire and ōtagire manuscripts. The Ashide shita-e manuscript is dated the first year of Eiryaku, or 1160, according to the colophon by its calligrapher, Fujiwara no Koreyuki (?–1175), who was a sixth-generation follower of Fujiwara no Yukinari. The underpaintings in this manuscript represent simple landscapes with motifs of plants and birds. In addition, the manuscript includes some written characters incorporated into the landscape motifs.[10] The text of the *Wakan rōei shū* is written continuously over the paintings; the columns of characters are superimposed on the landscapes, which appear as a background to the writing. The composition of the calligraphy otherwise follows the organization of other Heian period manuscripts, except for the greater variation in the length and arrangement of columns of kana. The kana sequences often begin from different levels and are written in irregular lengths, which contrast markedly with the regularity of the Chinese passages. The calligraphy in this manuscript also shares stylistic characteristics with other Japanese calligraphy of the late Heian period and features of the writer's personal style in the pronounced contrasts between dark and light ink tones, marked variations in the thickness of lines, and swift, energetic movements of the brush.

The superimposition of the calligraphy on landscapes and natural motifs places the calligraphy and the poetic imagery that it represents in an implicit relationship to the underpaintings and their pictorial representations of the natural world. Nature exists in these manuscripts in multivalent artistic manifestations that appeal synchronously to the reader's mind and heart.[11]

Before turning to later calligraphic interpretations of the *Wakan rōei shū*, I shall examine further the aesthetic ideals represented by the Heian period manuscripts. The Japanese courtiers' preference for calligraphy on highly decorated and colorful papers survives in full flower in these Heian period manuscripts, yet the widespread modern discomfort with ornament clouds our perception of the aesthetic significance of color and pattern in these works. Even in Japan, centuries of dominance by aesthetic ideals formulated in later historical periods—which has resulted, for example, in the isolation of segments of handscrolls to form hanging scrolls for display in the *tokonoma* (an alcove in the home for the display of art objects)—distances the viewer from the fully orchestrated splendor of the original work of art.

The selection of opulently decorated and colored papers for the eleventh- and twelfth-century calligraphic manuscripts of the *Wakan rōei shū* and other important poetry anthologies was not incidental but was a fundamental element of these works' complex aesthetic character. Color and pattern were an indispensable aspect of the daily lives of Heian period aristocrats. The sequential shifts of color and pattern forming the finest scrolls and books of Heian period calligraphy reveal a specific appreciation of color juxtaposition and harmony that was also expressed, for example, in the layered clothing of contrasting colors and patterns worn by women of the court. The finest calligraphy of literary, poetic, and religious texts in this period was fully integrated by juxtaposition or, more often, by superimposition, with color and ornament that were as essential to their artistic integrity as the timbre of a particular instrument is to an orchestral performance. For the Heian period aristocrat, the experience of reading poetry written in fine calligraphy on these opulently decorated scrolls must have been a particularly gratifying experience that simultaneously called up multiple associations from the content, imagery, and voice of the poetry itself, the visual beauty of the calligraphy, and the sumptuous and shifting color and ornament of the paper itself.

For calligraphers from the mid-Heian period onward, especially the aristocratic followers of lineages of masters descended from Fujiwara no Yukinari, the text of the *Wakan rōei shū* was an indispensable model for calligraphy in both Chinese and Japanese scripts. Although the full history of their passage to later generations is often obscure, some of the Heian period manuscripts of the *Wakan rōei shū* bear later documentation that attests to their ownership by prominent families of Kyoto aristocrats. The treasured Heian manuscripts undoubtedly served as models for connoisseurship and training for later generations of calligraphers, especially those who followed the courtly Sesonji lineage descended directly from Fujiwara no Yukinari, which continued for five centuries.

Interest in the complete text of the *Wakan rōei shū* for the production of artistic calligraphic manuscripts of the complete text appears to have reached a peak in the Heian period that would not again be matched. With the decline in the economic and political fortunes of Kyoto aristocrats that began in the twelfth century and continued through centuries of political rule by the warrior class, the refined complex of sensibility and connoisseurship supporting the production of the ornate calligraphic masterpieces of the Heian period receded. The complete text of the *Wakan rōei shū* was repeatedly copied for practical purposes such as reading and study, but calligraphic works written during the Kamakura period (1185–1333) and later often survive only in part and are generally written on papers plainer than those prevalent in the late Heian period. In addition, many later calligraphic works represent only selected quotations from the anthology in formats such as shikishi.

The evolution of calligraphic styles in the Kamakura period, and later, departed from the Heian period's emphasis on parity and harmony between the Chinese and Japanese scripts. These later works display a greater emphasis of visual contrasts between the passages written in Chinese and in Japanese. Chinese characters are often written in much larger scale and with greater spacing between characters, whereas the Japanese passages show freer compositional arrangements and occasionally incorporate Chinese characters— intended to be read according to Japanese pronunciations—as visual accents.

Calligraphers in Kyoto during the brilliant renaissance of the classical Japanese arts of the early seventeenth century consciously sought inspiration from the arts of the Heian period (figure 5.9). Many fine calligraphies based on poems of the *Wakan rōei shū* were produced in this period, often by members of the aristocracy, for whom the text had never lost its importance as a foundation of their training. The production of luxuriously decorated papers, which had declined after the Heian period, flourished once again.

A small folding screen in the Freer Gallery of Art is an example of the artistic revival during this period (figure 5.10). Six shikishi, each inscribed with a poem in Chinese and Japanese, were written by Konoe Nobutada (1565–1614), one of the Kan'ei Sampitsu, or "Three Great Brushes" of the Kan'ei era (1624–1644). Like many Kyoto calligraphers from the fourteenth century onward, Nobutada's training reflects the styles prevalent in the Shōren-in, a temple that served as a training center for calligraphers after its establishment as an artistic center by the abbot Son'en (1298–1356). The shikishi are decorated with gold and silver motifs depicting, for example, a bridge, bamboo, willow, snow, and mist. Nobutada's calligraphy is composed in large, evenly spaced characters that fill each sheet, giving the kana passages in particular an unusually substantial quality. Instead of the long, continuous columns typical of early manuscripts of the *Wakan rōei shū*, Nobutada's kana poems are written in four lines of relatively even length, following the format of the shikishi. Nobutada's bold approach to achieving the aesthetic balance between kana and kanji is essentially the reverse of that adopted by Heian period calligraphers. Instead of controlling the scale and expression of the Chinese calligraphy to balance the inherent delicacy of kana script, Nobutada enlarged and emboldened the kana, thereby giving each kana symbol the visual presence and substantiality of a Chinese character.

The pronounced individuality shown in Nobutada's work contrasts with the lyrical elegance of a handscroll with calligraphy by Imperial Prince Dōkō (fl. ca. 1650–1675), in the Hofer collection[12] (figure 5.11). Over landscapes executed in a combination of painted gold pigment and applied gold leaf, the elongated, elegant forms of Chinese characters and delicate sequences of kana appear to float.

In modern times, the *Wakan rōei shū* appears once again to have declined in importance as a source for artistic calligraphy, for reasons related to the decline in general knowledge of the anthology, as discussed in the Introduction, and perhaps in part because its value for defining the complex and subtle relationships between Chinese and Japanese poetry and calligraphy is less widely understood. Historically, most of the brilliant artistic renditions of this text were produced during the Heian period, when the importance of the text as a paradigm for beauty in poetry, calligraphy, and performance, was most fully recognized.

For subsequent generations of aristocratic calligraphers, however, the *Wakan rōei shū* remained resonant as a model for training in which they could experience the interdependence, complementarity, and ultimately the aesthetic harmony of the Chinese and Japanese calligraphic modes. Centuries of continuous care and appreciation for the magnificent calligraphic masterpieces from the Heian period have preserved these works remarkably well, so their aesthetic qualities of luxury and beauty that spoke at once to the mind and heart of the Heian courtier can still be experienced today.

Figure 5.1 *Kokinwakashū* (Kōyagire manuscript), vol. 19. Heian period, first quarter of eleventh century. Handscroll, ink on paper, 26.3 × 59.0 cm. Important Cultural Property. Tokyo National Museum, gift of Morita Ichirō.

Figure 5.2   *Wakan rōei shū* (Detchōbon manuscript). Attributed to Fujiwara no Yukinari (972–1027). Heian period, mid-eleventh century. Two volumes, ink on colored paper with mica, 20.0 × 12.1 cm. Imperial Household Agency (Kunaichō), Sannomaru Shōzōkan.

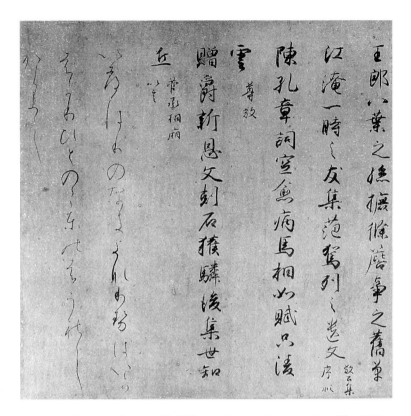

Figure 5.3   Segment from the Daiji (Large-character) manuscript of the *Wakan rōei shū*. Attributed to Fujiwara no Yukinari (972–1027). Heian period, eleventh century. Hanging scroll, ink on colored paper with mica, gold, and silver, 25.1 × 25.6 cm. Tokyo National Museum, gift of Morita Ichirō. Important Art Object.

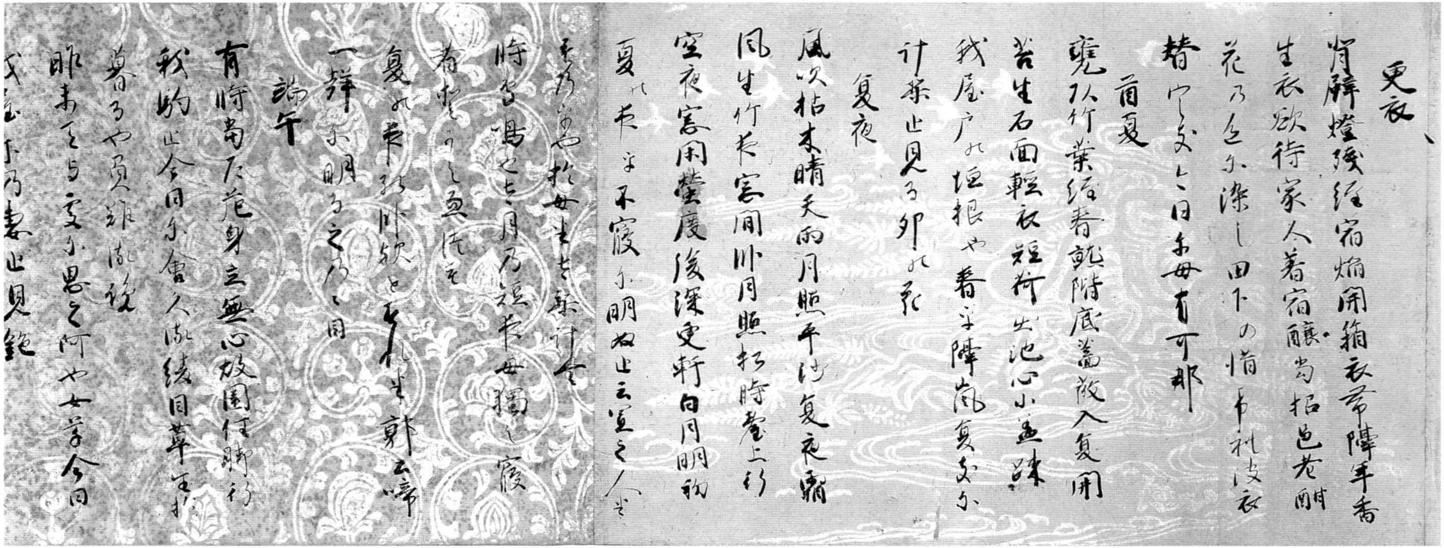

Figure 5.4 *Wakan rōei shū* (Kansubon manuscript). Attributed to Fujiwara no Kintō. Two handscrolls, ink on colored paper with mica, 25.8 × 1292.6 cm, 21.8 × 1133.2 cm. Imperial Household Agency, Sannomaru Shōzōkan.

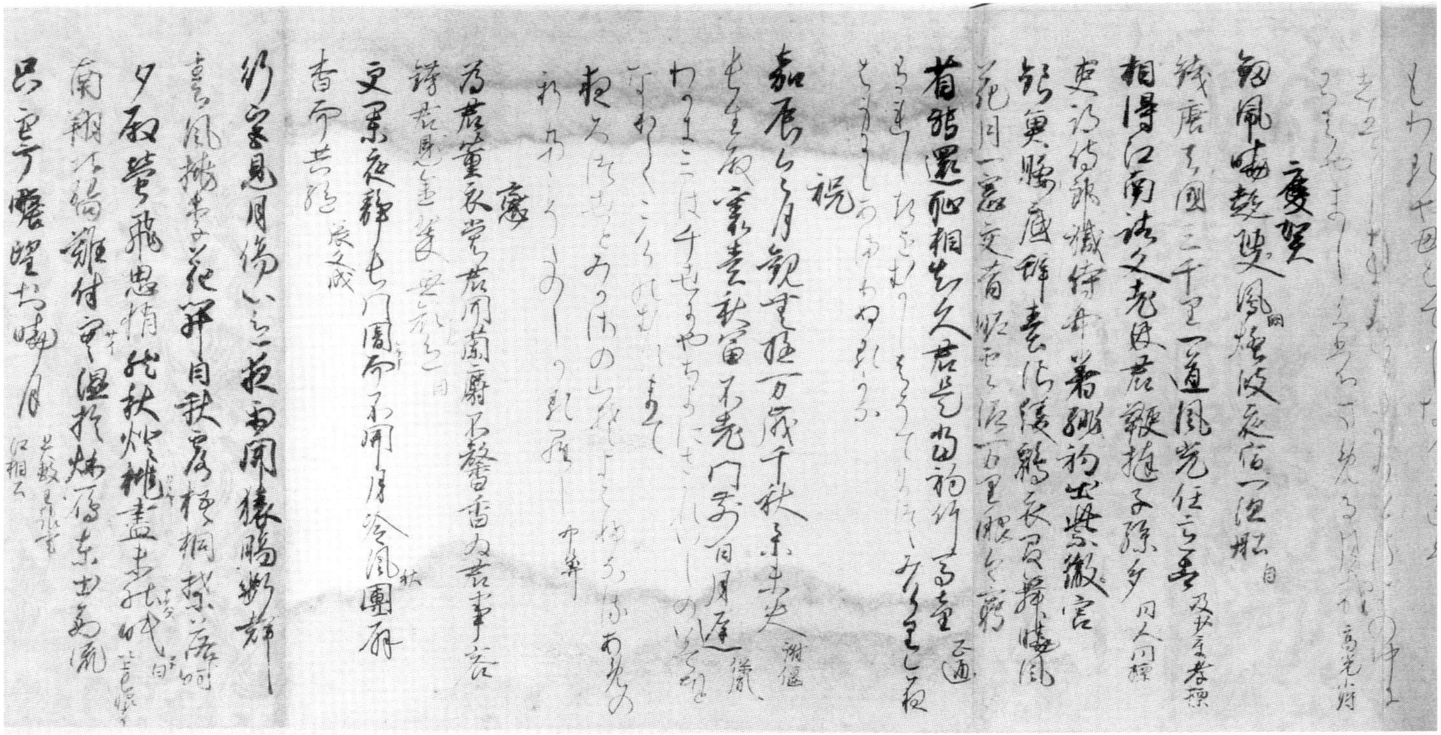

Figure 5.5   *Wakan rōei shū* (Masudabon manuscript). Heian period, twelfth century. Handscroll, ink on colored paper, 26.3 × 105.0 cm. Important Cultural Property. Tokyo National Museum.

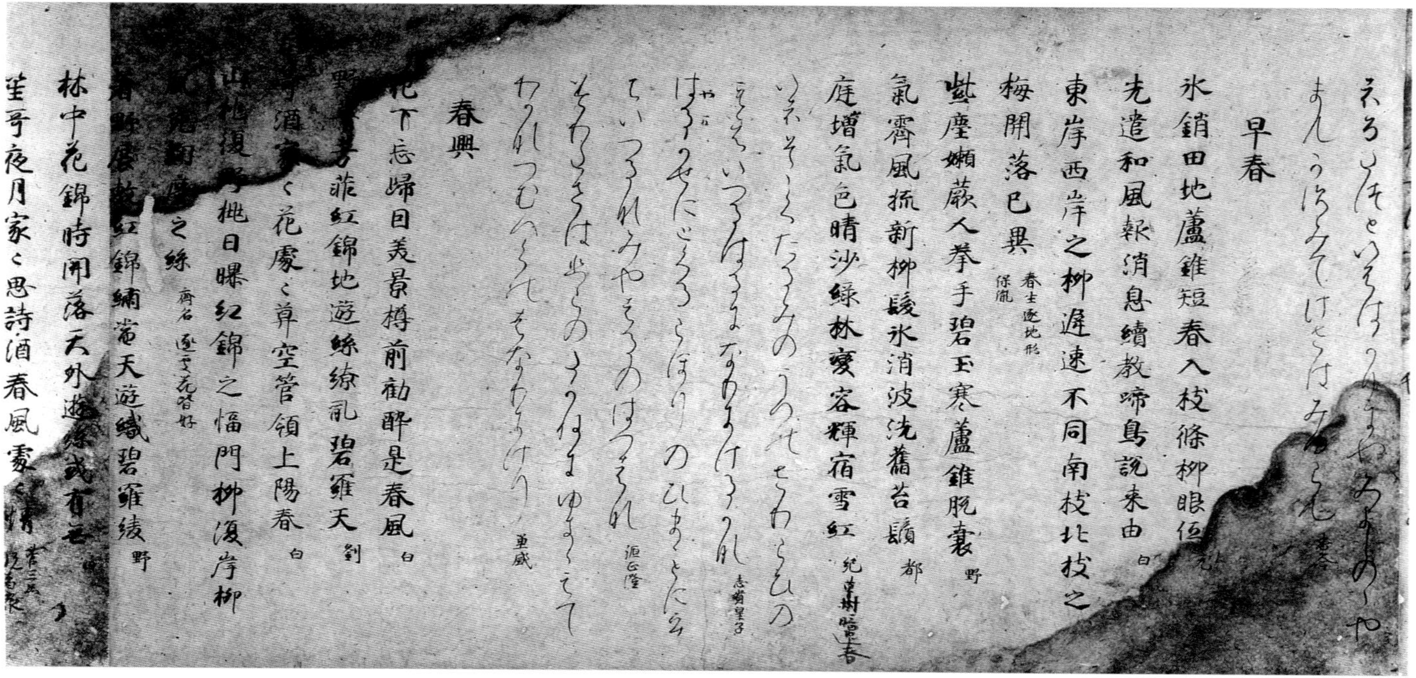

Figure 56 *Wakan rōei shū* (Kumogamibon manuscript). Attributed to Fujiwara no Yukinari (972–1027). Heian period, eleventh century. Two hand-scrolls, ink on colored paper. Imperial Household Agency, Sannomaru Shōzōkan.

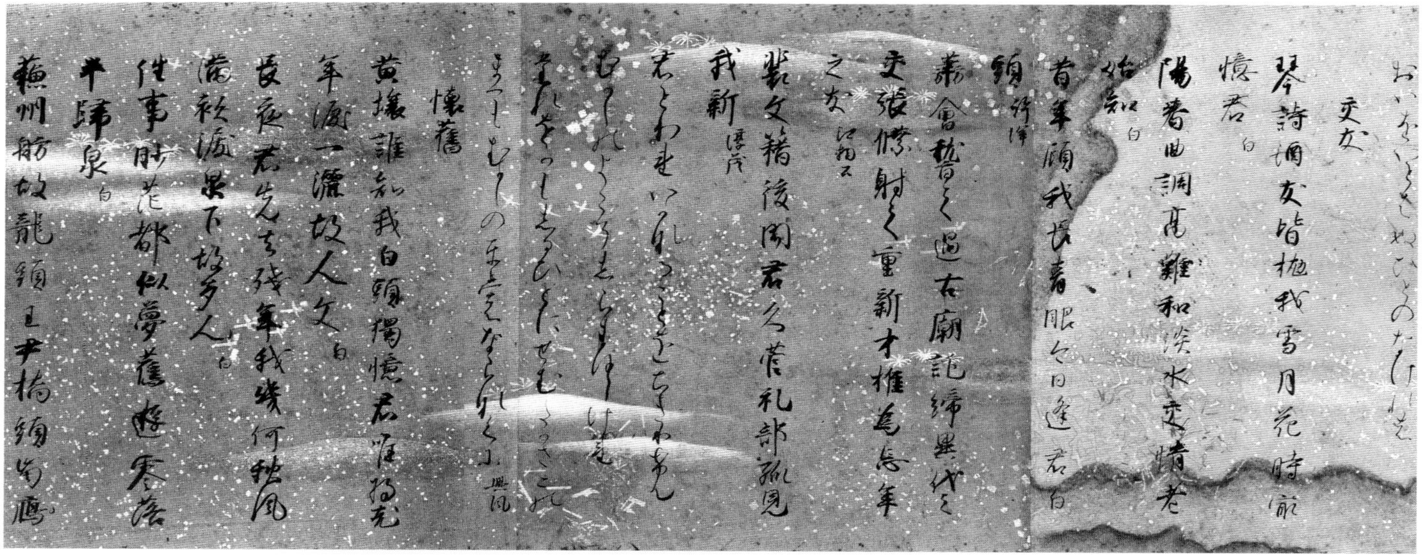

Figure 5.7 *Wakan rōei shū* (Atakagire manuscript). Heian period, eleventh century. Handscroll, ink on colored paper with gold and silver. Imperial Household Agency, Sannomaru Shōzōkan.

Figure 5.8 *Wakan rōei shō* (Ashide-e or Eiryakubon manuscript). Calligraphy by Fujiwara Koreyuki. Heian period, twelfth century. Two handscrolls, ink and color on paper, 28.0 × 1368.0 cm, 28.0 × 1423.0 cm. National Treasure. Kyoto National Museum.

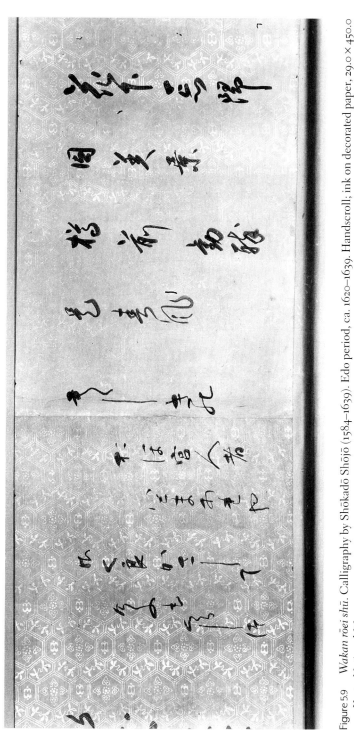

Figure 5.9 *Wakan rōei shū*. Calligraphy by Shōkadō Shōjō (1584–1639). Edo period, ca. 1620–1639. Handscroll; ink on decorated paper, 29.0 × 450.0 cm. Kyoto National Museum.

Figure 5.10　Folding screen with poems from the *Wakan rōei shū*. Calligraphy by Konoe Nobutada (1565–1614). Momoyama period (1568–1615). Ink on paper with gold and silver, (overall dimensions) 69.5 × 46.2 cm. Courtesy of the Freer Gallery of Art, Smithsonian Institution, Washington, D.C. Acc. No. 81.16.

Figure 5.11   Selected verses from the *Wakan rōei shū*. Calligraphy by Imperial Prince Dōkō (1612–1679). Early Edo period, third quarter of seventeenth century. Handscroll, ink on paper decorated with gold and gold leaf, height 23.9 cm. Courtesy of the Arthur M. Sackler Museum, Harvard University Art Museums, Loan from the Hofer Collection.

Notes

Introduction

1. An evocative translation of *No Traveler Returns* appears in Hosea Hirata's *The Poetry and Poetics of Nishiwaki Junzaburō: Modernism in Translation* (Princeton, NJ: Princeton University Press 1993), pp. 71–115.

2. See Earl Miner et al., *The Princeton Companion to Classical Japanese Literature* (Princeton, NJ: Princeton University Press, 1985), p. 32.

3. The study by Arthur Waley, *The Life and Times of Po Chü-i*, first published by Allen & Unwin in London in 1949, is only one of the sympathetic and lively treatments Po has received in the West.

4. See Jin'ichi Konishi, *The High Middle Ages*, vol. 3 of *A History of Japanese Literature* (Princeton, NJ: Princeton University Press, 1991), p. 27.

5. For detailed information on the life of Sugawara Michizane as well as translations of a number of his longer poems, see Robert Borgen, *Sugawara no Michizane and the Early Heian Court* (Cambridge, MA: Harvard University Press, 1986). Biographical details and excellent translations can also be found in Burton Watson's *Japanese Literature in Chinese* (New York: Columbia University Press, 1975), vol. 1, pp. 73–130. Stanleigh Jones translated the play *Sugawara and the Secrets of Calligraphy* (New York: Columbia University Press, 1985).

6. Donald Keene adeptly translated this charming and sophisticated tale, currently most readily available in J. Thomas Rimer, *Modern Japanese Fiction and Its Traditions* (Princeton, NJ: Princeton University Press, 1978), pp. 274–305.

7. A translation by Wilfrid Whitehouse of the *Ochikubo monogatari* is available, entitled *The Tale of Lady Ochikubo* (New York: Doubleday, 1971).

8. See Watson, *Japanese Literature in Chinese*, vol. 1, pp. 65–67.

9. Translation in ibid., pp. 57–64.

10. See Ivan Morris, *The Pillow Book of Sei Shōnagon* (New York: Columbia University Press, 1967), vol. 1, p. 167.

11. For Keene's perceptive comments on the *Collection*, see his *Seeds in the Heart: Japanese Literature from Earliest Times to the Late Sixteenth Century* (New York: Henry Holt, 1993), pp. 341–344.

12. This subject, so fascinating in itself, is too complex to discuss in detail here. But see the beautifully informed article by Yoshiaki Shimizu, "Seasons and Places in Yamato Landscape and Poetry," *Ars Orientalis* 12 (1981): 1–14.

13. For Watsuji's remarks on calligraphy, see *Zoku Nihon seishinshi kenkyū* (Tokyo: Iwanami shoten, 1962), pp. 414–419.

14. See Donald Keene, trans., *Essays in Idleness, the Tsurezuregusa of Kenkō* (New York: Columbia University Press, 1967), p. 75.

Chapter 1, Chinese Poets in the Wakan rōei shū

1. For an excellent introduction to the subject of early Japanese interest in Chinese literature, and early works in the Chinese language by Japanese writers, see Burton Watson, *Japanese Literature in Chinese*, vol. 1 (New York: Columbia University Press, 1975). Vol. 2 (1976) carries the story into the later periods.

2. George Sansom, *A History of Japan to 1334* (Stanford, CA: Stanford University Press, 1958), p. 135.

3. I consulted the edition of this text presented as an appendix to Kobase Kei-kichi's *Nihonkoku genzaisho mokuroku kaisetsu kō* (Tokyo, 1936). The pagination for the text is separate from that of the rest of the book and is followed here.

4. The literary anthologies are found on pp. 19–22 of the *Nihonkoku genzaisho mokuroku*.

5. This list is also given by Ōsone and Horiuchi in the *Wakan rōei shū*, p. 320. They note that as many as two-thirds of the passages by Chinese writers that appear in the *Wakan rōei shū* had already appeared in an earlier Japanese anthology of Chinese poetry, *Senzai kaku* (Fine verses of a thousand years), compiled by Ōe no Koretoki (888–963); see the *Wakan rōei shū*, p. 305. Donald Keene also discusses this point in *Seeds in the Heart: Japanese Literature from Earliest Times to the Late Sixteenth Century* (New York: Henry Holt, 1993), pp. 342–343, referring to the *Senzai kaku* as probably "the earliest Japanese collection of Chinese couplets." Of course, we cannot tell for certain from which source Kintō directly drew any given passage; indeed, many of these couplets appear to have been widely circulating among the courtiers and by Kintō's day may have constituted a kind of common literary heritage of the Heian court.

6. Yu Mao, *Sui-ch'u-t'ang shu-mu*, printed together with Yüeh K'o, *Chiu-ching san-chuan yen-ko-li* (Taipei: Kuang-wen shu-chü, 1968), pp. 66–83.

7. William Hung, *Tu Fu: China's Greatest Poet*, 2 vols.

(Cambridge, MA: Harvard University Press, 1952).

8. David Lattimore, entry on Tu Fu, in William H. Nienhauser Jr., Charles Hartman, Y. W. Ma, and Stephen H. West, eds., *The Indiana Companion to Traditional Chinese Literature* (Bloomington: Indiana University Press, 1986), p. 813.

9. Cheng Ch'ing-tu et al., *Tu chi shu-mu t'i-yao* (Chi-nan: Ch'i-lu shu-she, 1986), p. 1.

10. Shen Wen-cho, ed., *Su Shun-ch'in chi* (Shanghai: Chung-hua shu-chü, 1961), p. 200.

11. According to Kurokawa Yōichi, the first definite indication that a collection of Tu's poetry was available in Japan appears in *The Ōe Conversations*, a collection of anecdotes concerning literary and other matters compiled by Ōe no Masafusa (1041–1111), which postdates the *Wakan rōei shū*. He also observes that the *Senzai kaku* already contained six couplets drawn from poems by Tu Fu and that a kanshi poem by Sugawara no Kiyokimi (770–842) makes an apparent allusion to a poem by Tu. Thus, individual poems and lines by Tu must already have been trickling into Japan, although the absence of any reference to Tu in the *Nihonkoku genzaisho mokuroku* seems to indicate that the awareness of his work was still extremely limited. See Kurokawa Yōichi, *To Ho* (Tokyo: Iwanami shoten, 1959), vol. 2, p. 8. By the fourteenth or fifteenth century, such a poet as Zekkai Chūshin (1336–1405), a leading master of the Gozan bungaku (Literature of the five mountain temples) movement, consisting of Zen monks who wrote kanshi poetry, was described as carrying the works of Tu Fu with him into exile as his only possession (earlier in his life, Zekkai had actually visited China, from 1368 to 1376). In addition, Shinkei (1406–1475) characterized Tu Fu as "the greatest of the Chinese poets." See Keene, *Seeds in the Heart*, pp. 1076, 947. For more on Zekkai, see Marian Ury, *Poems of the Five Mountains*, 2nd rev. ed. (Ann Arbor: University of Michigan Center for Japanese Studies, 1992), pp. 81–87.

12. *Po Chü-i chüan*, in *Ku-tien wen-hsüeh yen-chiu tzu-liao hui-pien* (Peking?: Chung-hua shu-chü, 1965), p. 30. For a fuller discussion of Ou-yang's view of Po, see Jonathan Chaves, *Mei Yao-ch'en and the Development of Early Sung Poetry* (New York: Columbia University Press, 1976), pp. 78 ff.

13. *Po Chü-i chüan*, p. 399.

14. Watson, *Japanese Literature in Chinese*, vol. 1, pp. 79–80.

15. Robert H. Brower and Earl Miner, *Japanese Court Poetry* (Stanford, CA: Stanford University Press, 1961), p. 428.

16. Richard Bowring, *Murasaki Shikibu: Her Diary and Poetic Memoirs* (Princeton, NJ: Princeton University Press, 1982), p. 139.

17. William H. McCullough and Helen Craig McCullough, trans., *A Tale of Flowering Fortunes*, 2 vols. (Stanford, CA: Stanford University Press, 1980), vol. 2, p. 563.

18. For a complete translation of this poem, see Burton Watson, *The Columbia Book of Chinese Poetry* (New York: Columbia University Press, 1984), pp. 245–246.

19. Marian Ury, "The Ōe Conversations," *Monumenta Nipponica* 48 (Autumn 1993): 377–378.

20. See Chaves, *Mei Yao-ch'en*, pp. 52 ff, for Fang's analysis and full discussion.

21. See ibid., pp. 60 ff, for this, and the rest of the description of Wang Yü-ch'eng.

22. For a discussion of Michizane's Chinese writings and a selection of translations, see Watson, *Japanese Literature in Chinese*, vol. 1, pp. 73–122.

23. Quoted in Marian Ury, "Ōe Conversations," p. 380.

24. Arthur Waley, trans., *The Tale of Genji* (New York: Modern Library, 1960), p. 63.

25. Ibid., p. 77.

26. Ibid., p. 114.

27. *Po Chü-i chüan*, 19/12b.

28. For the date of *Genji*'s composition, see Keene, *Seeds in the Heart*, pp. 481–484; and for Murasaki's dates, see Bowring, *Murasaki Shikubu*, pp. 8–13.

29. Bowring, *Murasaki Shikibu*, pp. 67–69.

30. Ibid., pp. 90–91.

31. G. K. Chesterton, *Robert Browning* (London: Macmillan, 1903), pp. 98–99.

32. Quoted and discussed in Chaves, *Mei Yao-ch'en*, pp. 53–54.

33. *Ch'üan T'ang shih*, vol. 8, p. 6098.

34. Helmut Martin, ed., *Index to the Ho Collection of Twenty-Eight* Shih-hua, 2 vols. (Taipei: Chinese Materials and Research Aids Service Center, 1973), vol. 1, p. 21.

35. See Bodman's article on this book in Nienhauser et al., eds., *The Indiana Companion*, pp. 197–198, as well as his "Poetics and Prosody in Early Mediaeval China: A Study and Translation of Kūkai's *Bunkyō hifuron*" (Ph.D. diss., Cornell University, 1978). Keene discusses the importance of *Bunkyō hifuron*, in *Seeds in the Heart*, pp. 187–188.

36. This tentative conclusion was reached by comparing the passage as it appears in the *Wakan rōei shū* with the version recorded in the *Taishō Tripitaka*, vol. 46, p. 3.

37. For more on these poems, see the *Addendum on T'ang Dynasty* fu at the end of the Finding List.

Chapter 4, Singing the Wakan rōei shū

1. The translations in this chapter are mine unless otherwise noted.

2. Edwin A. Cranston, *The Gem-Glistening Cup*, vol. 1 of *A Waka Anthology* (Stanford, CA: Stanford University Press, 1993), p. 159.

3. See Eta Harich-Schneider, *A History of Japanese Music* (Oxford: Oxford University Press, 1973), p. 101.

4. Translation by Earl Miner, *An Introduction to Japanese Court Poetry* (Stanford, CA: Stanford University Press, 1968), p. 18.

5. Eta Harich-Schneider, *Rōei, the Medieval Court Songs of Japan* (Tokyo: Sophia University Press, 1965).

6. The rōei "Tōgan" (Eastern shore) was published on the third of the three-record set *Gagaku Taikei*, issued by Japanese His Master's Voice SJ 3003-1-3.

7. Poem translated by Jonathan Chaves, no. 345, *Wakan rōei shū*.

8. Poem translated by Jonathan Chaves, no. 242, *Wakan rōei shū*.

9. From a poem by Sugawara no Funtoki, translated by Jonathan Chaves, no. 744, *Wakan rōei shū*.

10. Harich-Schneider, *Rōei*, p. 43.

11. Text translated by Karen Brazell, *The Confessions of Lady Nijō* (London: Arrow Books, 1983, p. 139); poem by Sugawara no Michizane translated by Jonathan Chaves, no. 620, *Wakan rōei shū*.

12. Harich-Schneider, *Rōei*, pp. 173–174.

13. Translation based on that of Harich-Schneider, *Rōei*, p. 9.

14. Ibid., p. 8.

15. Ibid., p. 9.

16. Ibid., pp. 34, 35, 37.

17. Ibid., pp. 50–51.

18. Ibid., p. 101.

19. Translation by Jonathan Chaves.

20. Harich-Schneider, *Rōei*, pp. 118–119.

Chapter 5, The Art of Calligraphy and the Wakan rōei shū

1. Ivan Morris, in *The World of the Shining Prince: Court Life in Ancient Japan* (New York: Knopf, 1964), p. 209, cites the advice given by courtier Fujiwara no Morotada (918–969) to his daughter, Yoshiko: "First you must study penmanship. Next you must learn to play the seven-string zither better than anyone else. And also you must memorize all the poems in the twenty books of the *Kokin Shū*." Morris also cites numerous examples from literature of the Heian period illustrating the importance of poetry (pp. 177–183), calligraphy (pp. 183–186), and music (pp. 188–191) as skills to be cultivated by both men and women of the court.

2. Archaeological remains suggest that by the fourth century, Chinese characters were in limited use. An early example of the use of Chinese characters in Japan is the iron sword with an inscription inlaid along the blade in gold that was excavated from the Tōdaijiyama *kofun* (tumulus) in Tenri City, Nara Prefecture, a

registered Important Cultural Property, published in *Nihon no kōkogaku* (Tokyo: Tokyo National Museum, 1988), cat. no. 217 and p. 226.

Japanese writing with brush and ink has been found on both paper and wood. The use of wood slips or tags, a less costly alternative to paper for practical or administrative writing, was first discovered in 1961 in excavations at the Heijō Palace site in Nara. See Richard J. Pearson, *Ancient Japan* (Washington, DC: Arthur M. Sackler Gallery, 1992), pp. 267–268, 286–299.

3. Some of the fundamental problems of adapting the Japanese spoken language to the characters of the Chinese written language are discussed with particular reference to the *Kojiki* (Records of ancient matters, A.D. 712), by David Pollack in *The Fracture of Meaning: Japan's Synthesis of China from the Eighth Through the Eighteenth Centuries* (Princeton, NJ: Princeton University Press, 1986), pp. 15–43.

4. The major extant works of the Heian and Kamakura periods are fully illustrated in monochrome, described, and documented in detail in Komatsu Shigemi's *Kohitsu gaku taisei* (Tokyo: Kōdansha, 1990), vols. 13–15.

5. Ibid., vol. 13, p. 365.

6. Yoshiaki Shimizu and John M. Rosenfield, *Masters of Japanese Calligraphy: Eighth Through Ninteenth Centuries* (New York: Asia Society Galleries and Japan House Gallery, 1984), p. 48.

7. Shikishi with calligraphy mounted on folding screens are mentioned, for example, in the *Eiga monogatari*. The English translation is by William H. McCullough and Helen Craig McCullough, *A Tale of Flowering Fortunes: Annals of Japanese Aristocratic Life in the Heian Period* (Stanford, CA: Stanford University Press, 1980), vol. 1, p. 301.

8. Morris, *World of the Shining Prince*, pp. 187–188.

9. Egami Yasushi, "Atakagire ryōshi shita-e no tokushusei: Heian sezoku sansuiga to kyō-e no issetten (The art historical position of the painted decoration in the Ataka-gire version of the *Wakan rōei shū*) *Bijutsu kenkyū* no. 284 (November 1972): 121–140. Egami presents a well-supported argument for a close technical and stylistic relationship between the underpaintings in calligraphic manuscripts of poetry and those painted in gold and silver by specialists in the frontispieces of contemporaneous Buddhist sutras.

10. Julia Meech-Pekarik, "Disguised Scripts and Hidden Poems in an Illustrated Heian Sutra: Ashide and Uta-e in the Heike Nōgyō," *Archives of Asian Art* 31 (1977–78): 53–78, presents a detailed analysis of *ashide*, or the use of written characters in pictorial composition. Her analysis of the underpaintings in the Ashide manuscript of the *Wakan rōei shū* suggests that the illustrations are not directly related in content to the poems written over them.

11. Yoshiaki Shimizu, in "Seasons and Places in Yamato Landscape and Poetry," *Ars Orientalis* 12 (1981): 1–14, analyzes the meanings of pictorial representations of

Japanese landscapes as determined by literary and aesthetic meanings rather than as representations of the natural world.

12. John M. Rosenfield, Fumiko E. Cranston, and Edwin A. Cranston, *The Courtly Tradition in Japanese Art and Literature: Selections from the Hofer and Hyde Collections* (Cambridge, MA: Fogg Art Museum, Harvard University, 1973), pp. 144–145.

Bibliography

with Abbreviations for Finding List for Works by Chinese Writers

This bibliography provides the sources used in compiling the finding list for works by Chinese writers in the *Wakan rōei shū* and explains the abbreviations. It also lists the works consulted for chapter 1. In this book, *Wakan rōei shū* (WRS) stands for the *Shinchō Nihon koten shūsei* 新潮日本古典集成 edition, edited by Ōsone Shōsuke 大曽根章介 and Horiuchi Hideaki 堀內秀晃 and published in 1983. The *Nihon koten bungaku taikei* 日本古典文學大系 edition, number 73 in that series, also was consulted. Po Chü-i's works are cited in two special editions of his writings, abbreviated here as *Po* and *Po, prose*. Other T'ang poets are cited from the *Ch'üan T'ang shih* (CTS). Special editions of other T'ang poets also were consulted, for example, the editions of Tu Hsün-ho and Wen T'ing-yün listed here. Chinese official titles are translated in accordance with the standard renditions established by Charles O. Hucker, *A Dictionary of Official Titles in Imperial China* (Stanford, CA: Stanford University Press, 1985), with occasional simplifications or variations.

Bodman, Richard Wainwright. "Poetics and Prosody in Early Mediaeval China: A Study and Translation of Kūkai's *Bunkyō hifuron*" 空海, 文鏡秘府論 . Ph.D. diss., Cornell University, 1978.

Bowring, Richard. *Murasaki Shikibu: Her Diary and Poetic Memoirs*. Princeton, NJ: Princeton University Press, 1982.

Brower, Robert H., and Earl Miner. *Japanese Court Poetry*. Stanford, CA: Stanford University Press, 1961.

Chaves, Jonathan. *Mei Yao-ch'en and the Development of Early Sung Poetry*. New York: Columbia University Press, 1976.

Cheng Ch'ing-tu 鄭慶篤 et al., *Tu chi shu-mu t'i-yao* 杜集書目提要 . Chi-nan: Ch'i-lu shu-she, 1986.

Chesterton, G. K. *Robert Browning*. London: Macmillan, 1903.

Ch'üan T'ang shih (CTS) 全唐詩. 12 vols. Peking: Chung-hua shu-chü, 1960. The appendix in vol. 12 was compiled by a Japanese scholar, Ichikawa Kansai 市河寬齋 (1749–1820), apparently drawing on the WRS and other similar works, although there are some examples in the WRS that he seems to have missed.

Ch'üan T'ang wen (CTW). See Ma Hsü-ch'uan.

Fujiwara no Sukeyo. See Kobase Keikichi.

Han shu 漢書. Peking: Chung-hua shu-chü, 1962.

Hou Han shu 後漢書. Peking: Chung-hua shu-chü, 1965.

Hung, William. *Tu Fu: China's Greatest Poet*. 2 vols. Cambridge, MA: Harvard University Press, 1952.

Keene, Donald. *Seeds in the Heart: Japanese Literature from Earlist Times to the late Sixteenth Century*. New York: Henry Holt, 1993.

Kobase Keikichi 小長谷惠吉. *Nihonkoku genzaisho mokuroku kaisetsu kō* 日本國現在書目錄解説稿. Tokyo, 1936. Presents complete text of original work by Fujiwara no Sukeyo 藤原佐世 (847–897).

Kurokawa Yōichi 黑川洋一. *To Ho* (Tu Fu) 杜甫. Chūgoku shijin senshū 中國詩人選集. 2 vols. Tokyo: Iwanami Shoten, 1959.

Levy, Howard S. *The Dwelling of Playful Goddesses: China's First Novelette*. 2 vols. Tokyo: Howard S. Levy, 1965. The second volume is the complete, collated text of the original work.

Ma Hsü-ch'uan 馬緒傳. *Ch'üan T'ang wen p'ien-ming mu-lu chi tso-che so-yin* 全唐文篇名目錄及作者索引. Peking: Chung-hua shu-chü, 1985.

Martin, Helmut, ed. *Index to the Ho Collection of Twenty-Eight Shih-hua*. 2 vols. Taipei: Chinese Materials and Research Aids Service Center, 1973.

McCullough, William H., and Helen Craig McCullough, trans. *A Tale of Flowering Fortunes*. 2 vols. Stanford, CA: Stanford University Press, 1980. This is a translation of *Eiga monogatari*.

Mo-ho chih-kuan 摩訶止觀. Vol. 46 of *Taishō shinshū daizōkyō* (TSD) 大正新修大藏經. Tokyo, 1924–34.

Murasaki Shikibu (Lady Murasaki). See Bowring; Waley.

Nienhauser, William H. Jr., Charles Hartman, Y. W. Ma, and Stephen H. West, eds. *The Indiana Companion to Traditional Chinese Literature*. Bloomington: Indiana University Press, 1986.

Po Hsiang-shan shih-chi (Po) 白香山詩集. Ssu-pu pei-yao 四部備要 edition.

Po Chü-i chüan 白居易卷. Volume in series Ku-tien wen-hsüeh yen-chiu tzu-liao hui-pien 古典文學研究資料彙編. Peking (?): Chung-hua shu-chü, 1965. An anthology of traditional criticism on Po Chü-i.

Po-shih Ch'ang-ch'ing chi (Po, prose) 白氏長慶集. Ssu-pu ts'ung-k'an 四部叢刊 edition (so-yin-pen 縮印本).

Sansom, George. *A History of Japan to 1334*. Stanford, CA: Stanford University Press, 1958.

Shen Wen-cho 沈文倬 , ed. *Su Shun-ch'in chi* 蘇舜欽集 . Shanghai: Chung-hua shu-chü, 1961.

Shih chi 史記 . Peking: Chung-hua shu-chü, 1959.

T'an Cheng-pi 譚正璧 . *Chung-kuo wen-hsüeh-chia ta tz'u-tien* 中國文學家大辭典 . 2 vols. Taipei: Shih-chieh shu-chü, 1971.

TSD. See *Mo-ho chih-kuan.*

Tu Hsün-ho wen-chi 杜荀鶴文集. Shanghai: Ku-chi ch'u-pan-she, 1980. Facsimile of Sung dynasty edition.

Ury, Marian. "The Ōe Conversations." *Monumenta Nipponica* 48 (Autumn 1993): 359–380.

———. *Poems of the Five Mountains.* 2nd, rev. ed. Ann Arbor: University of Michigan Center for Japanese Studies, 1992.

Waley, Arthur, trans. *The Tale of Genji.* New York: Modern Library, 1960.

Watson, Burton. *The Columbia Book of Chinese Poetry.* New York: Columbia University Press, 1984.

———. *Japanese Literature in Chinese.* 2 vols. New York: Columbia University Press, 1975 and 1976.

Wen hsüan 文選 . 2 vols. Hong Kong: Shang-wu yin-shu-kuan, 1960.

Wen T'ing-yün 温庭筠 . *Wen Fei-ch'ing chi chien-chu* 温飛卿集箋注 , Ssu-pu pei-yao 四部備要 edition.

Yu hsien k'u 游仙窟 . Shanghai: Chung-kuo ku-tien wen-hsüeh ch'u-pan-she, 1955. The passage occurs on p. 2. See also Levy.

Yu Mao 尤袤 . *Sui-ch'u-t'ang shu-mu* 遂初堂書目 . Printed together with Yüeh K'o 岳珂 , *Chiu-ching san-chuan yen-ko-li* 九經三傳沿革例 . Taipei: Kuang-wen shu-chü, 1968.

Finding List for Works by Chinese Writers

This list provides the Chinese sources for writings by Chinese writers used in the *Wakan rōei shū* (WRS). See the Bibliography with Abbreviations for Finding List for Works by Chinese Writers for explanations of the abbreviations used here.

The following points should be kept in mind when consulting this list:

1. Because of the overwhelming predominance of works by Po Chü-i, we used special editions of his writings. We cite other T'ang poets from the *Ch'üan T'ang shih* (CTS) but cite separately earlier writings such as the dynastic histories.

2. Some poems in the *Wakan rōei shū* are erroneously attributed, a problem that extends to some of the attributions to Po Chü-i, even though he was the best-known Chinese poet in Japan. In addition, in China itself, it is not uncommon to find a single poem attributed to more than one poet, even in the pages of the *Ch'üan T'ang shih*. (An example is poem 790 in the *Wakan rōei shū*, attributed in the *Ch'üan T'ang shih* to both Sung Chih-wen—as in the *Wakan rōei shū*—and Liu Hsi-i.) Such problems parallel the better-known issue of problematic attributions in painting and calligraphy. In some cases, it is even possible that poems actually written by Japanese courtiers have been misattributed to Chinese writers.

3. Considerable quantities of Chinese literature have simply been lost, as is the case, again, with paintings and calligraphies. Some of the passages used in the *Wakan rōei shū* are no longer to be found in the *Ch'üan T'ang shih* or, apparently, anywhere else. Some of the poets whose

names appear may no longer be represented by surviving works even in China. Thus, it is likely that Fujiwara no Kintō may have had access to Chinese material that is no longer available to us. This seems to be particularly true of the T'ang dynasty *fu* to which he refers, not one of which is recorded in the *Ch'üan T'ang wen* (*CTW*). For this reason, we include a separate addendum for this material after the finding list proper.

4. The finding list also provides the complete titles of the poems excerpted in *Wakan rōei shū*, as these often help demonstrate the implications of some of the imagery or situations in the poetic couplets.

5. This list does not give alternative readings except when they are of particular interest or when alternative readings from the original source have been adopted. Even in China, the transmission of old texts has frequently led to alternative readings, which is why the collation of different versions of a text has traditionally been an important branch of Chinese scholarship.

6. A number of T'ang poetic couplets are described as not being found in the "original *Ch'üan T'ang shih*"; they may, however, have been recorded in a special appendix compiled by a Japanese scholar, which is found in volume 12 of the standard modern edition. This scholar specifically searched for lost Chinese couplets preserved in Japanese anthologies (see the Bibliography under *Ch'üan T'ang shih*).

Wakan rōei shū no.	*Source (if known)* (* = see addendum on T'ang *fu* at end)	*Title and Comments*
4 and 5	Po, hou, 10/10a	"The Pond to the West of the Prefectural Office." nos. 4 and 5 together are a complete quatrain.
9	CTS, vol. 6, p. 4601	"Sent to Lo-t'ien" (Po Chü-i)
10	Po, 17/3b	"Birth of Spring," from the series "Spring in Hsün-yang"
18	Po, 13/5a	"In Response to a Poem Sent to Me by Ko-shu Ta"

19	*CTS*, vol. 6, p. 4060	"Writing My Feelings on a Spring Day and Sending Them to the Two Mentors, Po the Twenty-Second and Yang the Eighth, in Loyang"
20	*Po, hou,* 9/6a	"Seeing off Secretary Ling-hu, Regent to the Eastern Capital, as He Leaves to Take up His Duties"
27	*Po,* 13/7b	"In Springtime, Dwelling Together with Lu the Fourth and Chou Liang at Hua-yang Shrine"
38	*CTS*, vol. 2, pp. 1257–58	"Ballad of Peach Blossom Spring"
45	*CTS*, vol. 6, p. 4577	"Visiting the Hsiang-yang Pavilion, Presented to the Commandery Governor, Minister of Works Yen; the Pavilion Is Located at the Northern Corner of the Residence of the Military Commissioner"
50	*Po, hou,* 1/18b	"Falling Flowers"
51	*Po, hou,* 10/4b	"In Response to Adviser Huang-fu"
52	*Po,* 13/7a	"On the Thirtieth Day of the Third Month, Inscribed on the Wall at Compassion Temple"
59	*CTS*, vol. 12 (appendix), p. 10210	"Seeing off Vice Censor in Chief Li of Huai-nan to Take up Military Duties." This poet not represented in the original *CTS*.
63	*	

64	*	
65	*CTS*, vol. 6, p. 4577	"Seeking out Editing Clerk Li in Early Spring." No. 96 derives from this same poem.
66	*Po, hou*, 15/4b–5a	"In Reponse to His Request, Echoing Ssu-an's Poem Inscribed on the Southern Villa, Which He Has Sent to Me; Also Presented to Meng-te"
67	*Po*, 18/8a	"River in Spring"
75	*Po, hou*, 12/8b	"In Early Spring, Remembering Suchou—Sent to Meng-te." In the second line, there is an alternative reading, "mountains" instead of "grasses."
80	*	
81	*CTS*, vol. 4, pp. 2674–75	"In the Palace, Sent to Secretary P'ei"; actually by Ch'ien Ch'i (fl. ca. 766).
87	*Po*, 18/7b	"Spring Has Arrived"
88	*CTS*, vol. 12 (appendix), p. 10185	"In Early Spring, Picnicking Under Newly Cleared Skies." This poem not included in the original *CTS*.
96	*CTS*, vol. 6, p. 4577	"Seeking out Editing Clerk Li in Early Spring." No. 65 derives from this same poem.
102	*Po, hou*, 10/14b	"Early Spring at the Pavilion of the Heavenly Palace"

103	*Po, hou,* 14/13b–14a	"Happy That the Young Willows West of the Little Tower Are Putting Forth Branches." Uses same rhyme category as the previous couplet.
104 and 105	*Po,* 17/16b–17a	"Inscribed on a Rock in the Gorges." Nos. 104 and 105 together are a complete quatrain.
113	*	
114	*Po, hou,* 12/9a	"Early Spring—Summoning Adviser Chang"
115	*Po, hou,* 14/2b	"Again Writing a Quatrain on the Theme 'In Search of Spring—Inscribed on the Gardens of the Various Households' "
126	*Po, hou,* 11/4a	"Visiting the Residence of Li-hsin of the Yüan Family"
127	*Po, hou,* 14/3b	"As Spring Arrives, I Often Go out to the Country Together with Adviser Li the Second, and So I Have Sent Him This Long-Verse Poem." "Long-verse" means that each line has seven, as opposed to five, characters.
133	*Po,* 16/14b	"In Response to a Poem Sent to Me by Supernumerary Yüan on the Thirteenth Day of the Third Month, in Which He Remembers Me While Visiting Compassion Temple"
137	*Po,* 16/7a	"Inscribed on the Riverside Residence of Yüan the Eighth"

144	*Po, hou,* 15/6a	"Early Summer—Morning Moods; Sent to Meng-te"
147	*Po,* 17/8a	"The Roses Are Just Now Opening, and the Spring Wine Is Just Ready, So I Have Summoned Liu the Nineteenth, Master Chang, and Ts'ui the Twenty-Fourth to Drink It Together with Me"
150	*Po, hou,* 5/4a,b	"Evening View from a River Pavilion—Summoning Guests"
151	*Po,* 19/11b	"Twelve Verses in Seven-Character Meter Sent to Seventh Elder Brother Wu, Gentleman of the Interior of the Ministry of War—: At the time it was early summer; upon returning from court, I closed up my study and, while residing there alone, spontaneously wrote this poem."
152	?	Not to be found in Po's collected works. In some editions, it is entitled "Late at Night, Returning to My Residence" and attributed to "Ki, the Remitter of Words."
159	*Po, hou,* 14/5a	"Beside the Pool, Pursuing Coolness." This is the first poem of a set of two.
160	*Po, hou,* 2/12a	"Night Scene Beside the Pool"
161	*Po,* 15/9a,b	"Suffering from the Heat—Inscribed on the Meditation Chamber of Master Heng-chi." Alternative reading for first character in *Po.*

168	Po, *hou*, 16/8b	"Harmonizing with [a Poem by] Secretary Yang, 'After Leaving My Position as Minister, on a Summer Day Taking an Excursion to the Water Pavilion at Yung-an and Inviting the Attendant Gentleman, Yang, of the Same Bureau to Accompany Me' "
171	Po, *hou*, 5/2b	"Returning Late from West Lake, Gazing Back Toward Solitary Mountain Temple— Presented to My Various Guests"
175	Po, 13/7b	"Autumn in the Countryside West of the Prefectural Seat— Sent in Presentation to Ma Tsao"
176	Po, 16/7a	"Lotus Beneath the Stairs"
177	CTS, vol. 8, p. 6089	"The Lotus Pond West of the Pavilion at Yün-yang Station in Late Autumn"
182	CTS, vol. 8, p. 6098	"Rising at Dawn, Taking a Boat from the Leng-chia Temple; Feelings Along the Way"
186	CTS, vol. 6, p. 4586	"Sitting at Night"
187	CTS, vol. 12 (appendix), p. 10186	"Presented to Supervising Secretary Yang in Ch'ang-chou." This is not in the original CTS.
192	Po, 4/1a	"Li Palace Is Tall"

193	*CTS*, vol. 12 (appendix), p. 10179	"Setting out from Blue Mud Inn and Traveling to the Mountain Pass at the Ferry West of Ch'ang-yü County." This is not in the original *CTS*.
194	*CTS*, vol. 8, p. 6085	"The Eastern Tower of Hsien-yang City Wall"
199	*Po, hou*, 13/9a	"The White-Feather Fan"
204	*Po*, 19/5b	"On the Day of the Establishment of Autumn, Climbing to Pleasure-Trip Gardens"
208	*Po, hou*, 9/15b	"Answering Su the Sixth"
209	*Po, hou*, 8/3a	"The Rear Chamber of the Palace Library"
212	?	"Seventh Night." This is not in Po's collected works.
221	*Po*, 14/2a	"Seeing off Wang the Eighteenth on His Return to the Mountains and Sent to Be Inscribed on the Temple of the Immortal Journey"
222	*Po*, 15/13b	"Attendant Censor Lu and Case Reviewer Ts'ui Held a Banquet for Me at Yellow Crane Tower; After the Banquet, We Viewed the Scene Together"
223	*Po*, 14/10b–11a	"Standing at Evening"
230	*Po*, 13/15a	"Inscribed on the Eastern Pavilion of Li the Eleventh"
233	*Po*, 3/3b–4a	"The Woman of Shang-yang Palace"

234	*Po,* 12/6b–9a	"The Song of Everlasting Sorrow." Nos. 779, 780, and 781 also derive from this poem.
235	*Po,* 15/10b–11a	"Swallow Tower—Three Poems." The couplet comes from the first of the three.
240 and 241	*	
242	*Po,* 14/3a	"On the Night of the Fifteenth of the Eighth Month, in the Forbidden City, on Night-Duty Alone, I Face the Moon and Think of Yüan the Ninth"
243	*Po, hou,* 15/5a,b	"On the Night of the Fifteenth or the Eighth Month, Together with the Other Guests Enjoying the Moon"
252	*Po,* 16/14b	"The Mid-Autumn Moon"
253	*CTS,* vol. 12 (appendix), pp. 10207–208	The only surviving couplet by this unknown figure; it is not in the original *CTS.*
254	*Po,* 18/6a	"Seeing off Retired Scholar Hsiao on His Trip to Ch'ien-an,"
261	*CTS,* vol. 4, p. 2811	"Written in the Eastern Suburbs on an Autumn Day." Erroneously attributed to Li Tuan in the *WRS;* actually by Huang-fu Jan (714–767).
266	*Po, hou,* 15/9b	"On the Eighth Day of the Ninth Month, in Response to a Poem Sent by Huang-fu the Ninth"
267	*CTS,* vol. 6, p. 4560	"Chrysanthemums"

286	*Po, hou*, 15/10a	"Late Autumn—Alone at Night"
287	*Po*, 15/14b–15b	"Freely Expressed Words, Five Poems—With Preface." The couplet comes from the fifth of the poems.
301	*Po*, 13/5b	"In the Autumn Rain—Sent to Yüan the Ninth"
302	*Po, hou*, 7/6b	"Boating on T'ai-hu Lake, Writing Down Events—Sent to Wei-chih." Wei-chih is Po's great friend Yüan Chen.
307	*	
308	*Po, hou*, 16/9b–10a	"Entering the Imperial City Early in the Morning—Sent to the Vice Director of the Regency, Wang"
309	*Po*, 13/12b	"Living at Leisure in Late Autumn"
317	*CTS*, vol. 1, p. 557	"Poem Singing of the Geese in the South." Erroneously attributed to the *Wen hsüan* (Literary anthology); actually by Wei Ch'eng-ch'ing (d. 706?).
318	*CTS*, vol. 6, 4127	"Climbing Ch'ing-hui Tower"
319	*CTS*, vol. 10, p. 7973	"On the Road to Chui-yang." The *CTS* reads *t'ieh* (pasted [against]) for *tien* (dotting) in the second line of the couplet, as does Tu's collected works.
327	*Po*, 14/6b	"Autumn Insects"; the complete text of the poem.

328	*Po, hou,* 14/8a,b	"Responding to a Poem Sent to Me by Meng-te, 'Sitting Alone in the Autumn Courtyard.'" The reading *chi* (anxious) has been adopted from *Po* in preference to the reading *k'u* (embittered) found in the WRS. The "Meng-te" referred to here and elsewhere is Po's good friend Liu Yü-hsi, himself a major T'ang poet also represented in the WRS.
334	*CTS,* vol. 9, pp. 6749–50	"Staying Overnight at Cloud-Edge Temple." The *CTS* reads *shu,* "familiar," for *hua,* "worn smooth," as does Wen's collected works, so that the first line of the couplet translates "Green moss along the path, well known of monks returning to the temple."
338	*Po,* 19/12b–13a	"Poem Chanted by the River at Evening"
341	*Po,* 16/3a	"Dawn View from the tower of Yü"
342	*Po,* 19/12b	"Hearing the Fulling Blocks at Night"
343	*CTS,* vol. 11, pp. 8765–66	"This Concubine's Lot Is Poor"; the poet's only surviving poem.
352	*Po, hou,* 5/6a	"Early Winter"
356	*Po, hou,* 17/3a	"Echoing the Poems of Palace Aide Li and Supervising Secretary Li on Spending a Snowy Night Drinking Together While Residing in the Mountains"

359	Po, 16/3a,b	"A Farewell Banquet in the River Tower"
362	Po, hou, 11/11a	"Playfully Inviting My Guests"
367	Po, 15/14a	"At Year's End, Scene While Traveling"
368	CTS, vol. 9, p. 6755	"At Prājña Temple, Parting from Master Ch'eng." The character shih (rock) in the name of the temple yields "Temple of the Great Rock," but it may well be an error for jo, an orthographically similar character. If the preceding character is written without its bottom component, the combination would be the common Chinese transliteration for the Sanskrit prājña, "wisdom."
374	*	
375	Po, hou, 6/2b–3a	"Things Experienced in the Snow—In Response to Wei-chih"
376	Po, hou, 14/9b	"In Response to a Poem Sent to Me During a Snowfall by Master Ling and Expressing Surprise That He and Meng-te Did Not Come to Visit Me Together"
387	Po, hou, 15/4b	"In Early Spring, Remembering a Trip to Ssu-an's Southern Villa and So Sending Him a Poem in Long Lines"
393	Po, hou, 16/4b	"Making Fun of an Old Monk for Venerating a Sutra"

397	*CTS*, vol. 12 (appendix), p. 10197	"Living in the Mountains." The poet is unknown and is not represented in the original *CTS*.
403	*	
405	*CTS*, vol. 6, p. 4560	"Living in Solitude"
410	*CTS*, vol. 12 (appendix), pp. 10206–207	"Inspiration Under Clear Skies" (or "Inscribed on the Retirement Villa of Graduate Tai Yüan [or Wan]"). The poet is unknown and is not represented in the original *CTS*.
416	*	
417	*	
418	*	
419	*Po*, 14/3a	"At Night in the Forbidden City—Writing a Letter to Yüan the Ninth"
421		"Living at Leisure in Hsin-ch'ang, Inviting Director Yang and His Brothers"
422	*CTS*, vol. 8, p. 6110	"Sent to My Elder, Yin Yao-fan"
430	*Po, hou*, 9/4a	"Echoing a Poem by Minister Ling-hu of Pien-chou, 'Recently within the official precincts I have planted one hundred bamboos and opened a wall to communicate with a newly built pavilion from which day and night I face the bamboo and enjoy them—informally inscribed in seven-character lines and five rhymes.'"

431	*CTS*, vol. 12 (appendix), p. 10185	"Bamboo Branches." This is not in the original *CTS*.
435	*Po, hou*, 6/4a	"In Early Spring, Remembering Wei-chih"
436	*CTS*, vol. 6, pp. 4590–91	"Spring Words"
443	*	
444	*	
445	*Po*, 16/7a	"Inscribed on the River Residence of Yüan the Eighth"
446	*Po, hou*, 16/8b–9a	"At Home Leaving Home"
447	*CTS*, vol. 6, p. 4062	"Echoing Lo-t'ien's Work, 'Seeing off a Crane, Presented to Minister P'ei in Farewell to His Crane' "
454	*	
455	*Po*, 18/6a	"Seeing off Retired Scholar Hsiao on His Journey to Ch'ien-nan"
456	*Po*, 15/13a	"In the Boat at Night — Sent to My Wife"
462	*	
463	*Po*, 3/7b	"The Five-String Plays"
464	*Po, hou*, 7/10a	"Again Replying to Liu Ho-chou"
465	*CTS*, vol. 8, p. 5620 (as Shih Chien-wu), and vol. 12 (appendix), p. 10184 (as Chang Hsiao-piao)	"Poem on Flute Music Heard at Night." Attributed to Chang Hsiao-piao in the WRS and to Shih Chien-wu in the original *CTS*.

470	*Wen hsüan*, vol. 1, p. 350	"Prosepoem on Letters"
471	*Po, hou*, 1/14a,b	"Inscribed After the Collected Works of Vice Governor Yüan—Two Poems." This is the complete text of the second poem.
472	*CTS*, vol. 6, p. 4651	"Sent to Hsüeh T'ao"
473	*CTS*, vol. 8, pp. 5755–56	"Perusing the Literary Collection of Editing Clerk Yang"
479	*	
480	*Po, prose*, ch. 61, pp. 336–37	"Eulogy on Wine, with Preface"; parallel prose passage from the preface.
481	*Po*, 17/5a	"While Drunk, Facing the Red Leaves"; the complete text of the poem.
482	*Po*, 18/6a	"Seeing off Retired Scholar Hsiao on His Way to Ch'ien-nan"
483	*Po, hou*, 9/3b	"Exchanging My Mirror for a Wine Cup"
484	*Po, hou*, 11/7a	"Lute and Wine"
491	*CTS*, vol. 12 (appendix), p. 10197	"Thousands-Feet-High Mountain." The poet, who also appears as Ho-lan Hsien, is unknown and not represented in the original *CTS*.
492	*Po*, 13/8b	"Visiting Cloud-Residence Temple—Sent to Landowner Mu the Thirty-Sixth"

499	*Shih chi*, vol. 8, p. 2545	"Biography of Li Ssu"; with some alternative readings.
500	*	
501	*Po*, 16/15b	"Climbing the Western Tower, Remembering Hsing-chien"
502	*CTS*, vol. 10, p. 7951	"In Autumn, Staying Overnight at Lin-chiang Stream." The *CTS* and Tu's collected works both read "return to the cold shore" for the second part of line 1, so that the entire line would read "Reflected fires from fishing boats return to the cold shore," which yields a far less interesting image than the conceit of "burning the ripples" found in the *WRS*.
503	*CTS*, vol. 12 (appendix), p. 10181	"Riding in a Boat." This is not in the original *CTS*.
510	*	
511	*Po*, 3/6a	"Spring at K'un-ming." The reading of *tuan* (short; translated "delicate" here) was adopted from *Po* in place of *ch'ang* (long, to grow long) in the *WRS* as the last character of the first line.
512	*Po*, 16/8a	"Seeing off a Guest on His Trip to Hunan"
513	*Po, pu-i, shang*/4a	"Seeing off Director Liu on His Journey to Take up Official Duties in Suchou"
514	*CTS*, vol. 10, p. 7968	"Playfully Sent to a Fisherman"

521	?	"Hearing That the Two Secretaries, Fei and Li, Were on Duty at the Silk-Thread Pavilion (the Secretariat)." This is not included in standard editions of Po's works. It is either a lost poem by him or an erroneous attribution.
522	Po, 14/4b–5a	"On the Fifteenth Day of the Eighth Month, at Night, Hearing That Elder Ts'ui, Supernumerary, Was on Solitary Night Duty at the Han-lin Academy, Drinking Wine and Enjoying the Moon, I Therefore Yearned for the Serene Scenery in the Forbidden City and Dashed off This Poem"
523	?	"On the Day I Passed the Examination, It Was Announced That They Had Defeated Tung-p'ing." This is not in the original CTS or in the appendix. It may be a false attribution, although it is consistent with a number of poems by Chang on the subject of passing the examinations.
530	*	
531	Po, hou, 12/7a	"Together with Various Guests, Inscribed on the Old Mansion of a Princess of the Yü Family"
540	CTS, vol. 6, p. 4560.	"Perching in Solitude"
541	Po, 17/3b	"Seeking Taoist Kuo and Not Finding Him at Home"

542	?	"Going Forth to Become a Hermit." This is also attributed to Po Chü-i but is not in the complete works of either poet or in the CTS. The actual author is not certain.
554	Po, 16/12a	"Beneath Incense Burner Peak I Have Newly Made My Mountain Residence; the Thatched Hut Has Just Been Completed—Informally Inscribed on the Eastern Wall." This couplet comes from the third of the four additional poems following the original one and entitled "Again Inscribed" (no. 618 from same series).
555	Po, 17/11a,b	"In My Mount Lu Thatched Hut on a Rainy Night, Living Alone; Sent to the Supernumeraries Niu the Second, Li the Seventh, and Yü the Thirty-Second"
556	CTS, vol. 10, p. 7974	"Climbing the Water Pavilion of the Ch'an Master of Stone Cliff"
565	Po, hou, 5/9a	"Spring—Written on the Lake"
572 and 573	Po, 15/3b–4a	"Wishing to Move in Next Door to Yüan the Eighth, I First Send Him This Poem"
578	CTS, vol. 9, p. 6374	"The Temple of the Fourth Patriarch." This is an erroneous attribution; it is actually by Chao Ku (ca. 810–ca. 856). The CTS text of this couplet reads "before this single lamp" for "inside this single boat."

579	*Po, hou,* 7/13b	"Staying Overnight at the Upper Cloister of Spirit-Cliff Temple"
587	*Mo-ho chih-kuan,* TSD, vol. 46, p. 3	*Treatise on the Great Cessation and Contemplation;* some alternative readings.
588	*Po, prose,* ch. 70, pp. 390–91	"An Account of the Collected Works of Master Po of Fragrant Mountain Temple While in Lo-yang"
589	*Po, hou,* 11/4b–5a	"Great Master Ju[-man] of Begging Bowl Pagoda Cloister." This is the first of five poems entitled "Sent to Monks."
604	*	
605	CTS, vol. 12 (appendix), p. 10183	"Sent to Recluse Tun-hsien of the Eastern Suburbs." This is not in the original CTS.
613	*Po, prose,* ch. 61, pp. 339–40	"Preface to the Lo[-yang] Poems"
614 and 615	*	
616	*Po, hou,* 9/16a	"I Don't Go Out the Gate"
617	*Po, hou,* 14/3a	"Plan for Growing Old"
618	*Po,* 16/12a,b	From the fourth of the poems described under no. 554, "Again Inscribed."
624	*Po, hou,* 5/5a	"In an Evening View from the River Tower, Nature's Scenes Were Fresh and Wondrous, So I Sang of My Enjoyment and Formed a Poem, Which I Send to Supernumerary Chang of the Bureau of Waterways"

631	*Po, hou*, 9/16a	"At Capital-View Station, Seeing off Ts'ui the Eighteenth"
641	*CTS*, vol. 8, p. 6106	"At Kua-chou, Left in Parting from Li Hsü"
650	*CTS*, vol. 8, p. 6103	"Sent to Mountain Man Wang"
655	*Po*, 4/1a,b	"The Mirror of a Hundred Refinings"
656	*Po, hou*, 12/9a	"Leisurely Chanting Beside the Pond." This is from the first of the two poems.
657	?	"Verse for Spring at Shang-yang Palace." This is not in the *CTS*.
666	*Po*, 4/3a,b	"The Peonies So Fragrant"
674	*Hou Han shu*, vol. 4, pp. 933–34	The *lun* (discussion) from the "Biography of Wang Liang."
675	*Han shu*, vol. 8, p. 2346	"Biography of Tsou Yang"
676	*Po, hou*, 9/2a,b	"Staying Overnight at the Hsing-hua Pond-Pavilion of Prime Minister P'ei"
681	*CTS*, vol. 12 (appendix), p. 10195	"Sent to Commissioner Li." The poet is unknown and unrecorded in the original *CTS*.
682	*CTS*, vol. 12 (appendix), p. 10189	"Echoing a Poem by the Old Man of Fu-feng." This is not in the original *CTS*.
683	*CTS*, vol. 8, pp. 6110–11	"Sent to Officer Yü of Ho-tung—Two Poems." This is from the first of the two poems. No. 735 also derives from these poems.

689	Po, hou, 12/8b	"In Early Spring, Remembering Suchou—Sent to Meng-te"
690	?	"To Secretary Li." The poet, a Buddhist monk also recorded as Chih-hsüan or Chen-hsüan, is not represented in the CTS.
697	Po, 14/12a,b	"Wang Chao-chün—Two Poems." This is from the first of the two poems.
705	Yu hsien k'u, vol. 2, p. 3	A Journey to the Dwellings of the Immortals
706	?	"Palace Poem." This is not in Yüan's collected works or in the CTS. The attribution is uncertain.
707	Po, 4/7a,b	"From the Well Bottom, We Draw the Silver Vase"
708	?	"Sent to a Beautiful Woman After Parting." This is not in Po's collected works or in the CTS. The attribution is questionable.
715	?	"It Is Hard for the Beauty to Emerge." The attribution is probably erroneous. It is also attributed to Sugawara no Funtoki, Shimada no Tadaomi, and anonymous.
718	CTS, vol. 12 (appendix), p. 10197	"To a Beautiful Woman I Yearn For." This is not in the original CTS.
722	Po, 15/14a,b	"Sitting Quietly—A Leisurely Poem"
723	Po, hou, 10/15b	"Rising Early"

724	*Po*, 18/1b–2a	"Presented to Old Man K'ang"
733	*Po, hou*, 8/8a,b	"Sent to Chief Musician Yin"
734	*Po, hou*, 6/1b–2a	"Supernumerary Chang the Eighteenth Has Sent Me Twenty-Five of His New Poems; in the Yamen Tower Beneath the Moon, I Chanted and Enjoyed Them All Night Long, and Then Inscribed This at the End"
735	*CTS*, vol. 8, pp. 6110–11	"Sent to Officer Yü of Ho-tung—Two Poems." This is from the second of the two poems. No. 683 also derives from these poems.
740	*Po, hou*, 1/14a,b	"Inscribed After the Collected Works of the Late Governor Yüan." This is the complete text of the first of the two poems of this title.
741	*Po, hou*, 12/4a,b	"Wei-chih, Tun-shih, and Hui-shu have Died One After the Other; I Have Been Left to Grieve in Solitude, and So I Have Written Two Quatrains." This is the complete text of the second poem.
742	*Po*, 17/16a,b	"On the thirtieth day of the third month of the tenth year, I parted from Wei-chih by the Li River. On the night of the eleventh day of the third month of the fourteenth year, I met him in the gorges. We stopped our boats at I-ling for three nights, and only then did we part. Whatever we left

742 (*cont.*)	*Po*, 17/16a,b	unsaid was to be completed in poetry, and so I have written this seven-character-meter poem in seventeen rhymes to send to him and also in the desire of recording the places I have encountered and the times I have experienced, so as to provide a prompt-book for conversations of future years."
743	*Po, hou*, 9/14a	"Inquiring About the Things of Chiang-nan"
750	*Hou Han shu*, vol. 6, p. 1474	"Discussion" (*lun*) from the "Biography of Chu Mu" (with some alternative readings)
751	*Hou Han shu*, vol. 2, p. 520	"Biography of Wei Hsiao"
752	*Wen hsüan*, vol. 1, p. 94	"Prosepoem on the Capital of Wu" by Tso Ssu (ca. 250–ca. 305) (with some alternative readings)
753	*Po, hou*, 9/10b–11a	"Toward the End of the Year Wu-shen [828], Singing of My Feelings." This is from the third of the three poems of this title.
754	CTS, vol. 9, p. 6120	"Sent to Li Yüan of Tang-t'u"
755	*Po*, 17/9a,b	"Drunken Chanting." This is from the first of the two poems of this title.
765	*Po*, 16/7b	"At Night, Staying Overnight at Chiang-p'u, I Learn That Yüan the Eighth Has Been Promoted, So I Send Him This Poem"

766	CTS, vol. 12 (appendix), p. 10185	"Passing the Examinations." This is not in the original CTS.
767	CTS, vol. 12 (appendix), p. 10184	"Seeing off Graduate Chang on His Return to Wu." This is not in the original CTS.
773	?	"Miscellaneous Words." This is not in the CTS.
777	Po, 3/5a	"The T'ai-hang Road"
778	?	This is not in the current redaction of Yu hsien k'u.
779, 780, 781	Po, 12/6b–9a	"The Song of Everlasting Sorrow." no. 234 also derives from this poem.
789	?	"Impermanence." This is presumably by Yen Wei (mid-8th c.), for whose name Lo Wei is an error, but it is not in the CTS.
790	CTS, vol. 1, p. 630 (as Sung Chih-wen), and vol. 2, pp. 885–86 (as Liu Hsi-i)	"Something on My Mind." This is attributed both to Sung Chih-wen and, under the title "Written on Behalf of an Old Man Lamenting His White Hairs," to Liu Hsi-i (651–ca. 678).
791	Po, hou, 9/10a	"Facing the Wine—Five Poems." This is from the second of the poems.
798	*	

* Addendum on T'ang Dynasty *fu* ["Prosepoem," "Rhyme Prose," "Rhapsody"] in the *Wakan rōei shū*

Twenty-three entries in the book derive from *fu* of the T'ang dynasty. The most comprehensive collection of T'ang *fu* is found in the *Ch'üan T'ang wen* (Complete prose works of the T'ang dynasty), a massive work completed in 1814. Although the *fu* is in fact a type of poetry, writings of this type were omitted from the CTS and were therefore included in *Ch'üan T'ang wen* (*CTW*) to compensate for that omission. Paul W. Kroll, writing in *The Indiana Companion to Traditional Chinese Literature* (ed. William H. Nienhauser Jr. et al., Bloomington: Indiana University Press, 1986, pp. 366–368), describes the *CTW* as "the repository for [T'ang] *fu*." It is perhaps remarkable, therefore, that not one of the T'ang *fu* on which Fujiwara no Kintō drew when compiling the WRS is to be found in the *CTW*, although some of the authors of the *fu* he used are represented there by other *fu*. (A useful reference work for researching this matter is the complete index and list of authors for the *CTW*, *Ch'üan T'ang wen p'ien-ming mu-lu chi tso-che so-yin*, compiled by Ma Hsü-ch'uan and published in 1985 by Chung-hua shu-chü in Peking.)

Although the compiler of the current finding list has not searched through all the possible Chinese sources, it appears that Kintō may have had access to many works that were subsequently lost in China itself. This should not be surprising when one considers the case of such a writer as Kung-ch'eng I, four of whose *fu* Kintō used. According to the *Monograph on Bibliography* in the *New History of the T'ang Dynasty*, compiled in the eleventh century by the great scholar Ou-yang Hsiu and his associates, Kung-ch'eng published a collection of his *fu* in no fewer than twelve chapters, and yet he is represented in the *CTW* by only one *fu*. Indeed, if one inspects the lists of books found in all the *Monographs on Bibliography* in all the official histories, one will find that vast amounts of literature have been lost down through the centuries, despite the early invention of printing in China. For this reason, the following list tries only to clarify certain details of attribution and the like and not to provide the Chinese sources.

Wakan rōei shū	*Name of fu*	*Comments*
63, 443	"Prosepoem, The Phoenix Is the Monarch"	Attributed to Chia Sung, a little-known late T'ang poet represented in the *CTW* by a single *fu*.
64, 417, 418, 510	"Prosepoem on the Dawn"	Attributed to Hsieh Kuan, an obscure T'ang poet represented in the *CTW* by no fewer than 23 *fu*, although this is not one of them. Not to be confused with the *fu* of the same name attributed to Chia Sung (see no. 416).

80	"Prosepoem on the Fine Rains Scattering Their Threads"	Erroneously attributed to various Japanese writers but assumed by the modern editors of the WRS to be a T'ang work. The Shinchō edition, without explanation, attributes it at one point (p. 429) to Tso Lao (chin-shih degree, 843), who is represented in the CTW by a single fu.
113, 604, 614, 615	"Prosepoem on Leisure"	Attributed to Chang Tu, a completely unknown figure. A man by this name who flourished in the mid-9th c. is recorded in T'an Cheng-pi's comprehensive biographical dictionary of Chinese writers (Chung-kuo wen-hsüeh-chia ta tz'u-tien, no. 1606), but he does not appear to be the same person. Chang Tu is not represented in in the CTW.
240, 241	"Prosepoem on the Night of the Fifteenth"	By Kung-ch'eng I (chin-shih degree, 871), represented in the CTW by a single fu.
307, 403	"Prosepoem on Sadness"	Attributed to Chang Tu; not to be confused with another fu of the same name by Kung-ch'eng I (see no. 500).
374, 798	"Prosepoem on Whiteness"	Attributed to Hsieh Kuan.
416	"Prosepoem on the Dawn"	Attributed to Chia Sung; not to be confused with the fu of the same name attributed to Hsieh Kuan (see nos. 64, 417, 418, 510).

444	"Prosepoem, The Crane in the Midst of a Flock of Chickens"	Attributed to Huang-fu Tseng, recorded in T'an Cheng-pi's biographical dictionary (no. 1311) but not in the CTW. The younger brother of Huang-fu Jan, the author of no. 261.
454	"Prosepoem on Purity"	Attributed to Hsieh Kuan.
462, 530	"Prosepoem on Lien-ch'ang Palace"	By Kung-ch'eng I.
479	"Prosepoem on Seeing off a Friend as He Returns to Ta-liang"	By Kung-ch'eng I.
500	"Prosepoem on Sadness"	By Kung-ch'eng I; not to be confused with the different work of the same name attributed to Chang Tu (see nos. 307 and 403).

Chinese Names and Terms

This list is limited to the names of writers whose works appear in the *Wakan rōei shū*, the names of books or writings from which the *Wakan rōei shū's* entries derive, and certain names and terms that appear elsewhere in this book. In the case of writers or books represented in the *Wakan rōei shū*, the numbers following the name indicate the entries in the *Wakan rōei shū* where selections from the writer or book are to be found. Books or writings are marked with an asterisk (*).

Chang Cho, Wen-ch'eng	張鷟 （文成）	(660–732)	705, 778 (?)
Chang Hsiao-piao	章孝標	(fl. ca. 826)	88, 431, 465, 473, 523, 766, 767
Chang Tu	張讀	(?T'ang dynasty)	23, 307, 403, 604, 614, 615
Chao Ku	趙嘏	(ca. 810–ca. 856)	578
Cheng Shih-jan	鄭師冉	(?T'ang dynasty)	410
Chia Sung	賈嵩	(?late T'ang dynasty)	63, 416, 443
Chiao-jan	皎然	(730–799)	
Ch'ien Ch'i	錢起	(722–780)	81
Chih-i	智顗	(538–597)	587
ch'ou	愁	"grief," "sadness"	
*Chou li	周禮	"The Rites of the Chou Dynasty"	
Ch'ü Yüan	屈原	(340?–278 B.C.)	
*Ch'üan T'ang shih	全唐詩	"Complete Poetry [*shih*] of the T'ang Dynasty"	

*Ch'üan T'ang wen	全唐文	"Complete Prose of the T'ang Dynasty"	
*Chuang Tzu	莊子	The writings of the great Taoist philosopher of the fourth century B.C	
Fang Hui	方回	(1227–1306)	
Fu Wen	傅溫	(?T'ang dynasty)	397
hai-su	駭俗	"startling and common"	
*Han Shu	漢書	"History of the Han Dynasty"	675
Ho-lan Sui (or Hsien)	賀蘭遂（暹）	(?T'ang dynasty)	491, 718
*Hou Han shu	後漢書	"History of the Latter Han Dynasty"	674, 750, 751
hsi	兮	"Ah!" (exclamation)	
Hsi K'ang	嵇康	(223–262)	
Hsieh Kuan	謝觀	(?T'ang dynasty)	64, 374, 417, 418, 454, 510, 798
Hsieh Yen	謝偃	(d. 643)	733
Hsi-k'un	西崑	(school of poetry)	
*Hsin Yüeh-fu	新樂府	"New Music Bureau Ballads"	
Hsü Hun	許渾	(791–854?)	177, 182, 187, 194, 422, 641, 650, 683, 735, 754
hu	壺	"jar," ceremonial bronze vessel type	
*Huai-nan Tzu	淮南子	"The Prince of Huai-nan"; eclectic philosophical compilation of the second century B.C.	
Huang-fu Jan	皇甫冉	(714–767)	261
Huang-fu Tseng	皇甫曾	(fl. ca. 756; younger brother of Huang-fu Jan)	444
*I ching	易經	"The Book of Changes"	
*I-wen chih	藝文志	"Monograph on Bibliography"	
jen	人	"person"	

keng-shen (Jpse: kōshin)	庚申	(cyclical calendrical term)	
Ko Hung	葛洪	(283–343)	
Kung-ch'eng (or-sheng) I	公乘億	(*chin-shih* degree, 871)	240, 241, 462, 479, 500, 530
Kuo P'u	郭璞	(276–324)	
Li Chiao	李嶠	(644–713)	81 wrongly attributed
Li Chia-yu	李嘉祐	(*chin-shih* degree, between 742 and 755)	193
Li Po	李白	(701–762)	
Li Shang-yin	李商隱	(813?–858)	
Li Tuan	李端	(d. ca. 787)	261 wrongly attributed
Lieh Tzu	列子	Writings attributed to a semilegendary Taoist figure; contains elements from the fourth century B.C. but was probably compiled in the fourth century A.D.	
Liu Hsi-i	劉希夷	(651–ca. 678)	790 (alternative attribution)
Liu-i shih-hua	六一詩話	"One-of-Six Comments on Poetry"	
Liu Yüan-shu	劉元叔	(?late T'ang dynasty)	346
Liu Yü-hsi	劉禹錫	(772–842)	19, 318, 447, 503
Lo Ch'iu	羅虯	(fl. ca. 874)	682
Lu, attendant censor	陸侍御	(?T'ang dynasty)	59
Lu Chi	陸機	(261–303)	470
Lu Hui	陸翬	(?T'ang dynasty)	681
Lun wen	論文	"Discussing Literature"	
Lun yü	論語	[Confucian] "Analects"	
Mo-ho chih-kuan	摩訶止觀	"Treatise on the Great Cessation and Contemplation"	
Monk Keng [or Hsüan]- hsüan	亘玄	(?T'ang dynasty)	690
Ou-yang Hsiu	歐陽修	(1007–1072)	
pa	八	"eight"	

pa	巴	(Ancient place-name—part of Szechwan)	
p'an, pan	磐，般	(orthographically similar characters; second + 若 = "prājña")	
Pan Chieh-yü	班婕妤	(fl. ca. 48 B.C), "Concubine Pan"	
P'an Yüeh	潘岳	(247–300)	
Pao Jung (or Yung)	鮑溶	(*chin-shih* degree, 809)	605
Pao p'u Tzu	抱朴子	"He Who Enbraces Simplicity," a philosophical text by Ko Hung	
pieh-chi	別集	"individual collections"	
Po Chü-i	白居易	(772–846)	4, 5, 10, 18, 20, 27, 50, 51, 52, 66, 67, 75, 87, 102, 103, 104, 105, 114, 115, 126, 127, 133, 137, 144, 147, 150, 151, 152, 159, 160, 161, 168, 171, 175, 176, 192, 199, 204, 208, 209, 212, 221, 222, 223, 230, 233, 234, 235, 242, 243, 252, 254, 266, 286, 291, 301, 302, 308, 309, 327, 328, 338, 341, 345, 352, 356, 359, 362, 367, 375, 376, 387, 393, 419, 421, 430, 435, 445, 446, 455, 456, 463, 464, 471, 480, 481, 482, 483, 484, 492, 501, 511, 512, 513, 521, 522, 531, 541, 554, 555, 565, 572, 573, 578, 579, 588, 589, 613, 616, 617, 618, 624, 631, 655, 656, 666, 676, 689, 697, 707, 708, 715, 722, 723, 724, 733, 734, 740, 741, 742, 743, 753, 755, 765, 777, 779, 780, 781, 781, 791 (includes erroneous or questionable attributions)

Po Hsing-chien	白行簡	(775–826), younger brother of Po Chü-i	
se-hsiang	色相	"form-and-attribute" (Buddhist technical term)	
shang	商	(note of the Chinese pentatonic scale)	
shih, jo	石，若	(orthographically similar characters; see under "p'an, pan")	
Shih chi	史記	"Records of the Historian"	
Shih Chien-wu	施肩吾	(*chin-shih* degree between 806 and 820)	465
Shih ching	詩經	"Book of Songs"	
shih-hua	詩話	"comments on poetry"	
Shih-shih	詩式	"Rules for Poetry"	
Shih-shuo hsin-yü	世說新語	"A New Account of Tales of the World"	
shuang	霜	"frost"	
shuang	雙	"paired"	
Ssu-ma Ch'ien	司馬遷	(ca. 145–ca. 85 B.C.)	
Ssu-ma Hsiang-ju	司馬相如	(179–117 B.C.)	
Su Shih, Tung-p'o	蘇軾（東坡）	(1037–1101)	
Su Shun-ch'in	蘇舜欽	(1008–1048)	
Sui-ch'u-t'ang shu-mu	遂初堂書目	"Catalog of Books in the Hall of Pursuing the Origin"	
sung	松	"pine tree"	
Sung Chih-wen	宋之問	(656?–712)	790
T'ang-shih san-pai-shou	唐詩三百首	"Three Hundred Poems of the T'ang Dynasty"	

*Tao te ching	道德經	The famous Taoist "Classic of the Way and Its Power," probably dating from the third century B.C.	
Ts'ao P'i	曹丕	(r. 220–227)	
Tso Lao	左牢	(chin-shih degree, 843)	80 (attribution unclear)
Tso Ssu	左思	(ca. 250–ca. 305)	752
tsung-chi	總集	"mixed anthologies"	
Tu Fu	杜甫	(712–770)	
Tu Hsün-ho	杜荀鶴	(846–907)	319, 502, 514, 556
Wang Chu	王洙	(997–1057)	
Wang Wei	王維	(701–761)	38
Wang Yü-ch'eng	王禹偁	(954–1001)	
Wei Ch'eng-ch'ing	韋承慶	(d. 706?)	317
*Wen hsüan	文選	"Literary Anthology"	[470], 752
Wen T'ing-yün	温庭筠	(ca. 812–870)	334, 368, 542
Yang Heng	楊衡	(fl. ca. 766)	657
Yang Shen	楊慎	(1488–1559)	
Yen Wei	嚴維	(mid-eighth century)	789
Ying Chan	郢展	(?T'ang dynasty)	253
*Yu hsien k'u	游仙窟	"A Journey to the Dwellings of the Immortals"	
Yu Mao	尤袤	(1124–1193)	
Yüan Chen	元稹	(779–831)	9, 45, 65, 96, 186, 267, 405, 436, 472, 540, 706
yung-wu	詠物	"singing of things" (a type of poem)	

Japanese Poets Writing Poetry in Chinese (*kanshi*)

The following poets are represented in the *Wakan rōei shū*. Full names and, when available, dates of birth and death are included. The numbers following the name of each poet indicate the entries in the *Wakan rōei shū* itself. An asterisk (*) is given to those poets whose *waka* also are included in the *Wakan rōei shū*. Positive attributions for some of these poems are difficult to establish. Useful details concerning attributions can be found in both the Ōsone and Horiuchi volume (1983) and in volume 73 of the *Nihon koten bungaku taikei* (1965).

Compiler of the anthology: Fujiwara no Kintō 藤原公任 (966–1041)

Emperor Daigo	醍醐天皇	(r. 901–923)	179, 353
Fujiwara no Atsumochi	藤原篤茂	(d. ca. 793)	2, 41, 347, 432, 474, 629
Fujiwara no Kokufū	藤原國風	(dates uncertain)	663
Fujiwara no Korechika	藤原惟成	(974–1010)	662
Fujiwara no Koreshige	藤原伊周	(953–989)	411
Fujiwara no Masaki	藤原雅材	(fl. ca. 960)	653, 654 attributed
*Fujiwara no Yoshitaka	藤原義孝	(954–974)	793
Fujiwara no Yukifuji	藤原行葛	(fl. ca. 960)	399
Prince Kaneakira	兼明親王	(914–997)	98, 256, 287, 292, 433, 760
Ki no Arimasa	紀在昌	(fl. ca. 950)	178, 372, 694
Ki no Haseo	紀長谷雄	(845–912)	14, 43, 82, 188, 196, 210, 244, 262–264, 268, 335, 369, 377,

Japanese Poets Writing Poetry in Japanese (*waka*)

The following poets are represented in the *Wakan rōei shū*. Full names and, when available, dates of birth and death are included. The numbers following the name of each poet indicate the entries in the *Wakan rōei shū* itself. An asterisk (*) is given to those poets whose *kanshi* also are included in the *Wakan rōei shū*. Positive attributions for some of these poems are difficult to establish. Useful details concerning attributions can be found in both the Ōsone and Horiuchi volume (1983) and in volume 73 of the *Nihon koten bungaku taikei* (1965).

Abe no Hironiwa	安法法師	(659–732)	93
Abe no Nakamaro	安倍広庭	(698–770)	258
Anbō Hōshi	安部仲丸	(dates uncertain)	429
Ariwara no Motokata	在原元方	(ca. 900)	3
Ariwara no Narihira	在原業平	(825–880)	123, 366 attributed
Asuka no Miko	明日香皇子	(?–834)	183 attributed
Atsumi no Ōkimi	厚見女皇	(ca. 750)	142
Chūsan	仲算	(935–976)	776
Dengyō Daishi	伝教大師	(767–822)	602
Egyō	惠慶	(early eleventh century)	167
Fujiwara no Kanesuke	藤原兼輔	(877–932)	112, 434
Fujiwara no Kiyotada	藤原清正	(?–958)	33, 306, 453
Fujiwara no Koretada	藤原伊尹	(934–972)	539
Fujiwara no Michinaga	藤原道長	(966–1027)	603 attributed
Fujiwara no Michinobu	藤原道信	(972–994)	294

Fujiwara no Nobuomu	藤原信臣	(ca. 900)	527
Fujiwara no Okikaze	藤原興風	(fl. ca. 900)	49, 739
Fujiwara no Sanekata	藤原実方	(?–998)	704
Fujiwara no Saneyori	藤原実賴	(900–970)	281
Fujiwara no Tadafusa	藤原忠房	(?–928)	333
Fujiwara no Takamitsu	藤原高光	(?–994)	764
Fujiwara no Tameyori	藤原為賴	(?–998?)	732, 749
Fujiwara no Tokihira	藤原時平	(871–909)	692
Fujiwara no Toshiyuki	藤原敏行	(?–907)	206, 272
Fujiwara no Yatsuka	藤原八束	(714–766)	277
*Fujiwara no Yoshitaka	藤原義孝	(954–974)	229
Gembin	玄賓	(818–?)	612
Bishop Hemjō	遍昭	(816–?890)	181, 610, 623, 717, 797
Lady Ise	伊勢	(?877–?940)	62, 86, 284, 326, 452, 519
Kakinomoto no Hitomaro	柿本人麿	(fl. 710)	35, 218, 238, 314, 787
Emperor Kazan	花山天皇	(968–1008)	101
Ki no Tomonori	紀友則	(?–606?)	100, 324, 344, 383
Ki no Tsurayuki	紀貫之	(?872–945)	7, 37, 57, 58, 110, 131, 155, 219, 305, 316, 337, 351, 358, 361, 420, 538 variant, 570, 577, 796
Kiyohara no Fukayabu	清原深養父	(fl. 910)	343
Kiyohara no Motosuke	清原元輔	(908–990)	202, 285
Kiyowara no Motozane	清原元真	(fl. 960)	639
Emperor Kōkō	光孝天皇	(r. 884–887)	665
Kūya	空也	(903–972)	601
Mansei	滿誓	(ca. 700)	795
Mibu no Tadami	壬生忠見	(ca. 950)	185, 442, 497 attributed
Mibu no Tadamine	壬生忠岑	(fl. 898–920)	8, 26, 31 attributed, 169
Minamoto no Kintada	源公忠	(889–948)	132, 184, 688
Minamoto no Masazumi	源當純	(fl. 900)	16
Minamoto no Muneyuki	源宗于	(?–939)	427, 564
Minamoto no Saneakira	源信明	(910–970)	402
Minamoto no Shigemitsu	源重光	(923–998)	198
Minamoto no Shigeyuki	源重之	(?–ca. 1000)	146
*Minamoto no Shitagō	源順	(911–983)	149, 70

*Miyako no Arinaka	都在中	(dates uncertain)	325
Emperor Murakami	村上天皇	(r. 946–967)	600, 748
Nakatsuka	中務	(?920–980)	74, 166, 201, 203, 265, 401
Nawamaro	繩丸	(fl. 740)	135
*Ōe no Asatsuna	大江朝綱	(886–957)	696
Ōnakatomi no Yorimoto	大中臣賴基	(ca. 940)	157
Ōnakatomi no Yoshinobu	大中臣能宣	(921–991)	32, 158, 336, 490, 526 variant
Ono no Komachi	小野小町	(fl. ca. 833–857)	441 attributed
*Ono no Takamura	小野篁	(803–852)	648
*Ono no Yoshiki	小野美材	(902–?)	280
Ōshikōchi no Mitsune	凡河内躬恆	(fl. 898–922)	28, 56, 95, 124, 220, 239, 273, 299, 461, 731, 786
Ōtomo no Yakamochi	大伴家持	(?–785)	340
Reikeiden no Nyōgo	麗景殿女御	(930–1008)	73
Sakanoue no Korenori	坂上是則	(fl. 905–925)	382
Semimaru	蟬丸	(ca. 920)	763
Shiki no Miko	志貴皇子	(?–716)	15, 211
Shirome	白女	(ca. 875?)	640
Sone no Yoshitada	曾禰義忠	(fl. 1075)	520
Sosei	素性	(fl. 859–897)	72, 125, 290, 553, 630, 788
*Tachibana no Naomoto	橘直幹	(fl. ca. 950)	638
Taira no Kanemori	平兼盛	(?–ca. 900)	17, 79, 143, 278, 395 attributed, 498, 649, 680
Takamuko no Kusawaru	高向草春	(dates uncertain)	509 attributed
*Prince Tomohira	具平親王	(964–1009)	260
Wani	王仁	(ca. 300)	664
Yamabe no Akahito	山部赤人	(ca. 730)	25, 36, 94, 451

Other Works in the Columbia Asian Studies Series

Two Plays of Ancient India: The Little Clay Cart and the Minister's Seal, tr. J. A. B. van Buitenen 1968

The Complete Works of Chuang Tzu, tr. Burton Watson 1968

The Romance of the Western Chamber (Hsi Hsiang chi), tr. S. I. Hsiung. Also in paperback ed. 1968

The Manyōshū, Nippon Gakujutsu Shinkōkai edition. Paperback ed. only. 1969

Records of the Historian: Chapters from the Shih chi of Ssu-ma Ch'ien, tr. Burton Watson. Paperback ed. only. 1969

Cold Mountain: 100 Poems by the T'ang Poet Han-shan, tr. Burton Watson. Also in paperback ed. 1970

Twenty Plays of the Nō Theatre, ed. Donald Keene. Also in paperback ed. 1970

Chūshingura: The Treasury of Loyal Retainers, tr. Donald Keene. Also in paperback ed. 1971

The Zen Master Hakuin: Selected Writings, tr. Philip B. Yampolsky 1971

Chinese Rhyme-Prose: Poems in the Fu Form from the Han and Six Dynasties Periods, tr. Burton Watson. Also in paperback ed. 1971

Kūkai: Major Works, tr. Yoshito S. Hakeda. Also in paperback ed. 1972

The Old Man Who Does as He Pleases: Selections from the Poetry and Prose of Lu Yu, tr. Burton Watson 1973

The Lion's Roar of Queen Śrīmālā, tr. Alex and Hideko Wayman 1974

Courtier and Commoner in Ancient China: Selections from the History of the Former Han by Pan Ku, tr. Burton Watson. Also in paperback ed. 1974

Japanese Literature in Chinese, vol. 1: *Poetry and Prose in Chinese by Japanese Writers of the Early Period*, tr. Burton Watson 1975

Japanese Literature in Chinese, vol. 2: *Poetry and Prose in Chinese by Japanese Writers of the Later Period*, tr. Burton Watson 1976

Scripture of the Lotus Blossom of the Fine Dharma, tr. Leon Hurvitz. Also in paperback ed. 1976

Love Song of the Dark Lord: Jayadeva's Gītagovinda, tr. Barbara Stoler Miller. Also in paperback ed. Cloth ed. includes critical text of the Sanskrit. 1977

Ryōkan: Zen Monk-Poet of Japan, tr. Burton Watson 1977

Calming the Mind and Discerning the Real: From the Lam rim chen mo of Tsoñ-kha-pa, tr. Alex Wayman 1978

The Hermit and the Love-Thief: Sanskrit Poems of Bhartrihari and Bilhaṇa, tr. Barbara Stoler Miller 1978

The Lute: Kao Ming's P'i-p'a chi, tr. Jean Mulligan. Also in paperback ed. 1980

A Chronicle of Gods and Sovereigns: Jinnō Shōtōki of Kitabatake Chikafusa, tr. H. Paul Varley. 1980

Among the Flowers: The Hua-chien chi, tr. Lois Fusek 1982

Grass Hill: Poems and Prose by the Japanese Monk Gensei, tr. Burton Watson 1983

Doctors, Diviners, and Magicians of Ancient China: Biographies of Fang-shih, tr. Kenneth J. DeWoskin. Also in paperback ed. 1983

Theater of Memory: The Plays of Kālidāsa, ed. Barbara Stoler Miller. Also in paper-
  back ed.   1984
The Columbia Book of Chinese Poetry: From Early Times to the Thirteenth Century,
  ed. and tr. Burton Watson. Also in paperback ed.   1984
*Poems of Love and War: From the Eight Anthologies and the Ten Long Poems of
  Classical Tamil*, tr. A. K. Ramanujan. Also in paperback ed.   1985
The Bhagavad Gita: Krishna's Counsel in Time of War, tr. Barbara Stoler Miller
  1986
The Columbia Book of Later Chinese Poetry, ed. and tr. Jonathan Chaves. Also in
  paperback ed.   1986
The Tso Chuan: Selections from China's Oldest Narrative History, tr. Burton
  Watson   1989
Waiting for the Wind: Thirty-six Poets of Japan's Late Medieval Age, tr. Steven
  Carter   1989
Selected Writings of Nichiren, ed. Philip B. Yampolsky   1990
Saigyō, Poems of a Mountain Home, tr. Burton Watson   1990
The Book of Lieh-Tzū: A Classic of the Tao, tr. A. C. Graham. Morningside ed.
  1990
*The Tale of an Anklet: An Epic of South India — The Cilappatikāram of Iḷaṅkō
  Aṭikaḷ*, tr. R. Parthasarathy   1993
Waiting for the Dawn: A Plan for the Prince, tr. and introduction by Wm. Theodore
  de Bary   1993
*Yoshitsune and the Thousand Cherry Trees: A Masterpiece of the Eighteenth-
  Century Japanese Puppet Theater*, tr., annotated, and with introduction by
  Stanleigh H. Jones, Jr.   1993
The Lotus Sutra, tr. Burton Watson. Also in paperback ed.   1993
*The Classic of Changes: A New Translation of the I Ching as Interpreted by Wang
  Bi*, tr. Richard John Lynn   1994
Beyond Spring: T'zu Poems of the Sung Dynasty, tr. Julie Landau   1994
The Columbia Anthology of Traditional Chinese Literature, ed. Victor H. Mair
  1994
Scenes for Mandarins: The Elite Theater of the Ming, tr. Cyril Birch   1995
Letters of Nichiren, ed. Philip B. Yampolsky; tr. Burton Watson et al.   1996
Unforgotten Dreams: Poems by the Zen Monk Shōtetsu, tr. Steven D. Carter   1997
Sutra on the Expositions of Vimalakirti, tr. by Burton Watson   1997

MODERN ASIAN LITERATURE SERIES

Modern Japanese Drama: An Anthology, ed. and tr. Ted. Takaya. Also in paperback
  ed.   1979
Mask and Sword: Two Plays for the Contemporary Japanese Theater, by Yamazaki
  Masakazu, tr. J. Thomas Rimer   1980

Yokomitsu Riichi, Modernist, Dennis Keene   1980
Nepali Visions, Nepali Dreams: The Poetry of Laxmiprasad Devkota, tr. David
     Rubin   1980
Literature of the Hundred Flowers, vol. 1: *Criticism and Polemics,* ed. Hualing
     Nieh   1981
Literature of the Hundred Flowers, vol. 2: *Poetry and Fiction,* ed. Hualing Nieh
     1981
Modern Chinese Stories and Novellas, 1919 1949, ed. Joseph S. M. Lau, C. T. Hsia,
     and Leo Ou-fan Lee. Also in paperback ed.   1984
A View by the Sea, by Yasuoka Shōtarō, tr. Kären Wigen Lewis   1984
Other Worlds; Arishima Takeo and the Bounds of Modern Japanese Fiction, by Paul
     Anderer   1984
Selected Poems of Sŏ Chŏngju, tr. with introduction by David R. McCann   1989
The Sting of Life: Four Contemporary Japanese Novelists, by Van C. Gessel   1989
Stories of Osaka Life, by Oda Sakunosuke, tr. Burton Watson   1990
The Bodhisattva, or Samantabhadra, by Ishikawa Jun, tr. with introduction by
     William Jefferson Tyler   1990
The Travels of Lao Ts'an, by Liu T'ieh-yün, tr. Harold Shadick. Morningside
     ed.   1990
Three Plays by Kōbō Abe, tr. with introduction by Donald Keene   1993
The Columbia Anthology of Modern Chinese Literature, ed. Joseph S. M. Lau and
     Howard Goldblatt   1995
Modern Japanese Tanka, ed. and tr. by Makoto Ueda   1996

STUDIES IN ASIAN CULTURE

*The Ōnin War: History of Its Origins and Background, with a Selective Translation
     of the Chronicle of Ōnin,* by H. Paul Varley   1967
Chinese Government in Ming Times: Seven Studies, ed. Charles O. Hucker
     1969
The Actors' Analects (Yakusha Rongo), ed. and tr. by Charles J. Dunn and Bungō
     Torigoe   1969
Self and Society in Ming Thought, by Wm. Theodore de Bary and the Conference
     on Ming Thought. Also in paperback ed.   1970
A History of Islamic Philosophy, by Majid Fakhry, 2d ed.   1983
Phantasies of a Love Thief: The Caurapañcāśikā Attributed to Bilhaṇa, by
     Barbara Stoler Miller   1971
Iqbal: Poet-Philosopher of Pakistan, ed. Hafeez Malik   1971
The Golden Tradition: An Anthology of Urdu Poetry, ed. and tr. Ahmed Ali. Also in
     paperback ed.   1973
Conquerors and Confucians: Aspects of Political Change in Late Yüan China, by
     John W. Dardess   1973

The Unfolding of Neo-Confucianism, by Wm. Theodore de Bary and the Conference on Seventeenth-Century Chinese Thought. Also in paperback ed.   1975

To Acquire Wisdom: The Way of Wang Yang-ming, by Julia Ching   1976

Gods, Priests, and Warriors: The Bhṛgus of the Mahābhārata, by Robert P. Goldman   1977

Mei Yao-ch'en and the Development of Early Sung Poetry, by Jonathan Chaves   1976

The Legend of Semimaru, Blind Musician of Japan, by Susan Matisoff   1977

Sir Sayyid Ahmad Khan and Muslim Modernization in India and Pakistan, by Hafeez Malik   1980

The Khilafat Movement: Religious Symbolism and Political Mobilization in India, by Gail Minault   1982

The World of K'ung Shang-jen: A Man of Letters in Early Ch'ing China, by Richard Strassberg   1983

The Lotus Boat: The Origins of Chinese Tz'u Poetry in T'ang Popular Culture, by Marsha L. Wagner   1984

Expressions of Self in Chinese Literature, ed. Robert E. Hegel and Richard C. Hessney   1985

Songs for the Bride: Women's Voices and Wedding Rites of Rural India, by W. G. Archer; eds. Barbara Stoler Miller and Mildred Archer   1986

A Heritage of Kings: One Man's Monarchy in the Confucian World, by JaHyun Kim Haboush   1988

COMPANIONS TO ASIAN STUDIES

Approaches to the Oriental Classics, ed. Wm. Theodore de Bary   1959

Early Chinese Literature, by Burton Watson. Also in paperback ed.   1962

Approaches to Asian Civilizations, eds. Wm. Theodore de Bary and Ainslie T. Embree   1964

The Classic Chinese Novel: A Critical Introduction, by C. T. Hsia. Also in paperback ed.   1968

Chinese Lyricism: Shih Poetry from the Second to the Twelfth Century, tr. Burton Watson. Also in paperback ed.   1971

A Syllabus of Indian Civilization, by Leonard A. Gordon and Barbara Stoler Miller   1971

Twentieth-Century Chinese Stories, ed. C. T. Hsia and Joseph S. M. Lau. Also in paperback ed.   1971

A Syllabus of Chinese Civilization, by J. Mason Gentzler, 2d ed.   1972

A Syllabus of Japanese Civilization, by H. Paul Varley, 2d ed.   1972

An Introduction to Chinese Civilization, ed. John Meskill, with the assistance of J. Mason Gentzler   1973

An Introduction to Japanese Civilization, ed. Arthur E. Tiedemann   1974
Ukifune: Love in the Tale of Genji, ed. Andrew Pekarik   1982
The Pleasures of Japanese Literature, by Donald Keene   1988
A Guide to Oriental Classics, eds. Wm. Theodore de Bary and Ainslie T. Embree;
    3d edition ed. Amy Vladeck Heinrich, 2 vols.   1989

INTRODUCTION TO ASIAN CIVILIZATIONS

Wm. Theodore de Bary, General Editor

Sources of Japanese Tradition, 1958; paperback ed., 2 vols., 1964
Sources of Indian Tradition, 1958; paperback ed., 2 vols., 1964; 2d ed., 2 vols., 1988
Sources of Chinese Tradition, 1960; paperback ed., 2 vols., 1964
Sources of Korean Tradition, paperback ed., vol. 1, 1997

NEO-CONFUCIAN STUDIES

Instructions for Practical Living and Other Neo-Confucian Writings by Wang Yang-ming, tr. Wing-tsit Chan   1963
Reflections on Things at Hand: The Neo-Confucian Anthology, comp. Chu Hsi and
    Lü Tsu-ch'ien, tr. Wing-tsit Chan   1967
Self and Society in Ming Thought, by Wm. Theodore de Bary and the Conference
    on Ming Thought. Also in paperback ed.   1970
The Unfolding of Neo-Confucianism, by Wm. Theodore de Bary and the Confer-
    ence on Seventeenth-Century Chinese Thought. Also in paperback ed.   1975
Principle and Practicality: Essays in Neo-Confucianism and Practical Learning,
    eds. Wm. Theodore de Bary and Irene Bloom. Also in paperback ed.   1979
The Syncretic Religion of Lin Chao-en, by Judith A. Berling   1980
The Renewal of Buddhism in China: Chu-hung and the Late Ming Synthesis, by
    Chün-fang Yü   1981
Neo-Confucian Orthodoxy and the Learning of the Mind-and-Heart, by Wm.
    Theodore de Bary   1981
Yüan Thought: Chinese Thought and Religion Under the Mongols, eds. Hok-lam
    Chan and Wm. Theodore de Bary   1982
The Liberal Tradition in China, by Wm. Theodore de Bary   1983
The Development and Decline of Chinese Cosmology, by John B. Henderson
    1984
The Rise of Neo-Confucianism in Korea, by Wm. Theodore de Bary and JaHyun
    Kim Haboush   1985
Chiao Hung and the Restructuring of Neo-Confucianism in Late Ming, by Edward
    T. Ch'ien   1985

Neo-Confucian Terms Explained: Pei-hsi tzu-i, by Ch'en Ch'un, ed. and trans.
   Wing-tsit Chan   1986
Knowledge Painfully Acquired: K'un-chih chi, by Lo Ch'in-shun, ed. and trans.
   Irene Bloom   1987
To Become a Sage: The Ten Diagrams on Sage Learning, by Yi T'oegye, ed. and
   trans. Michael C. Kalton   1988
The Message of the Mind in Neo-Confucian Thought, by Wm. Theodore de
   Bary   1989